TEACHING THROUGH
SELF-INSTRUCTION

LEARNING THROUGH
SELF-INSTRUCTION

TEACHING THROUGH
SELF-INSTRUCTION

How to Develop Open Learning Materials

REVISED EDITION

DEREK ROWNTREE

Kogan Page, London/Nichols Publishing, New York

First published in England in 1986.
This revised edition first published in 1990 by
Kogan Page
120 Pentonville Road
London N1 9JN.

Printed and bound in Great Britain by
Biddles Ltd, Guildford.

British Library Cataloguing in Publication Data
A CIP Catalogue record for this book is available from the British Library.

ISBN 1 85091 957 7

First published in the USA in 1986.
This revised edition first published in 1990 by
Nichols Publishing, an imprint of GP Publishing Inc.,
PO Box 96, New York, NY 10024.

Library of Congress Cataloging-in-Publication Data
Rowntree, Derek.
    Teaching through self-instruction/Derek Rowntree.--Rev. ed.
    p. cm.
    Includes bibliographical references.
    ISBN 0-89397-356-4
    1. Distance education. 2. Self-culture. I. Title.
LC5800.R68   1990
371.3--dc20   89-49775   CIP

CONTENTS

1. GETTING TO GRIPS WITH SELF-INSTRUCTION

Self-instructional teaching seems to be cropping up everywhere these days. Keen-eyed connoisseurs of the absurd will have noticed that even the infant hero of the film *Superman* was kept usefully occupied by a distance learning course throughout his intergalactic journey from Krypton to Smallsville.

And, in the real world, correspondence colleges continue to flourish; more and more schools, colleges and universities are requiring students to do some of their learning from specially-prepared teaching materials (and some, like Britain's Open University, have thousands of students working from self-instruction only); and much professional, vocational and industrial training is now dependent upon pre-packaged teaching.

I assume you are reading this book because you are interested in teaching through self-instruction. Teachers and trainers are becoming increasingly involved with self-instruction -- not least because it enables them to reach learners they would otherwise be unable to reach, but also because it offers benefits that are not obtainable from classroom instruction. These teachers and trainers may know self-instruction by any of a variety of pet names, like:

- distance education
- packaged learning
- open learning
- flexistudy
- independent/individualized learning
- flexible learning
- home study
- supported self study
- computer based training
- computer aided instruction/learning

- directed private study
- programmed instruction/learning
- correspondence education
- learning by appointment
- resource-based learning...and so on

I shall not go into detail about each of these forms of self-instruction. You will know which one you are likely to be involved with -- perhaps it even goes by yet another name in your institution. And what I have to say in this book is relevant to **any** kind of self-instruction.

TWO BASIC DISTINCTIONS

Although I do not intend to describe every variety of self-instruction, there are a couple of basic distinctions I must make clear:

Distance v On-site Self-instruction

Some forms of self-instruction cater for learners who are learning "at a distance". That is to say, the learners will not be in regular contact with the teachers who design the courses. Indeed they may have little or no face-to-face contact with any teachers at all -- or even with other learners. "Correspondence education" is typical of this form, and so is much "open learning".

Other forms of self-instruction are used on the premises of the institution that is sponsoring the course -- e.g. in a college laboratory, a civil service office, or the staff room in a retail store. With such "on-site" self-instruction, learners may still see little or nothing of the teachers who produced the course. But at least they may be able to meet one another, a tutor, and perhaps a more experienced colleague who can support their studies. In this category we may encounter, for example, "learning by appointment", much "open learning", and a wide variety of package-based training schemes.

Whether "on-site" or "at-a-distance", learners working with self-instruction have one important thing in common. Because they have much less contact with a teacher than "normal" learners do, they rely very heavily on **specially prepared teaching materials**. That is, the teaching will have been largely pre-planned, pre-recorded, and pre-packaged. It will be presented in instructional texts, audiotapes, videotapes, computer packages, work-based projects, and so on.

Self-instruction v "Conventional" Instruction

With normal or "conventional" instruction, learners meet together regularly in classes, and much of their learning is done face-to-face with a teacher or trainer. Admittedly, they may also spend a considerable amount of time learning on their own -- more perhaps than they spend in class. But this will usually involve them in using materials that **already** exist, e.g. books and journals. That is, their private study materials will not have been created especially for them, with **their** particular courses needs in mind. Furthermore, their teachers may make little or no attempt to structure that side of their studies.

Self-instruction, on the other hand, depends on materials specially written -- or at least specially selected and modified -- with particular course objectives in mind. Furthermore, they will be structured in such a way that learners can do most, if not all, their learning from the materials alone. The materials must carry out all the functions a teacher or trainer would carry out in the conventional situation -- guiding, motivating, intriguing, expounding, explaining, provoking, reminding, asking questions, discussing alternative answers, appraising each learner's progress, giving appropriate remedial or enrichment help...and so on.

A self-instructional system may, of course, encourage learners to make occasional contact with a tutor. It may even **demand** that they do so. But the contact will be slight, compared with that in conventional instruction. For instance, learners working at a distance may have no contact other than by mailing occasional assignments to a tutor and getting the tutor's written comments some time later. Of course, they may also be expected to speak to the tutor on the telephone from time to time. They may even be expected to meet tutors for a seminar or tutorial occasionally, or even for a weekend workshop or residential summer school.

Similarly, on-site learners may find that a series of self-instructional sessions is topped and tailed by a group meeting with a tutor. They may also be expected to complete regular progress tests that are checked (perhaps in their presence) by a tutor or by a more experienced colleague or their line manager acting as a "mentor". One-to-one remedial tuition may be available for learners who are having special difficulties with the self-instructional materials.

Apart from tutors, mentors and materials, learners can learn a great deal from one another. This will be especially the case in professional training and in aesthetic or social areas -- e.g. in sales training, literary criticism, or child-rearing. Here, learners benefit from the realization that other people's values and beliefs and experiences lead them to see things differently. But face-to-face interaction with their peers may not be readily available to learners working with self-instruction -- especially when they are learning at a distance, perhaps dispersed over a wide geographical area. So self-instructional materials may need to compensate for lack of contact with other learners as well as with tutors.

Finally, it is worth remarking that even a largely "conventional" course or teaching system may incorporate **some** self-instruction. Thus, the learners may take one or two courses in packaged form, while the bulk of their courses are conventional. Similarly, even within an otherwise conventional course, the teacher or trainer may prepare or obtain self-instructional materials to help learners with some of the topics that are difficult to teach to a group -- perhaps because different learners master different bits of them at different speeds, or because they require demonstrations that not everyone in the group would be able to see at the same time.

> SELF-INSTRUCTION MAY BE AN **ALTERNATIVE**
> TO OTHER FORMS OF TEACHING. BUT IT CAN
> ALSO BE **COMBINED** WITH THEM.

WHAT CAN YOU EXPECT FROM THIS BOOK?

Before we get into the details of developing self-instructional materials, I'd better let you know what I'm trying to do in this book. I'll say a few words about what I'm assuming your interest might be, about what my own background is, and about the aims and objectives of this book and how you might wish to use it.

Who are You?

I assume you are someone who needs **practical** advice on teaching with self-instruction. You may be, for example:

* a school-teacher, helping students learn from specialist materials that were largely produced, perhaps, by other teachers;

* a college or university lecturer developing an open learning scheme;

* a trainer in business or the civil service, producing training packages for the benefit of trainees who

cannot easily be brought together to form a class; or

- an author or editor in an organization preparing self-instructional materials to meet clients' needs.

The ideas I discuss in this book should be of value to people in any of the above groups -- and maybe in others I have not thought about. Throughout the book, I shall often use the word "**tutor**" to stand for teacher/lecturer/ coach/ tutor/trainer/instructor/author, etc. -- just as I shall use "**learner**" to stand for any kind of student, trainee, or reader engaged in a systematic search for understanding and competence.

I assume that you have some experience as a teacher or trainer. This book is not an introduction to teaching as such. It is a guide to applying what you know of teaching to a new enterprise. All the same, if you are to make your teaching "public" in the form of self-instructional materials, you may find yourself agonizing over aspects of teaching and learning that you have never needed to pay much attention to before.

Who am I?

I have been working in self-instruction for more than 25 years -- writing materials myself, running training workshops for intending writers, editing or rewriting the work of other writers, and helping teachers and trainers rethink their courses in terms of distance learning and other forms of self-instruction and open learning.

Throughout the 1960s, I was concerned with programmed learning. I wrote programmes, and helped others to write them, in a wide variety of topics, some for use in schools and colleges, some in industrial or professional training. My first book (*Basically Branching*, 1966) was actually a forerunner to this one, being a guide to writing programmed learning materials.

Towards the end of the 1960s, like many of my colleagues at the time, I realized that the principles of programmed learning might have wider applications in helping people learn. I put them to use, and extended them, in developing the new approach that became known (unfortunately, I think) as "educational technology".

Since 1970, I have been pursuing that approach in Britain's Open University -- the world-famous pioneer in distance learning in post-secondary education. Here I have been concerned with understanding the processes of teaching and learning through self-instruction in order to develop effective material and systems myself, and help others to do so. The teaching I have been involved with ranges from year-long courses in literature, history or psychology for undergraduates to short packs and courses (15-100 hours of learning time) for family doctors, managers, and social workers.

I have taught in secondary school, teacher-training college, polytechnic and university, and have been a consultant on training to many industrial or public service organizations (from family planning, through coal mining to the Police and Civil Service). So my ideas about self-instruction relate to a wide variety of learning situations. Similarly, my experience with a wide range of subject-matter has assured me that I can give useful advice to a teacher or trainer planning self-instruction, whatever his or her chosen topic.

The Aims and Objectives of this Book

The overall aims of this book are to help you gain sufficient confidence to start producing self-instructional materials and to help improve your ability to teach with such materials.

In terms of specific objectives, I want to help you work towards improvement in the following areas:

- Formulating aims and objectives for whatever materials you plan to produce.

- Identifying the skills, knowledge and expectations that learners will possess before starting upon your materials.

- Being realistic about the constraints within which you and your learners must work.

- Choosing the subject content of your materials and deciding how it might best be sequenced to help the learners learn.

- Selecting appropriate teaching media and deciding how they may be effectively combined.

- Using the media effectively to produce self-instructional teaching from which the learners do learn.

- Devising assessment tests or situations that will give a fair indication of how your learners have developed in competence.

- Evaluating your materials by critical analysis and by trying them out on learners.

- Improving your materials (and the system within which they are used) in the light of evaluation.

This book is meant to raise questions -- questions you will recognize as so important that you must seek out answers that are right for you in your situation. In other words, I am trying to provide a stimulus to your thinking and decision-making -- which is likely to continue developing over a period of several months, or even years. I am not offering a set of hand-me-down, ready-made, all-purpose solutions. There are none.

How to Use this Book

One thing we do know about self-instructional materials is that we can't rely on learners paying attention to suggestions we make under a heading like the one above. Different people use the same material differently.

All I want to do here is assure you that there is no need for you to read the chapters in the order in which I've presented them. Of course, I think that order is reasonably logical, and many readers will be content to start at the beginning and work their way through to the end. But I have taken care to write the later chapters in such a way that you'll be able to follow them even if you have not worked through earlier ones.

So, have a quick skim through the book to see what is dealt with where. (Note particularly the sample pages of self-instructional material in Chapter 5). Then, if you don't feel like following my sequence, feel free to plunge into whichever chapters or sections deal with the issues that concern you most at present. The other chapters can wait until you're ready for them.

The book may also be used as the basis for a series of workshops, under the guidance of someone more experienced in producing self-instructional materials. Or it may serve simply as the common reference point for a group of colleagues learning the art of self-instruction together by discussing common problems and commenting on one another's work. Either way, learn what you can from other people's approaches -- but don't expect any of them to be entirely right for your needs.

> THERE IS NO ONE RIGHT WAY TO DEVELOP
> SELF-INSTRUCTIONAL MATERIALS.
> BUT THERE ARE LOTS OF WRONG WAYS.
> I HOPE THIS BOOK WILL HELP YOU AVOID THEM.

2. ORGANIZING FOR COURSE DEVELOPMENT

To avoid undue discussion here, let's say that a course is a planned sequence of "learning experiences", occupying several learning sessions, and involving some form of assessment of the learner's progress. Thus, a course may occupy the learner for a few hours only or for several months; and the assessment may be done by you (the course developer), by a tutor who may or may not be guided by you, by some external body, or simply by the learner. You may be responsible for producing all of such a course or just for part of it.

WHO IS TO PRODUCE THE COURSE?

Either you will be producing the course on your own or you will be working with one or more colleagues

Individual Authorship

Working on your own may appear to have certain clear advantages, along with a number of disadvantages.

Advantages:

- You will have maximum freedom as to content, treatment, sequence, level, schedule, etc.

- The course is more likely to form a coherent whole, with no obvious gaps or undue repetitions.

- You will not need to use up time in discussions with other authors, or emotional energy in defending your chosen content and method.

- So, you may produce the course in less time than if several people were working together.

- Since you will know the course as a whole you should be better able to adapt and up-date parts of it in response to evaluation.

Disadvantages:

- You may feel exposed and isolated, especially if self-instruction is a new venture in your organization or department.

- You may feel that bias or limitations in your subject-matter knowledge or teaching experience may lead to the course being less effective than you would wish.

- You may feel you lack technical experience in such areas as typography, graphics, or audio-recording.

- You may feel you cannot carry out all the tasks connected with producing the whole course within the time period available.

Perhaps you could overcome some of the disadvantages by obtaining some **informal** help. That is, while retaining full responsibility for the course yourself, you could invite comments and advice -- which you would be free to disregard! -- from other subject-matter experts and educational specialists, or from editors and designers.

You could even commission other authors to produce materials for **your** course, working to a more-or-less precise specification that you have negotiated with them. You may retain the right not to use their material or to edit it as you choose. For some readers of this text, I expect, the boot will be on the other foot. That is, **you** may have been engaged on just such a basis to contribute to someone else's course.

Course Teams

When colleagues join together in a more democratic, equal-status group to produce a course, they form what is generally known as a course team. Course teams were pioneered by the Open University and have become popular elsewhere. A team may include one or more of the people listed below:

- *Convenor/Chair.* Person responsible for overall quality of the course (both in subject-matter content and in educational effectiveness) -- and for getting it produced within a budget. May also be a course author and may have no formal power over other team members.

- *Course authors.* Subject specialists, maybe from more than one department or organization who will be responsible for planning the course, writing texts, devising audio-visual materials or practical exercises, as well as producing assessment and examination materials and perhaps preparing to act as tutors once the course is being used by learners. Some may be seen as part of the "central" or "core" course team, some as "externals", with the latter perhaps having little influence on how the course develops.

- *Media producer.* Professional with special skills in the technical production of video material, audiotape, computer software, etc.

- *Educational technologist/developer.* Professional with a special interest in the improvement of teaching and learning who may be able to give authors disinterested help, as a "critical friend" -- e.g. in clarifying their educational purposes, in choosing appropriate teaching strategies or media, and in improving the course as a result of evaluation.

- *Transformer.* A skilled communicator who can liaise with any subject specialists whose writing is obscure, winkling out their key ideas and re-expressing them in ways the learners will be able to understand.

- *Editor.* Professional who can help authors in polishing their texts, ensure consistency of usage among authors, and prepare final drafts for printing (including copyright clearance).

- *Graphic designer.* Professional who advises authors on layout, typestyle and the overall graphic design of their texts, as well as suggesting how to supplement or even replace text with illustrations and executing whatever illustrations are agreed on.

- *Secretary/co-ordinator.* Administrator who handles day-to-day routine -- arranging meetings, keeping course team members informed between meetings, chasing authors who have missed deadlines, etc. -- leaving the convenor freer to concentrate on the management and quality control of the course.

In deciding whether to set up a course team of the type mentioned above, we again have both potential advantages and potential disadvantages to consider:

Advantages:

- Sharing the work means the course can be produced more quickly.

- Individuals may work faster because they know their colleagues have expectations of them.

- Discussion and mutual criticism can be stimulating and improve the quality of the course.

- Course team members can specialize, to some extent, in those aspects of course production each is best at and/or enjoys most.

- The individual is saved from feeling isolated and alone in facing potential hostility or lack of support from people not concerned with the course.

Unfortunately, course team operation is sometimes ruled out or else spoiled by one or more of the following:

Disadvantages:

- Specialists of the kind listed earlier are not available or the project cannot afford them.

- Course team members may dislike having criticisms, or even suggestions, from colleagues.

- Individuals may waste too much time in personal or ideological dispute and in trying to insist on the course being just as they think it should be.

- Individuals can opt out of unpopular tasks -- e.g. writing assessment materials -- and shrug off responsibility for the course as a whole.

- Individual authors may dislike the pressure of having to negotiate their own roles, contribute to frequent meetings, and abide by majority decisions -- especially those that impose deadlines by which work must be produced.

- It can be difficult to find a convenor with the right management skills to handle such a group, especially when his or her responsibility is unaccompanied by any formal authority.

CO-ORDINATING GROUP ACTIVITY

It is worth noticing that such disadvantages can begin to appear (as can the advantages) even when the "course team" consists of no more than two authors trying to work together as equal partners.

Despite the potential disadvantages of course team operation, many organizations have now found ways of minimizing them, while making the most of the advantages . It is possible to have many hands making light work rather than too many cooks spoiling the broth. Unless you are working entirely on your own, some means needs to be found by which members of the working group (whether democratic equal-status members or not) can co-ordinate their activities:

Decision-making

Numerous decisions have to be made during the development of a course -- e.g. about whether particular content should be included or whether certain materials are of an acceptable standard. Who is to make such decisions? Here are three possibilities:

- The convenor makes decisions on behalf of group.

- Decisions are made by consensus among the group (or certain "core" members of it) after discussion.

- Each member makes decisions about his/her "own" area of the course, taking account of group discussions.

Some types of decision may best be taken by one method, some by another. But the sooner the "ground-rules" are discussed, the less chance is there for bickering and resentment to spring up later.

Another issue: Will the author(s) of each individual section be separately named on the relevant materials? Or will the course team take **collective** responsibility for all sections, with the authorship of individual sections being left unstated?

Communications

How is the course team to communicate with itself? Even if the members of the team are acquainted with each other (and some may not be), they may never have worked together with the intimacy that successful course creation is likely to demand.

So what can be done to ensure that all are on much the same wavelength, sensitive to (if not always sharing) one another's assumptions, values, perspectives, terminology, intentions, and so on? How are they to get to trust and accept one another? How are they to profit from one another's insights and experience? How are they to judge what may realistically be expected from one another?

There are at least two ways of encouraging useful communication -- meetings and documentation:

Meetings. How often can/should the team get together? With what purpose? Some of your meetings may be strictly business occasions -- e.g. brainstorming sessions or discussions of schedules of the first draft of a member's plans or course materials. Some may be professional in a wider sense -- e.g. a seminar, perhaps with outsiders invited, on a topic related to the course, or a visit to a factory, farm or college. Some may be purely social -- e.g. parties, lunches, visits to theatres, concerts or football matches. Some meetings may be a mixture. In fact, any meeting of two or more members of the course may be expected to contribute towards getting the course developed or the team members better acquainted.

Documentation. Groups and committees everywhere are regularly accused of producing too much paperwork. Nevertheless, if more than a couple of people are involved in producing a course, they'd be well advised not to stint on paper. Every important decision -- e.g. about schedules, or intended content, or allocation of tasks -- should be written down and circulated to all members.

Every member should also receive a copy of the "specification", outlining the content and treatment, etc., proposed for each section and, later, a copy of each draft of every member's materials. Even if it has been agreed that not everyone will produce detailed comments on each draft, **all** should see any materials that might influence them in how they'd want to plan their own. In fact, those members who are going to produce detailed comments on a draft might well receive **two** copies. They could then give their annotated copy back to the author, keeping one copy as a reminder.

Allocating Tasks

Try to reach early agreement as to what tasks will need to be performed and how they might be shared out fairly.

Who will do what? Try not to overlook tasks such as:

- writing study guides and assignment questions;
- setting tests and examinations;
- commenting on one another's materials
- briefing other teachers;
- publicizing the course; and so on.

If early decisions are not made, someone is likely to end up doing more than a fair share -- and vital tasks may be neglected until it is too late to do them properly. In particular: Who will be responsible for looking after the course once it is **in operation** -- and making whatever adjustments and improvements may be necessary?

Constraints

Each member of the group needs to know the constraints within which he or she is to work. How much freedom does each one have to determine content and treatment? How much learner-time is each responsible for? Does each one have sufficient time available to spend on the course at all the relevant stages of production?

Does the group have enough resources, especially of author-hours, to produce a course of satisfactory quality? Every hour of learner-time may take 50-100 (or more) hours of course team time to develop.

What teaching media are available? What physical facilities for meetings, laboratory preparation of materials, workshop testing of prototype equipment, etc? Can specialist help be brought in? Is there money available for revising the course (and reprinting) after it has been in use for a while? And so on.

The Production Schedule

Agree on a schedule for production so that individuals know when their contributions are expected. This is especially vital if some authors need to see drafts of another's work before they can proceed with their own. Ensure there is time for each author to have his or her plans and draft materials studied and critically commented upon by **at least** one other member of the group -- and perhaps by experts outside it -- before they are finalized.

Make contingency plans against the possibility that production might slip behind schedule. Are there parts of the course, for instance, that might be jettisoned? Or are there extra resources that might be drawn on, however reluctantly, in an emergency?

It may not be good for group morale, however, to dwell too long on discussing how possible failures might be retrieved. Far better for the group to assure itself that its forward planning is as thorough and realistic as possible, so as to minimize nasty surprises up ahead. For instance, course teams routinely **under**-estimate the amount of time individuals will need to produce acceptable materials. Though it is possible that some of us would be too discouraged to write anything at all if we ever admitted to ourselves at the outset just how long it was really likely to take us!

Figure 2.1 overleaf shows some key events for a typical schedule, and also how individual authors and the full course team might need to interact. Several of the activities shown will be going on at once. For example, few course teams will be able to wait to see and approve **all** first drafts (D1s) before work starts on **any** second drafts (D2s). Thus, a given course team meeting may be discussing a D3 of one section of the course, a D2 of another, and a D1 or even a revised specification of a third. Authors need to know, for each piece of work they are responsible for, where their personal deadlines appear on the overall schedule.

Figure 2.1:   Key Events in a Production Schedule

Full Course Team (CT)   **Individual Authors**

- Decides overall aims, objectives and structure of course.

- Decides which authors are responsible for which sections/tasks.

- Write specifications or outlines, detailing the content and treatment for each section, on basis of earlier CT discussion.

- Discusses specification and agrees changes.

- Write first draft (D1) of each section's materials, incorporating changes agreed by CT.

- Discusses Dls, comparing them with amended specifications and with one another.

- Suggests more changes (probably minor ones).

- Write second drafts incorporating agreed changes.

- Arranges for D2s to be tested by typical learners and critically appraised by outside experts in the subject.

- Discusses D2s in light of learners' feedback and experts' comments.

- Agrees further changes.

- Write third drafts (D3).

- Discusses and approves D3.

- Suggests any "fine tuning" changes.

- Liaise with editor and designer in getting final "handover draft" of materials printed, taped, or otherwise reproduced by the agreed date.

Even the much-simplified example of a schedule in Figure 2.2 below shows that complications can arise when different authors are responsible for different amounts of material -- especially when each may need different amounts of time to produce any given amount of material; and may be completing their drafts in some order different from that in which they will ultimately be studied by the learners.

Figure 2.2:   Part of a Simple Schedule for Course Production

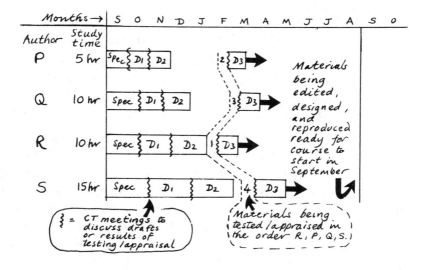

The schedule above, for instance, shows a 40-hour course being produced by four authors, P, Q, R, and S, responsible for, respectively, 5, 10, 10, and 15 hours' worth of learning materials. If all four start together, we see that authors P and Q will, at one point, have a break of two months or more before they can start on their D3s. This is because learners must study Author R's D2 material before theirs, yet it will not be available for testing until some time after theirs. If it were not essential for learners to read the D2s in a set sequence then, of course, P's and Q's material could be tested earlier; they could thus get their D3s completed earlier, so spreading the load on editor, designer and production facilities. As it is, P and Q might be asked to use some of their slack time in giving assistance to S who looks like the most hard-pressed member of the course team.

Needless to say, the sample schedule above does not pretend to illustrate all the problems that can emerge in attempting to draw up such a plan. It is simply meant to show that such scheduling **can** indeed throw up problems and issues about which decisions need to be taken early in our course planning.

COULD YOU ADAPT AN EXISTING COURSE?

In view of the many costs and complexities involved in developing a course from scratch, we are bound to ask this question: Can you take over a course that has **already** been produced by some other institution?

In the past, this has generally been discouraged by the "not-invented-here" response. (If we didn't produce it ourselves, then it can't be any use to our learners!) But financial cutbacks have led many organizations to take a more hospitable view. Someone else's course materials and/or system **may** be suitable for your learners. If so, consider using them. The staff-time you'll save by not producing your own version might better be invested in developing self-instructional courses in worthwhile topics that no-one has yet effectively dealt with.

Figure 2.3 suggests some questions to ask about any existing course you think might be worth adapting to suit your organization. Remember that, even if the course turns out not to be suitable as a whole, **parts** of it may be. (So indeed may existing books, videos, audiotapes, etc., that were not produced with self-instruction in mind at all. I'll say more about building such material into your own courses in Chapter 5.)

Figure 2.3: Questions to Ask About Adapting a Course

- *How suitable?* Are its objectives, methods and outcomes appropriate to our learners?

- *How effective?* Does it achieve satisfactory results?

- *How big?* How much time, staff and resources does it need? How many topics? What range of learners?

- *How complete?* Does it need extra supporting material?

- *How complex?* Is it difficult for teachers and learners to work with?

- *How flexible?* Is there room for teachers and learners to adapt it to their special needs?

- *How different?* Is it sufficiently different from other available approaches -- e.g. in results, methods, costs?

- *How replicable?* Are there any special features -- e.g. unusual teachers or local facilities -- that we could not match?

- *How compatible?* Would it fit in with or interfere with the rest of our existing system?

- *How ready?* Can it be started this month/year?

- *How "samplable"?* Could we give it a trial run and abandon it if unsatisfactory? Or would the decision have to be all-or-nothing -- e.g. if it involved heavy investment in capital equipment?

- *How expensive?* What are the initial costs and the running costs -- both in time and money, and for both the organization and the learners?

- *How comparable?* How does it compare, on all the above factors and any others we think important, with the course we might produce for ourselves?

COURSE MAINTENANCE

Finally, whether you are adapting a course or producing one from scratch, we must come back to a question I mentioned earlier: How will the course be maintained **in use**? In particular, who is to be responsible for its week-by-week operation, once learners have begun studying it? Maybe the full, original course team will still be involved; maybe only one or two of its members -- with or without some new helpers. At all events, the **maintenance** of the course should be planned quite early.

There are plenty of tasks that the "maintenance team" may need to undertake during the life of the course. Here are some of them; you may be able to think of more:

- Supervising the storage and delivery to learners of the course materials.

- Arranging for the production of new copies of the course materials as stocks run low.

- Tutoring, both by correspondence and face-to-face.

- Selecting, training, and backing up the work of other people who are supporting the learners.

- Producing new assessment materials and/or examination papers (together with notes of guidance for assessors) for each run of the course.

- Liaising with people who have an interest in the competences developed by our learners -- e.g. their employers and accrediting bodies.

- Publicizing the course and recruiting learners for it.

- Liaising with other organizations who wish to adopt or adapt the course for their own learners.

- Dealing with problems and queries raised by learners (and perhaps by tutors or mentors) concerning difficulties they are having with the course.

- Providing learners with a statement that they have worked through the course -- e.g. a "letter of course completion"; or with an indication of their level of achievement -- e.g. an examination grade or a list of the competences they have demonstrated.

- Evaluating the effects and effectiveness of the course, both by continuous monitoring and by occasional special studies -- e.g. of learning habits or of drop-out.

- Making minor improvements to the course, in the light of evaluation and changing circumstances, for the benefit of current learners -- e.g. by giving them details of current events or issues relevant to the course, and by correcting errors in the materials.

- Identifying areas of the course where more substantial improvements might be made for the benefit of future learners.

- Maintaining records concerning the operation of the course.

AGREE ON COURSE TEAM ROUTINES AND

RESPONSIBILITIES AS **EARLY** AS POSSIBLE

-- BEFORE IT IS TOO LATE.

3. PLANNING YOUR TEACHING -- LEARNERS AND CONTENT

As we know, self-instruction differs from conventional instruction in a variety of ways. Three of the most significant, from the **teacher's** point of view, are:

- *The need to "teach in one's hand"* -- to **anticipate** how future learners one may never meet might come to terms with the subject, and so write down in advance all the necessary explanations and encouragements that one would be giving almost unconsciously if one were working with them face to face.

- *The "public" nature of the teaching.* What may have formerly been a private, transient communication between teacher and learners, behind a closed classroom door, is now to be embodied, recorded and "published" as a package of materials which colleagues (and rivals) as well as learners can peruse and evaluate.

- *The relative inflexibility of self-instruction.* That is, once the materials have been developed and committed to paper or tape or computer tape, it may be prohibitively costly, in time and money, to change them or substitute others for them in response to unexpected needs and difficulties among the learners.

If we are working with colleagues, there is an additional factor -- our plans and decisions must be made **explicit.**

A FRAMEWORK FOR PLANNING

These factors seem to press us towards one inevitable aim -- that of making sure our materials are as effective as humanly possible before we finalize them. That, in turn, depends not only on teaching experience and imagination but also on open and thoughtful planning. I suggest a systematic framework for course planning that revolves around four inter-connected aspects. These are shown in Figure 3.1 below:

Figure 3.1: Four Aspects of Systematic Planning

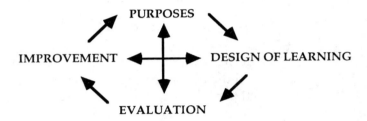

In planning any self-instructional teaching -- whether a long course or a brief package -- all four aspects must be given proper attention. We can begin our planning with any one of them. For instance, a new course may arise out of the evaluation of a previous one. But we cannot think about any one of the four aspects for long without needing to ask how the other three might be affected. The four aspects can be presented as four questions:

1. What are we trying to accomplish with this teaching?

2. What activities must we get learners to engage in if we are to accomplish this satisfactorily?

3. How shall we evaluate the effects and effectiveness of the course or package we have produced?

4. In the light of evaluation, how can we improve the teaching and learning, e.g. by modifying 1, 2 or 3?

KEEP ALL FOUR QUESTIONS IN MIND BEFORE, DURING AND AFTER PRODUCING YOUR TEACHING MATERIALS.

Courses and Lessons

Now I must introduce a new piece of terminology. The four questions we've just looked at are equally relevant whether you are planning a course that will occupy the learner for months, or sizeable sections within such a course, or as little as an hour's worth of learning (which may or may not be part of a package or a lengthy course).

Whatever the size of course or package you are planning, it may help you to think in terms of what I shall call **lessons**. By this, I mean the minimum amount of material that provides for a self-contained and coherent chunk of learning. I would usually plan for such "lessons" to occupy the average learner for about **one hour**.

Each lesson would then represent the minimum amount of material a learner might usefully tackle at a single study session. This notion is useful both to learners in scheduling their learning sessions and to the developers of materials in planning their teaching. You may prefer a term like "session" or "unit" to indicate your smallest building brick of self-instruction -- but here I use the term "lesson" because we all, whether in education or training, have an immediate image of the kind of time-span and coherence of learning implied by the term.

Subject- v Learner-oriented Approaches

Teachers differ in how they like to approach the planning of their teaching. To some extent, their habitual approach depends on whether they think chiefly of their **subject-matter** or chiefly of the **learners**. Figure 3.2 below presents two lists of ways you might start planning. One is largely subject-oriented, the other learner-oriented. Neither list is exhaustive.

Figure 3.2:   Two Sets of Approaches to Planning

SUBJECT-ORIENTED

- Study any relevant examination syllabus and question papers from previous years.

- Review your own knowledge of the proposed subject.

- Discuss it (e.g. by interviewing or by brainstorming) with other subject experts.

- Analyse similar courses elsewhere.

- Read textbooks pitched at what you regard as the appropriate level.

- Read more advanced books and articles on the subject.

- Review films, television and audiotapes, articles in newspapers and popular journals.

- Select books (or other source materials) around which the teaching will be organized.

- Identify and analyse the key concepts of the subject.

LEARNER-ORIENTED

- Establish and analyse the aims and learning objectives.

- Ask prospective learners what topics or competences they would like to tackle.

- Discuss with prospective learners their existing knowledge and experience of the subject area.

- Think of learning activities that learners logically must, or just usefully could, engage in.

- Analyse the knowledge, skills and attitudes displayed by "master performers" (or just very competent performers) in your field.

- Recall where people have previously had learning difficulties, or fallen into error, in the subject.

- Consider how learners' attainments as a result of the course or lesson might sensibly be assessed.

- Study other people's reports of learners' work on related courses in previous years.

FOR EFFECTIVE PLANNING, YOU WILL PROBABLY NEED TO TRY AT LEAST SOME APPROACHES FROM **BOTH** LISTS.

Seven Major Questions

There are at least seven major questions we need to ask in planning a self-instructional course or lesson:

1. Who will be the learners?
2. What are the aims and objectives?
3. What will be the subject-content?
4. How will the content be sequenced?
5. What teaching methods and media will be used?
6. How will learners be assessed?
7. How will the course or lesson be evaluated with a view to improvement?

These questions will all be looked at in this chapter or the next. However, as you may have noticed from the book's contents pages, questions 5, 6 and 7 are discussed at greater length later, in Chapters 11, 13 and 14.

WHO WILL BE THE LEARNERS?

What do you know about the learners who will be studying your course? What do you need to know? Are you developing materials and a system that will cope with whatever variety of learners happen to be attracted? Or do you have to produce comparatively inflexible materials -- e.g. to fit the requirements of a particular examining body -- and then recruit only those learners who can be expected to cope with the demands of your system?

To some extent, most courses can be flexible; to some extent, all learners must do some coping. If you wish to emphasize flexibility, you may need to build in alternative content or treatment to suit individual differences. If you need to rely on coping, you will need to think of **selection tests** -- what competences do learners need **before** they can begin on your materials?

There are four types of information you might need about your prospective learners:

Demographic.   How many of them? What age range? Both sexes? Marital status? Employed? What occupations?   Home area? etc.

Motivation. Why are they going to take your course? How is it related to their work? Why choose **self-**instruction? What do they want to get from the course? What are their hopes and fears? etc.

Learning factors.   How intelligent and capable are they as learners? Have they had prior experience with self-instruction and especially, if appropriate, with learning "at a distance"? Prior level of general educational attainment? Attainment in whatever abilities will be needed in coping with your teaching? Do they have adequate time and facilities available for study? etc.

Subject background.   What knowledge, skills and attitudes do they already have regarding the subject of your course? Do they have personal interests and experiences that are relevant? (Such information may help you decide on ways into the subject and may provide you with useful anecdotes, examples and analogies.)

Needless to say, by the above criteria, your learners may well be a very mixed bunch -- especially if they are adults. All the same, it is worth trying to write a "thumbnail sketch" of your typical learner. Better still if you can get a colleague to do so also, and compare notes. Figure 3.3 opposite is an example of such a thumbnail sketch of the typical learner on a business management course for farmers and horticulturalists. To have in mind such a picture of your typical learner may be useful -- but only up to a point (e.g. your writing would need to recognize that **some** of the farmers may be women).

Figure 3.3: Thumbnail Sketch of "Typical" Learner

The typical learner runs a small farm or market garden. He is male, between 30 and 40 years of age, and is married with one or two children living at home. He left school at 16 with a few examination certificates and has done no systematic studying since. His most regular reading will be at *Daily Mail* level.

He will not be worried about the cost of books or travelling to course meetings and will be ready to obtain playback machines for audio- and video-cassettes if he does not have them already. However, he is unwilling to commit himself to attending even occasional class meetings at a fixed time (because of the unpredictable demands of his work); and, in fact, this is why he is choosing a distance learning course.

He is enrolling for the course in hope of improving his efficiency and profitability and avoiding hassle from his bank manager, accountant and tax inspector. He will be perfectly capable of learning on his own, provided the materials are flexible enough for him to find his own level and he is allowed fairly ready access (at least by telephone) to a tutor or other learners if he gets into difficulties. The tutor will need to be scrupulous in providing support rather than criticism.

Needless to say, the learner is very familiar with the subject-matter of the course; he will be scathing about anything he regards as "unrealistic" in our examples or suggestions, and will not stick with the course unless it remains clearly relevant to what he perceives as his needs.

Finding Out

With self-instructional courses and packages, especially when learners are studying at a distance, we need to obtain information about them **before** they begin. Otherwise it cannot affect the teaching as much as it

Figure 3.4:   Questionnaire for Prospective Learners

Questionnaire (Put a tick in the box alongside each answer you choose)

1. **What is your sex?**
    (a) Male
    (b) Female

2. **How old are you?**
    (a) Less than 20
    (b) 20-25
    (c) 25-30
    (d) 30-40
    (e) 40-50
    (f) Over 50

3. **Why do you want to take this course?**
    (a) Because you think it will be interesting
    (b) Because you want to be able to plan better meals for yourself or your family
    (c) Because you want to be able to help or supervise other people who plan meals but without wanting some professional qualification
    (d) Because you want to get some sort of professional qualification in dietetics
    (e) Because you have been told to by your employer or a teacher
    (f) Because it completes your timetable of courses for a qualification not primarily in dietetics
    (g) Some other reason (please specify)

4. **What is the most important reason for wanting people to eat a reasonably balanced diet?**
    (a) To make sure they get enough to eat
    (b) To make sure they get the right sort of food
    (c) To keep them healthy
    (d) To make sure that the food is appetising
    (e) To ensure variety in meals
    (f) To make sure their bodies get enough of each of their requirements
    (g) To avoid waste of food and unnecessary expense

5. **Do you think your own present diet is adequately balanced?**
    (a) Yes
    (b) No
    (c) Don't know

6. **Do you think it is important to be able to judge how well a diet is balanced?**
    (a) Yes
    (b) No
    (c) Don't know

7. **Have you ever planned and prepared a meal for others?**
    (a) Yes, regularly
    (b) Yes, occasionally
    (c) No – only part of a meal
    (d) No – only helped others to do so
    (e) No – only watched others do so
    (f) No – never

8. **Which of the following have you studied in the last three years?**
    (Tick as many as apply)
    (a) Cookery
    (b) Elementary biology
    (c) Elementary physics and/or chemistry
    (d) Basic arithmetic
    (e) Elementary statistics
    (Write in any examinations you have passed in any of these subjects and the year you passed them.)

9. **How many different classes of nutrient are found in food?**
    (a) 1   (b) 2   (c) 3
    (d) 4   (e) 5   (f) 6
    (g) 7   (h) More than 7

Here is a list of terms used in connection with nutrition.
(Put the appropriate letters in the boxes below.)

A	Ascorbic Acid	G	Fibre	M	Obesity
B	Beri-beri	H	Iron	N	Pellagra
C	Brassica	I	Kwashiorkor	O	Protein
D	Carbohydrate	J	Methionine	P	Scurvy
E	Energy	K	Mineral	Q	Tryptophan
F	Fat	L	Nicotonic acid	R	Vitamin
				S	Water

Questions 10-14

10. Which of the above constitute major classes of nutrient?

11. Which of the above are names of diseases caused by a deficiency of some ingredient in food?

12. Which of the above are major sources of energy?

13. Which of the above, apart from 'vitamin' itself, are either vitamins, sources of vitamins, or are associated with vitamin deficiency?

14. Which of the above, apart from 'protein' itself, would you associate directly with protein or protein deficiency?

should. There are three main ways of building up a picture of your prospective learners:

- Rely on your previous experience of those learners, or broadly similar ones, or on that of colleagues.

- Meet some of the prospective learners and discuss with them (individually or as a group) what you have in mind to teach, and what they already know/feel about the subject and what they would like from the course.

- Send a questionnaire to prospective learners, trying to elicit the information you need. If this can be followed up by discussion with learners, whether face-to-face or on the telephone, so much the better.

Figure 3.4 shows a sample questionnaire compiled by a colleague of mine, Roger Harrison, for a distance learning course on Diet and Nutrition. He has since spotted certain weaknesses -- e.g. the possibility that too many "technical" questions, like 9-14, might scare off some potential learners, especially if they got the impression that the implied knowledge were being expected as an entry requirement. The purpose of the questioning could, however, be made clear in an accompanying letter.

> DON'T USE A QUESTIONNAIRE IN EARNEST
> UNTIL YOU'VE TRIED OUT A **PILOT** VERSION.

WHAT AIMS AND OBJECTIVES?

It is useful to start thinking about aims and objectives as early as possible in the process of planning a course or an individual lesson within it. The difference between aims and objectives is as follows:

Aims. -- a general statement of what you hope the course (or lesson) will achieve, perhaps expressed in terms of what you, the teacher, will be presenting to the learner.

Objectives. -- a statement of what learners should be able to **do** or do **better** as a result of having worked through the course (or lesson).

Examples

Aims (from different courses/lessons):

- To explain the concept and importance of energy; to provide practice in carrying out surveys and experiments relating to energy studies; to encourage a sense of concern about the depletion of fossil fuel reserves; and to give guidance on the planning of an energy policy.

- To introduce the learner to healthy eating habits.

- To foster an appreciation of the novels of D.H.Lawrence.

Objectives. (Note: It is customary to preface a list of objectives with some such phrase as "By the end of this course/lesson, learners should be able to, or have improved in their ability to...").

- 1. List the various forms of energy.
  2. Describe how one form may be converted into another.
  3. Distinguish between energy and power.
  4. Identify the chief energy flows in a given situation.
  5. etc...

- 1. List the principal components of a balanced diet and describe the function of each in the body.
  2. Name six diseases caused by inadequate or unbalanced diet.
  3. Calculate the amounts of energy, protein, certain vitamins, and calcium and iron in a given diet, using tables of food composition.
  4. etc...

- 1. Relate Lawrence's viewpoint to his or her own experiences.
  2. Analyse the literary elements that have provoked his/her involvement.
  3. Make and justify a personal statement as to Lawrence's "meanings".
  4. Seek out and read more of Lawrence's writings than are set for assignments.
  5. etc...

Look also at the aims and objectives for the book you are reading now (pages 15 and 16).

Writing Objectives

In writing objectives we are trying to indicate what successful learners should be able to **do** (or say) to **demonstrate** that they have learned. So it is better to avoid introducing objectives with words like those on the left below. (They hint at non-observable states of mind.) Instead, begin an objective with a verb like those on the right below:

AVOID words like:	**USE** words like:
know...	state...
understand...	describe...
really know...	explain...
really understand...	list...
be familiar with...	evaluate...
become acquainted with ...	pick out...
have a good grasp of...	distinguish between...
appreciate...	analyse...
be interested in...	summarize...
acquire a feeling for...	show diagrammatically...
be aware of...	compare...
believe...	apply...
have information about...	assess...
realize the significance of...	suggest reasons why...
learn the basics of...	give examples of...
obtain working knowledge of...	carry out...
believe in...	demonstrate...
etc...	etc...

Types of Objectives

Objectives can be classified in many different ways. I find it most useful to do so on the basis of the kind of benefit that learners are expected to get from a course or lesson:

* ***Knowledge.*** How do you want learners to demonstrate the knowledge they have gained from the course/lesson? -- e.g. *"The learner should be able to explain the significance of 'half-life' in the prescribing of drugs"*.

* ***Skills.*** How would you wish learners to be able to demonstrate their ability to apply their knowledge of the subject-matter? -- e.g. *"The learner should be able to diagnose the patient's ailment"*. Skills can be intellectual, physical, or social (or a mixture).

* ***Attitude.*** What attitudes or beliefs or dispositions would you wish the learner to develop in respect of the subject of the course/session? -- e.g. *"The learner should show a desire to find out how the patient feels about the illness and the treatment proposed"*.

Note that many objectives may combine two or all three of the aspects listed above.

The Value of Objectives

Don't expect to be able to finalize your objectives before you start writing your course materials. (Unless they have been given to you ready-made by someone else.) But I would recommend you to start thinking about them as early as possible and expect to revise them from time to time as your planning proceeds. This should help you in four main ways:

Communication. Objectives can help make clear your educational intentions -- to yourself, to colleagues and, eventually, to the learners.

Content and sequence. Thinking out objectives can help you to distinguish between possible and essential content and to identify ways of sequencing it.

Media and methods. An awareness of your objectives can help you decide on the most appropriate teaching media and the most appropriate learning activities.

Assessment and evaluation. Objectives can help you decide on suitable ways of testing what learners have gained from the course/lesson and of evaluating the effects and effectiveness of your materials.

Course v Lesson Objectives

Once you know your objectives for the course as a whole, you will need to know how they relate to the objectives for individual lessons. Learners will be expected to achieve some objectives as a result of a particular lesson -- e.g. *"learn to distinguish between ridges and valleys on a contour map"*. Others they will be expected to get better and better at, lesson by lesson -- e.g. *"learn to visualize the physical features of an unknown region from a topographical map"*.

So, lesson objectives can be arrived at by asking:

- Which of the course objectives will be **fully attained** during this lesson? and

- Which of the course objectives (or which aspects of which) will learners **improve** their ability in during this lesson?

WRITING OBJECTIVES IS MEANT TO HELP YOU PLAN YOUR TEACHING. WHETHER YOU MIGHT LATER WANT TO SHOW THEM TO LEARNERS IS A SEPARATE ISSUE.

DECIDING ON CONTENT

What are the main topics, concepts and principles to be covered in your course/lesson? Many thoughts about content will arise in the process of thinking about objectives. Some of the other approaches already listed in Figure 3.2 (page 38) should also be a rich source of ideas. Two further approaches may be useful -- concept analysis and diagramming.

Concept Analysis

Concepts are the basic elements of our teaching. In various combinations they make up the "main ideas" we'll be trying to teach in our lessons. Even within this chapter I have already touched on concepts such as "motivation", "objectives", "assessment", and "media".

We need to be alert to the kinds of difficulties and confusions that attach to the concepts we plan to teach. One way of thinking about these is to apply some of the techniques of concept analysis. I have space here only to mention them; but the list below should be reasonably suggestive:

- *Isolate the concepts* -- from the facts, principles, examples, etc., of our subject-matter.

- *Define each concept* -- dictionary-type definitions to begin with, perhaps.

- *Examine model examples* -- to sharpen the definition by deciding which features of the examples are essential to the concept by identifying features that would negate it.

- *Examine border-line examples* -- to clarify our understanding of the crucial features of the concept by considering cases where it "almost" applies or applies only "in a way".

- *Consider invented examples* -- testing the concept by inventing imaginary cases that might really stretch the features we have identified for the concept.

- *Compare social contexts* -- to consider the extent to which people from different places and/or/ times might disagree with our examples and non-examples.

- *Compare personal contexts* -- in recognition that the concept will have different personal associations for different individuals (which may or may not hinder communication).

- *Examine related concepts* -- studying one concept leads us to see how it fits into the surrounding network of concepts.

- *Elucidate the principles* -- concepts are related to other concepts in the form of principles (rules, theorems, axioms, laws, generalizations, statements) which constitute the "message(s)" of the subject-matter and give rise to the "teaching points".

There is, of course, no need to work through all of these techniques with every concept in your course. Life is too short. Usually a concept will be clarified sufficiently for teaching purposes after you have been through three or four of them. But all are at hand for the main concepts that are to underpin your course -- like "self-instruction" and "activities" in this book.

Diagramming Your Subject-matter

Many teachers find they can best get to grips with their course content by drawing a picture of it. Of the many possible forms of course diagram we might discuss, I have picked out just five that I have found particularly useful:

Spray diagram. To draw this widely-used form of diagram, we start with the name of a topic from our course or lesson and write it at the centre of a sheet of paper or chalkboard. Then we spray out lines from the centre -- one for each aspect of the topic that occurs to us. These lines will then be branched to illustrate sub-aspects, and so on. Figure 3.5 is a spray diagram showing relationships among the ideas in a book chapter whose content is listed in Figure 4.4 (on page 71).

Figure 3.5:   A Spray Diagram (based on *Learn How to Study* by D. Rowntree, Macdonalds, 1976)

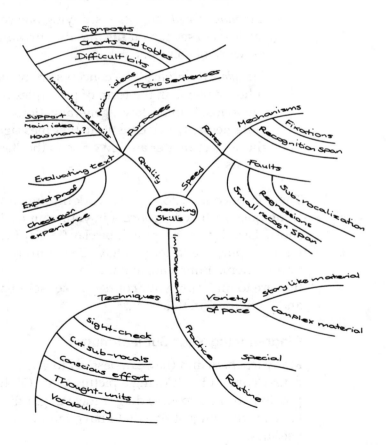

Concept map. A similar, but looser form of diagram is produced when we simply start with the name of a key topic or concept (e.g. "educational technology") and draw lines from it to a number of related concepts. Then we write in the names of concepts related to these and join them up with lines also. Figure 3.6 is such a concept map of the field of educational technology as seen by my colleague, David Hawkridge.

Figure 3.6:   A Concept Map of Educational Technology (from D. Hawkridge, *British Journal of Educational Technology*, 12, 1, Jan 1981, pp. 4-18.

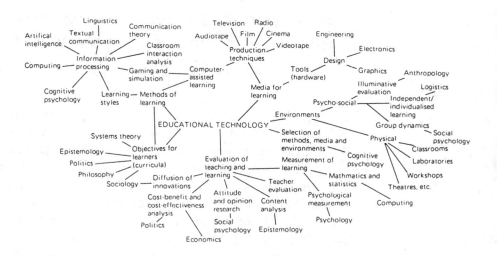

In this kind of diagram, as David Hawkridge says: "lines connect words, reflecting connections of some kind without revealing exactly what. Moreover, many other lines could be added to show additional connections".

Furthermore, he points out that the map of educational technology "could be drawn differently...by other educational technologists". I bring your attention to this perhaps obvious remark because many people setting out to draw a concept map seem to get obsessed with uncovering the "true, underlying structure" of the subject.

Even if such a structure exists, there is no need for that degree of dedication. Drawing such diagrams is a personal and subjective activity. Its purpose is simply to help you sort out your own understanding about how the concepts within your field connect up. So long as you find it helpful in your own course planning, there is no need to worry that others might have mapped the territory differently.

AS WITH OBJECTIVES, YOU MAY OR MAY NOT WISH TO DISCUSS YOUR DIAGRAMS WITH YOUR LEARNERS.

Figure 3.7 shows the first sketch of a concept map I drew up for a course on diet and nutrition. I started with "Food" in the middle and then began to identify chains of connected concepts. I put down the ideas more or less as they came to mind, without wondering too much about whether all would be needed in the eventual course, or what else might be needed in addition. Again, I drew lines wherever there seemed to be a connection, of whatever kind -- though the broken lines indicate links I was less sure about than others.

I admit, of course, that other people would map the field differently. But so might I on another occasion. The fact is, the diagramming served its purpose, at the time, as a course planning device. It enabled me to see my way around the field **as I perceived it.**

Figure 3.7: Initial Concept Map for a Course on Diet and Nutrition

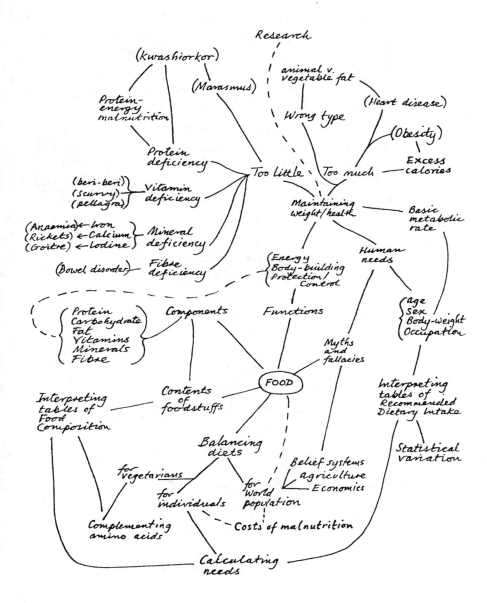

Statement network. Sometimes a much more structured diagram may emerge from this kind of process. Figure 3.8 is a well-developed network showing the relationships between climatic factors and the growth of trees. In this case, arrows link causes with effects. The column of double arrows down the centre indicates the primary chain of causation. To the right of it are factors affecting food storage, while the direct effects of growing-season climate on growth are to the left of it.

This chart can be seen to incorporate principles -- that is **statements** involving the concepts -- as well as the concepts themselves. For example, "Less root growth causes less water absorption" or "Rapid evaporation and low soil moisture lead to increased water stress in the tree".

Figure 3.8:   A Cause-Effect Network for Tree-ring Growth

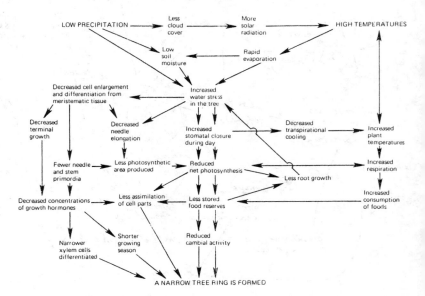

Algorithms. This is another form of diagram in which the arrows express very explicit connections between ideas. Such a diagram can be invaluable in sorting out a subject-area in which the emphasis is on classifying cases or examples, or deciding what action to take, on the basis of a number of yes/no decisions as to whether each of a limited number of characteristics applies in a particular case.

For instance, if you want to classify a soil specimen as loam, clay, sand, or whatever, you'll need to notice what combination of attributes it possesses from among such attributes as grittiness, silkiness, and resistance to deformation. (See Figure 9.4 on page 186 for an algorithm that deals with this task.) Similarly, diagnosing patients' ailments may depend on which combination each patient presents from a range of standard signs and symptoms. Figure 3.9 overleaf shows part of an algorithm concerned with the diagnosis of blood-vessel disorders in patients whose limbs have turned an unusual colour.

Working out an algorithm is a useful way of exploring subject-matter that can be boiled down to Yes-No decision-making. Such charts are useful not only as course planning devices; they may also be used as part of the teaching.

Indeed, you may sometimes decide to provide an algorithm **instead** of teaching. Why teach in advance a procedure that is used so rarely that learners are likely to have forgotten it before it is next needed -- especially if it can easily be "looked up" when it is needed? Better perhaps to provide them with a job-aid in the form of an algorithm.

Figure 3.9:   Part of a Medical Diagnosis Algorithm

(Redrawn from Lewis and Woolfenden, *Algorithms and Logical Trees,* Algorithms Press, 1969)

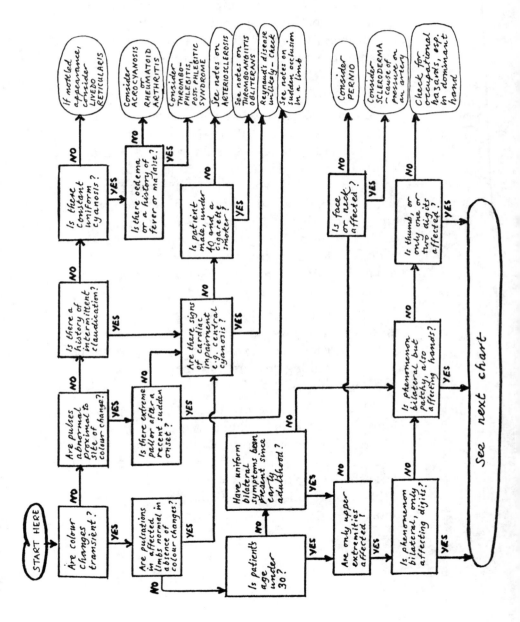

Matrix. This is the final form of diagram I want to mention here. A matrix may suggest itself when you are dealing with a body of knowledge that can be classified and discussed with more than one set of categories in mind. For example, in planning a course for school governors, I found the following matrix was useful:

Figure 3.10:   **Part of a Matrix for a Course for School Governors**

LEVEL of concern

	School	Local	National
Curriculum			
Staffing			
Pupils			
Organization			
Resources & Finance			
Community			

TYPE of concern

This matrix helped the course team be systematic in asking what are the **school** aspects, the **local** aspects, and the **national** aspects of each of the six topics: "curriculum", "staffing", "pupils", and so on. (In fact, we had a third categorization to juggle with also -- how do governors of "voluntary" schools differ from those of "county" schools in all of those concerns? -- but I have refrained from turning the matrix into a 3-dimensional block.) For an example of a filled-out matrix, depicting a complete course, see Figure 8.1 on page 166.

A final caution. As you will appreciate, a great variety
of diagrams can be drawn to represent a subject area.
There are many other kinds of diagram I could have
shown; indeed, there are others we must look at later in
the chapter. Furthermore, you may well have your own
ways of diagramming that are more suited to your
particular purposes.

Like any tool in educational planning -- like
schedules and objectives, for instance -- diagrams can be
a useful servant or a dangerous master. Their purpose is
to help you generate ideas. If some form of diagramming
seems helpful on a particular project, then use it. If
different forms seem suitable for different parts or
phases (e.g. matrix followed by concept maps) then use
more than one. But don't let the diagrams dictate to you.

For example, the matrix in Figure 3.10 gives
eighteen possible categories of course content to think
about. It would be dangerous, however, to assume that
every cell of the matrix must necessarily have something
in it. Some cells may be empty and some may be
considerably fuller than others. Nor should we allow the
neat boxes of the matrix to blind us to the possibility that
some important topics may lie outside its boundaries or
even be obscured by this quite powerful way of carving up
the conceptual territory.

Finally, remember it is the **process** of drawing such
diagrams that is meant to be helpful, rather than the final
product. It may be, on occasion, that your diagrams will
be so revealing of the structure of your subject (as with an
algorithm, for instance) that you will want to share them
with your learners. On the other hand, you may think it
more to the point to help your learners develop their own
pictures of the subject-matter.

Enough is Enough

However you decide on the possible content of your course, **don't overload it**. Too many self-instructional courses contain far more content than learners can possibly cope with in the time available. And nothing causes them more dismay, especially if they are working "at a distance". Unlike on-site learners, they cannot easily pick up hints from you or from fellow-learners as to which bits of the content can safely be ignored when time presses. Under stress, their learning may become superficial, or they may drop out altogether.

So, don't feel obliged to include everything you happen to know about the subject area, however much that might amaze your friends and affright your enemies. Tell your learners what they need to know to attain acceptable learning objectives, and no more than that. Given such a solid foundation, they will then be able to seek out any further content they feel they need, under their own steam and in their own time.

> IT MAY BE BETTER FOR LEARNERS TO
> FULLY UNDERSTAND **HALF** THE CONTENT
> YOU WOULD IDEALLY LIKE TO INCLUDE
> THAN TO HALF UNDERSTAND ALL OF IT.

Learners' Own Content

Finally, before we leave the subject, it is worth noting that some self-instructional courses require learners to decide **their own** content -- at least for some portion of their time on the course. Thus, for example, after several packaged lessons in a poetry course, learners might be asked to gear their next week's work to preparing an essay on a poet of their own choice.

Taken further -- perhaps involving practical work -- such a learning task may be called a **project**. Here, instead of working through course materials, learners will be guided in some kind of investigation of their own. They may, for example, carry out a noise survey in a factory or document the history of a local building. Such a topic would need to be agreed with a tutor or mentor, who would also advise on useful approaches and sources and would eventually comment on the results.

This kind of course would save money on preparing and producing teaching materials; but extra might need to be spent on providing human support to learners. How far the approach might be justified would depend on the nature of your objectives and on the degree to which your learners are able and willing to take responsibility for what and how they learn.

Finally, the potential learners you talk to before writing your package (see page 43) can often provide you with invaluable content. Especially if you are writing a job-related lesson, their anecdotes about experiences in that job can be used directly as illustrative examples and as case studies for discussion.

These last few paragraphs serve to highlight two questions that reflect back on the whole of this chapter:

WHAT DO YOU ALREADY KNOW ABOUT YOUR LEARNERS? AND WHAT DO YOU STILL NEED TO FIND OUT?

4. PLANNING YOUR TEACHING
-- SEQUENCE AND METHODS

Having identified your learners and thought about aims and objectives and content, you still have four questions to consider at the planning stage:

- How will the content be sequenced?
- What teaching methods and media will be used?
- How will learners be assessed?
- How will the teaching be evaluated and improved?

We shall look at all four questions in this chapter; and all but the first will be explored further in later chapters.

SEQUENCING THE LEARNING

Once you've got some notion of possible content, you need to think about sequencing it. How might the ideas best be ordered within your course or lesson? How do you identify a sensible teaching sequence? To the best of your ability, you must ensure that the ideas your learners meet early in the teaching are those that will help -- or at least not interfere with -- their later learning.

Your problem here is akin to that of many novelists or playwrights at a similar stage of their writing. Like them, you need some kind of vision of your course or lesson **as a whole**. What you are looking for is the equivalent of "narrative drive" or **storyline** -- a broad flow of ideas, sufficiently coherent for you to be able to begin writing with some confidence about where you are heading -- but not so rigid a framework that it prevents your material from developing in useful but unforeseen directions once you've got going.

It may help, when trying to envisage your storyline, to be aware of some of the kinds of sequence that I have noticed in self-instructional materials:

Varieties of Sequence

Here are some of the possible types of sequence that may
be needed within your course. More than one type will
usually be evident within any one course, and sometimes
within one lesson.

Topic-by-topic. This approach involves the study of a
number of related themes or topics which (after an initial
introduction to the overall purpose of the course) could
have been studied in **any** order. **Within** the lesson(s) on
each topic, however, other types of sequencing would
probably be needed.

Chronological sequence. In such a sequence,
happenings, events, or discoveries over a period of time
are presented in the order in which they occurred.
Chronological sequence may be necessary in dealing with
the development of groups or institutions, or of economic
or social theories, or of scientific discoveries -- wherever
understanding of one event or of one stage depends on
the understanding of what had occurred previously. I
have recently used chronological sequence in writing
lessons about a staff appraisal system. Here, the
sequence followed that of the separate activities that
managers and staff engage in at intervals over the
"reporting year".

Place-to-place. This is the spatial equivalent of
chronological order. Start talking about one place , and
work your way from place to adjacent place. In writing
about ailments of the human body, for example, you
might start with the head and work down to the toes.

Concentric circles. This is a variant on place-to-place
in which one "place" is included in the next, and that in
another, and so on. For instance, colleagues and I

developed a management course in which the sequence of the blocks was as follows:

1. You as a manager.
2. You and your team.
3. Your team within the organization.
4. Your organization within the wider world.

Beginning with the basic techniques required of a manager, the course goes on to discuss how these need to be blended with interpersonal issues in co-ordinating the activities of the members of the manager's team. Then on to how the work of the team is affected by the structure and culture of the organization. And finally to how the work of the organization is affected by social, legal and economic changes in the outside world.

Causal sequence. This kind of sequence is also closely related to the chronological. Learning based on a causal sequence will follow a chain of cause-and-effect for an event or phenomenon -- so that when learners reach the end of the chain they can explain the final effect, the event or phenomenon itself. It applies where you are teaching cause-and-effect relationships -- especially if your objective is that the learners should be able to work out and explain such a relationship.

This kind of sequencing might be relevant in meteorology or in geomorphology, where the learner is exploring the cause-and-effect relationships that result in different weather patterns or in different landscape formations. You might use a diagram like that shown in Figure 3.8 (page 54) to trace the possible causal chains.

Structural logic. Here we are talking about a sequence dictated by the logical structure of the subject. Sometimes it is clear that a certain topic cannot be learned without prior understanding of some other topic.

For instance, in basic arithmetic, the idea of multiplication will not make sense unless you have already learned addition. And in order to carry out division you need first to be able to subtract.

Most subjects have a certain amount of "structural logic" in them -- either in the connnection between one major topic and the next or at least **within** such topics. Conversely, what we often take to be "the" inner logic of a subject is sometimes nothing more sacred than the order in which we once happened to have learned it ourselves!

Problem-centred sequence. You may sometimes be able to structure a course, or lessons within it, around the exploration of an issue or problem. If you present your learners with a problem and then engage them in developing solutions or interpretations, you may be providing them with a realistic context in which to learn the essential knowledge and skills of the subject.

For instance, an in-service course for family doctors might focus on the problem of *"What do patients really want from doctors?"* A technology course on the properties of materials might have a section based on the problem *"What is the most suitable material from which to mass-produce car bodies?"*

Spiral sequence. In this kind of sequence, learners will meet a concept again and again during their progress through the course -- each time at a more complex or demanding level. This may appeal to you if your subject is of a kind where learners cannot get deeply into any one topic or concept unless they already have **some** familiarity with most of the others. Thus you may decide to give your learner a brief tour of the main conceptual landmarks before coming to examine them closely and, later still, going on to analyse them in yet greater depth.

At each new level, the learner will treat the concepts in more sophisticated ways, relating them to a growing network of more recently acquired understandings.

An example from elementary physics: The concept of "force" might first be introduced as "push" or "pull"; then discussed in terms of acceleration, using graphs; and, later on, it might be represented symbolically.

Backward chaining. Whenever objectives involve the learning of sequences (or "chains") of activity or decision-making -- whether simple chains (like tying a knot) or complex (like applying a problem-solving routine), it may be useful to teach the **final** step in the chain first. You might then teach the second to last step, and so on.

For example, you might teach your learners to interpret the results of a chemical test before you teach them how to carry out such a test. And you might then teach them to do such tests (which they can already interpret) before teaching them how to select the appropriate test. Figure 4.1 below shows how such a sequence would work with a chain of five steps:

Figure 4.1: Sequencing a Five-step Chain

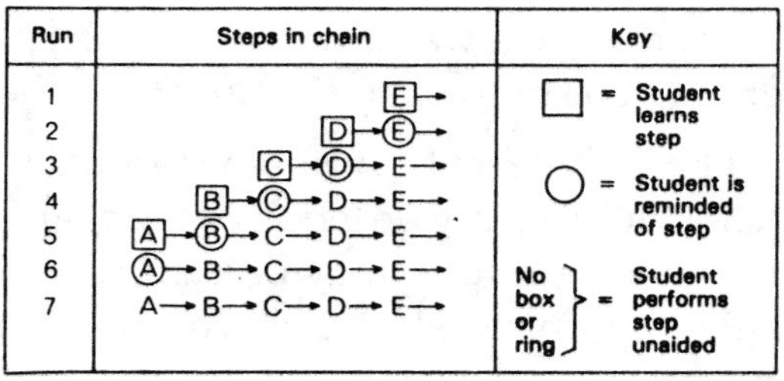

Such backward chaining offers an unusual advantage -- it can provide your learners with the satisfaction of mastering the final stages of the job at the outset of instruction. This can also help motivate their further learning because they now see the relevance of each new step they then need to learn in order to reach the stages they have already mastered.

Logic v Psychologic

Whatever types of sequence you go for, do so on the grounds of how you believe they will appeal to your learners and help them learn. Don't just follow the traditional "logic of the subject" as enshrined in the textbooks or training manuals. That would be the logic of people who are already expert in the subject. It might or might not appeal to newcomers.

What you should be looking for is not so much the best logical order as the most satisfying psychological order. For instance, despite the usual advice to go from simple to complex, concrete to abstract, learners may sometimes enjoy starting with something fairly complex -- e.g. as a challenge or as an indication of what the basic work will be leading up to. (Backward chaining would be one example.) Similarly, while one might traditionally start at the beginning of some chronological subject-matter and work towards the present, the psychological order might be to work **backwards** from the present.

I hope you feel I have been reasonably "psychological" in my ordering of the chapters in this book. if not, I am sure you will read them in the order you find most appropriate! (That's what our learners often do, no matter how carefully we've tried to think out the "ideal" sequence.) I leave you to decide what kinds of sequencing I have used within chapters -- and whether it is logical, psychological, both, or neither.

From Topics to Teaching Points

Within the subject-area you have defined -- whether by concept analysis, diagramming, or any less formal methods -- you should be able to identify the main topics. Figure 4.2 shows the main topics I picked out from my concept map for diet and nutrition (Figure 3.7 on page 53). It is a hierarchy (yet another form of diagram!). That is, it shows which topics must be explored before certain others can be understood ("structural logic"). Clearly, knowledge about "components of food" appeared to me as the cornerstone of understanding here.

Figure 4.2:   A Hierarchy for Diet & Nutrition Course

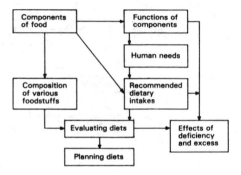

In Figure 4.3 below, I took the analysis one stage further, looking for linear sequences through the topics. In fact, I identified at least two. After an introduction to "the components of food", learners might work down the left-hand side of the diagram first, as far as "analysing sample diets", and then down the right-hand side as far as "interpreting tables of recommended dietary intakes" (always following the broken line) -- or they might work through the right-hand set of topics first (following the solid line). Either way, they must have followed both chains of topics **before** going on to "evaluating diets". Yet a third possibility is for the sequence to take, as it were, a "middle path" -- pursuing dietary needs and dietary sources both at the same time, combining ideas from both sets of topics.

Figure 4.3: A Flow Diagram for Diet & Nutrition Course

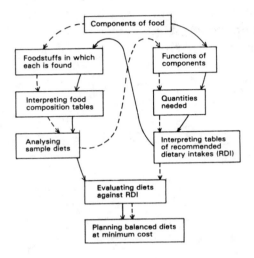

Teaching point outlines. In fact, a list of ordered topics may not provide a clear enough framework upon which to begin writing. Preferably, once you have decided on the topics you'll be tackling within each lesson, you should decide what **teaching points** you want to make about each topic. These should be arranged in sequence as a **teaching point outline.**

Your "teaching points" are the main statements you want to make about the subject-matter -- e.g. definitions, factual observations, relationships, judgements, and so on. For instance, you might begin your teaching point outline for a lesson on diet and nutrition by drawing on the topic "components of food" as follows:

- Food has six main components
- These components are:
- They can be divided into the following categories...

At this juncture we would need to decide whether to draw our next teaching point from the topic "functions of food" or from the topic "foodstuffs in which each is found". Alternatively, we might draw on both, making our next point an integrative statement, e.g.

- In order to balance a diet, you need to know how much of each component is required, and how to obtain it.

For a completed example of a teaching point outline, see Figure 4.4 which formed the basis for one chapter in a self-instructional book about studying. Compare it with the spray diagram in Figure 3.5 (page 50). If you have not already diagrammed your subject-matter, this kind of teaching point outline can be produced (as can a concept map, for that matter) by starting out with a number of topics -- e.g. "speed of reading", "quality of reading", "improving reading" -- and deciding what statements you want to make about each.

Once you have got your list of statements arranged in what seems like a sensible order, you can use it as a framework for your writing. Each teaching point may form the basis for a paragraph or two (rarely more). Remember, however -- as with all aids to course planning -- not to let your teaching point outline dictate to you. Be prepared to delete, add, re-write and re-sequence your teaching points as you get ahead with the writing of your lessons. The process of writing may bring to mind points that had escaped you earlier.

Incidentally, AFTER you have written a lesson, it can be a useful check on the lesson's structure to read through it -- or get someone else to -- making a list of the teaching points you have **actually** covered, paragraph by paragraph. This can reveal all kind of gaps and overlaps.

The Learner's Own Sequence

One final thought before we leave the subject: the sequence in which you finally decide to present your ideas may not be the sequence in which some learners choose to tackle them. Even within an individual lesson, some may begin by reading the final few pages -- and then skim through the rest of the text, stopping wherever they see something that catches their interest. They may or may not then go on to work through the text, paragraph by paragraph from the first page. And within a course, some learners may choose to start with the lessons they expect to be most rewarding (or most threatening) rather than follow the published sequence.

With some courses and subjects, it may be quite practicable for learners to decide their own sequences. With others, the way you've written the course materials will make this difficult, if not dangerous. You need to decide whether to encourage learners in choosing their own sequences -- e.g. by clear content lists, section headings, index, etc. (see Chapter 8) -- or whether to warn them against it.

> IF YOUR COURSE CONTAINS A **PROJECT** (SEE PAGE 59) LEARNERS WILL BE REQUIRED TO DECIDE NOT ONLY THE SEQUENCE BUT ALSO THE CONTENT OF THEIR STUDIES.

Figure 4.4: A Teaching Point Outline (based on
Learn How to Study by D. Rowntree, Macdonalds, 1976)

1. Despite "experience" few college students read as well as
    they might. (Too slow, can't concentrate, forget.)

2. For *better* reading (improved comprehension):
    (a) Apply SQ3R to get sense of purpose.
    (b) Look for topic sentence in each paragraph:
         (i)   Usually first or last sentence, and
         (ii) Contains the *main idea* of the paragraph.
    (c) Look for important *details*:
         (i)   e.g., proof, example, or support for main idea.
         (ii) Usually at least one to each main idea.
    (d) In hunt for main ideas and important details:
         (i)   Watch out for signposts: visual (Layout and typestyles)
               & verbal (Clue words and phrases).
         (ii) Study all charts and tables.
         (iii) Don't skip difficulties.
    (e) *Evaluate* the text:
         (i)   Be sceptical (expect author to prove).
         (ii) Look for applications in your own experience.

3. Towards *faster* reading: (most people could read half as
    fast again and still understand just as well).
    (a) During reading:
         (i)   Eyes jerk left to right in series of *fixations*.
         (ii) At each fixation, brain decodes group of words, making up
               its *recognition span*.
    (b) *Poor* readers:
         (i)   Have small recognition spans, therefore make many
               fixations.
         (ii) Regress frequently (backward glances).
         (iii) Read aloud (or make sub-vocal noises).

4. Can improve reading (speed *and* understanding).
    (a) Five basic steps:
         (i)   Check whether you need specs.
         (ii) Stop saying words aloud.
         (iii) Consciously try to read faster.
         (iv) Read in thought-units (2 or 3 words at a time).
         (v)   Build up vocabulary (reading, speaking, writing (by
               reading widely, learning Greek and Latin roots, noting
               new words, using dictionary, making glossaries.
    (b) Practice (absolutely essential), e.g.:
         • Nightly sessions (15 to 30 min.): time yourself (w.p.m.).
    (c) Vary your reading pace:
         (i)   Faster for "story-like" material and main ideas.
         (ii) Slower for complex argument and for important detail.

CHOOSING YOUR TEACHING MEDIA

Although Chapter 11 deals with media in some detail, I include a few paragraphs here. This is to persuade you that choice of media is worth thinking about **early** in your course planning. The most urgent question for consideration is likely to be:

TO WHICH MEDIA DO YOU AND
YOUR LEARNERS HAVE **ACCESS**?

Available Media

In most self-instructional courses -- whether on-site or at a distance -- the main medium is **print** (the written word, together with pictures). This may be supported by **audio-visual** material -- especially audio-cassette tapes, and slides or filmstrips. Occasionally, moving pictures in the form of video or film will be available. In some cases, video or audio teaching will be broadcast.

Practical work can be arranged, if necessary by providing learners with their own "kits" of material and equipment, or by enabling them to use laboratory or work-shop facilities at some convenient location. **Computers** may be available. **Personal interaction** -- between learners or between learners and a tutor -- may be possible, at least occasionally, either face-to-face or on the telephone or using "computer conferencing".

Figure 4.5 is a list of four broad categories of media. I leave you to decide which of them might be available for your course.

The Functions of Media

If you were meeting your learners in class, you would be performing a number of teaching functions. Since you are **not** meeting them face-to-face (or not often), you will need to make your chosen media perform these functions **instead of you**, viz:

Figure 4.5:　Types of Media

PRINT
- Textbooks and "readers" -- already published, or else specially written.
- Specially written commentaries or supplements to already published material.
- Specially written "correspondence texts" or "tutorials-in-print" (see Chapter 5).
- Worksheets (or media notes) for use with audiotape or videotape material, practical work, etc.
- Study guides, tests, notes on assignment requirements, bibliographies, etc.
- Maps, charts, photographs, posters, etc.
- Newspapers, journals and periodicals.
- Handwritten materials passing between learners and tutor.
- Computer-learner "conversations".
- Computer conferencing.

AUDIO VISUAL

- Audio-cassettes (or discs).
- Radio broadcasts.
- Slides or filmstrip.
- Film or film loops.
- Video-cassettes.
- Television broadcasts.
- Computer displays.

PRACTICAL WORK

- Materials, equipment, specimens for learner's individual use -- e.g. home experiment kits.
- Field-work or other use of learner's local environment -- e.g. social or ecological surveys, collection of local plant specimens, etc.
- Work in local offices, farms, workshops, etc.
- Assignments based on learner's place of work.

HUMAN INTERACTION

At-a-distance
- Telephone conversation between learner and tutor (supplementing written communications).
- Learner-learner telephone conversations (or exchange of letters).
- Several learners in telephone contact at the same time, with or without a tutor, by means of a "conference call".
- "Real time" computer conferencing.

Face-to-face
- Learners' self-help groups.
- Contacts with local people with relevant knowledge or skills
- Occasional seminars, tutorials, lectures by tutors or other group organizers.
- One-day, one week, weekend, or other short duration group sessions (residential or otherwise.)

- Catching the learners' interest.
- Reminding them of earlier learning.
- Stimulating new learning.
- Explaining, and provoking thought.
- Getting learners to respond actively.
- Giving them speedy feedback to their responses.
- Encouraging them to practise and review.
- Helping learners assess their own progress.

Types of Learning Stimuli

Between them, the various available media can provide several different types of stimuli to learning. These appeal to different senses or ways of understanding in our learners. The different stimuli are:

The written word	--	print, typescript and handwriting.
Pictures	--	diagrams, photographs, maps.
Recorded sound	--	music, speech, etc., that can be listened to away from the presence of the person who produced it.
Human interaction	--	responsive communication with other people, either face-to-face or on the telephone.
Real objects and events	--	and (if they are merely being observed rather than interacted with) real people.

For certain learning objectives, some types of stimuli are essential. For example, learners could not be expected to learn how to read blueprints without pictorial help. Nor could they learn to identify soil specimens -- e.g. as sandy, loam, or clay -- without getting their hands on some real specimens.

For other objectives, one stimulus may simply be preferable to another, though either might be serviceable. For instance, learners' attitudes can be affected by the written word -- but human interaction is likely to affect them more deeply.

Several types of stimulus can be combined in a particular medium. For example, both the written word and pictures can be contained in a book; a video-tape can combine pictures (still or moving), recorded sound, and (as captions) the written word; practical work can combine real objects or events and human interaction; and so on.

The Essential Questions

Here is a set of key questions to ask yourself when choosing media:

- Which media are available to me **and** to the learners?

- Do any of our learning objectives imply **particular** types of stimuli and particular media?

- If so, how and to what extent (e.g. what proportion of the learner's time) would I wish to use each of the preferred media?

- What would it cost me **and** the learner (in money, time and flexibility) to use these preferred media?

- Would less expensive media be **acceptably** effective?

- Do the chosen media offer the learner sufficient **variety** of stimulus and activity?

- How can I **combine** media for maximum effect -- e.g. audio-tape plus real specimens)?

ASSESSMENT AND EVALUATION

These two topics are also given chapters of their own later in the book. Again, however, I am spending a few paragraphs on each here -- simply to emphasize that you should consider them early in the planning of a course.

Assessing Your Students

As part of your planning, you should decide on:

(a) an assessment strategy for the course as a whole; and

(b) an appropriate way of assessing learners on each lesson, within this overall strategy.

Key questions. Here are some of the key questions you might consider:

- What knowledge, skills and attitudes will be assessed?

- At what points in the course will they be assessed? -- e.g. Sometimes the learners can usefully be assessed lesson by lesson, while with some objectives we need to know whether learners can **integrate** what they have learned over a **number** of previous lessons.

- How will learners be assessed? This is an important question to ask early on because some forms of assessment, e.g. a project report, will influence how the course is to be taught.

- Who will think up the assessment activities and prepare any necessary materials? -- e.g. assignment questions, exam papers, observers' checklists, guidance notes for markers, etc.

- By whom will the assessment be carried out? -- e.g. by the individual learner, other learners, the person who produced the course, a tutor, a line manager, an external examiner, etc.

- Will the assessments "count" towards any form of certification? -- e.g. a certificate of "course completion", course grade, diploma, or degree.

- If different standards of learner performance are to earn different grades, how will these standards be decided upon?

- What kind of feedback will learners be given as a result of assessment? -- e.g. marks, grades, comments on their strengths and weaknesses, model answers, etc. And will it be in time to help them improve before they finish the present course?

- Can data from assessment be used to improve the course for present or future learners?

> N.B. EVEN IF YOUR LEARNERS WOULD REJECT ANY
> KIND OF FORMAL ASSESSMENT (e.g. ON A HOBBY
> COURSE), YOU WILL STILL NEED TO PROVIDE THEM
> WITH THE MEANS OF **SELF**ASSESSMENT.

Assessment is discussed further in Chapter 13.

Evaluating Your Teaching

Evaluation is dealt with more fully in Chapter 14. However, like assessment and the choice of media, it is not an issue that can be safely left until after you've produced your course or lesson. Right from the start, you need to be thinking about how you will check on its effects and effectiveness -- with a view to making modifications and improvements, where necessary.

As with assessment, you need an overall strategy for evaluating the course, within which, plans can be made for evaluating each individual lesson or type of learning activity. What kinds of data will be sought and how might it be collected? There are two main areas about which you may want to collect evidence:

1. *Subject-matter credibility:* Is the course content accurate, relevant, up-to-date, balanced, etc.?

2. *Educational effects/effectiveness.* Can the course enable acceptably productive learning within the time learners have available? What unexpected problems/opportunities (e.g. educational, managerial, financial) arise during its operation?

There are four main ways of collecting evidence. Crudely speaking, the first two mentioned below will be chiefly concerned with 1 above, and the second two with 2. But all four are likely to yield at least some insights about both subject-matter and educational factors:

*   *Critical commenting.* What arrangements will be made for one or more members of the course team to prepare critical but constructive comments on the materials produced by each of the other members? Have realistic amounts of time been budgeted for this activity?

*   *Commenting by external readers/assessors.* These may be external to your institution or just to the course team. By whom are such people to be chosen? How will they be rewarded? What guidance will they be given as to the nature and depth of commenting required?

*   *Developmental testing.* What plans are there for trying out materials on typical learners in time to modify and improve before producing a final version?

*   *Continuous monitoring.* Once the course is in operation, how can the knowledge you gain in running it be used to make further improvements and refinements? Who will take responsibility for "maintaining" the course?

A LESSON SPECIFICATION

So, I'll assume that, for the course within which you are writing, decisions have been made, and properly documented, about:

- Prospective learners
- Aims and objectives
- Content
- Sequence
- Media
- Assessment
- Evaluation

I'll further assume that you are responsible for developing one or more sections of the course. These I would recommend you to think of as sets of "lessons", each lesson being meant to occupy the learner for, say, 1-2 hours. Experience indicates that both learners and teachers find this amount of learning time to be the most convenient and manageable unit when planning how to get to grips with the course content.

Before launching into the first draft of your first lesson, you should ideally produce a **specification**. This will be essential as a means of conveying your intentions to fellow-authors if you are working in a course team. But even if you are working alone, you may find a specification worth drafting to remind yourself of your own earlier intentions.

The specification for each lesson, or set of lessons, within a course might usefully indicate the following:

- Proposed title of lesson
- Name of author(s)
- Dates by which materials are to be made available -- e.g. for commenting by colleagues, for developmental testing, and for final production.

- Names of any course team colleagues who have been specifically enlisted as commenters.
- Names of external readers/assessors.
- Relationship of material to rest of course -- e.g. any prerequisite knowledge/skills/attitudes expected of learners. Entry test needed?
- Aims and objectives.
- Outline of content -- main issue, concepts, processes, procedures, etc., to be included.
- Sequence -- list of main teaching points in order, or a flow diagram.
- Teaching media to be used -- e.g. textbook plus study guide, audio-cassette, practical work, etc.
- Chief types of learner activity -- e.g. reading, problem-solving, workplace project, etc.
- Types of assessment required -- e.g. job-based practicals, learner-marked tests, tutor-assessed essays, etc.
- Estimated learning time, including assessment.
- Support system planned or suggested -- e.g. role of tutors, mentors, self-help groups, etc.
- Evaluation plans -- e.g. how might materials (and support system) be tested and improved?

You should now be ready to begin writing your first lesson, the subject of Chapter 5.

> BUT TRY NOT TO SPEND TOO MUCH TIME PREPARING YOUR LESSON UNLESS YOU KNOW THAT THE **REST** OF THE COURSE HAS BEEN AGREED IN OUTLINE OR YOU ARE QUITE CONFIDENT THAT YOUR LESSON **CANNOT** LATER BE DECLARED "SURPLUS TO REQUIREMENTS".

5. WRITING A SELF-INSTRUCTIONAL LESSON

Having thought about the purposes and content of your self-instructional lesson, you should now be ready to begin writing it. In this book I am assuming that the chief medium you will be using is **print** -- written words and (still) pictures. Print is the most-used medium of self-instruction and, in any case, all my advice about it can easily be adapted for use with other media also. (In Chapter 11, I do give some advice on using other media.)

TEACHING THROUGH SELF-INSTRUCTION

Teaching a learner through self-instruction is different from any other kind of teaching you may have done. It is not like lecturing -- where the learner is there in front of you and can ask you to clarify a point or give more examples. Nor is it like a classroom lesson or a demonstration, where you can see that the learner needs extra help or practice. You won't be around to advise the learner on how to tackle the work -- and, if the learner is studying alone, nor even will other learners. So:

> EVERYTHING YOU MIGHT HAVE WANTED TO SAY TO LEARNERS WORKING IN YOUR PRESENCE NEEDS TO BE THOUGHT OF AND PUT DOWN IN WRITING INSTEAD.

Unfortunately, even the kind of writing required is quite different from anything most teachers and trainers will have done previously. It is not like writing lecture notes, journal articles, training manuals or textbooks.

Lecture notes are clearly not written with solo learners in mind; and journal articles are usually written for fellow-specialists rather than learners. Training manuals and textbooks may seem closer to the mark. But they are usually written for teachers, or for learners working closely with a teacher. Usually they will provide learners only with a **reminder** of the bare bones of the course content -- and with a source of exercises to which the teacher will provide the answers. That is, they are rarely written as a **substitute** for the teaching.

The Tutorial-in-Print

It is vital that you keep in mind the learners you are writing for. But do not imagine them as part of a lecture audience -- nor as textbook readers whose teacher is hovering somewhere in the vicinity. Imagine instead that you are **tutoring** one individual learner for between one and two hours. Everything you might want to say to this individual will need to be written down -- forming what I have called a **tutorial-in-print**.

This is what you will need to do in your tutorial-in-print if you are to teach your individual learners:

- Help the learners find their way into and around your subject -- by-passing or repeating sections where appropriate.

- Tell them what they need to be able to do before tackling the material.

- Make clear what they should be able to do on completion of the material -- e.g. in terms of objectives.

- Advise them on how to tackle the work -- e.g. how much time to allow for different sections, how to plan for an assignment, etc.

- Explain the subject matter in such a way that learners can relate it to what they know already.

- Encourage them sufficiently to make whatever effort is needed in coming to grips with the subject.

- Engage them in exercises and activities that cause them to work with the subject-matter -- rather than merely reading about it.

- Give the learners feedback on these exercises and activities -- enabling them to judge for themselves whether they are learning successfully.

- Help them to sum up and perhaps reflect on their learning at the end of the lesson.

How Much to Write?

Perhaps I ought rather to say "How **little?**" Newcomers to self-instruction are often surprised that learners take so long to work through their materials. It is rare to find an author who **under**-estimates the amount of material learners can get through in a given time.

When reading for entertainment -- say the latest Jacky Collins or John le Carré -- people may be able to read two or three hundred words per minute. But research indicates that people **studying** a self-instructional text will read much more slowly. As **learners**, they will be pausing to take notes, or to answer questions, or simply to reflect on how their own experience or beliefs relate to the ideas in the text. They may even need to read certain sections several times.

As a **very** rough-and-ready estimate, you might reckon on your average reader working through self-instructional materials at the rate of about:

50-100 WORDS PER MINUTE, OVERALL.

For a one-hour tutorial-in-print, this suggests a **total** of (50 x 60, to (100 x 60) = 3000 to 6000 words.

With straightforward, narrative material (like this), some of your readers may exceed 100 words per minute. But with a complex, closely-reasoned argument -- especially when the ideas are new to your learners and take some coming to terms with -- their speed may drop to 50 words per minute, or less.

As for the questions, exercises and activities you build into your text -- and these are essential in self-instruction -- they can reduce the reader's overall speed yet further. Some activities may be particularly time-consuming. For instance, just the **four** following words -- "Now interview six customers" -- would be quite enough to keep your learners busy for an hour or more.

So, one cannot simply give a formula figure for the number of words that learners might be expected to cope with in a given time period. It depends on what you are wanting them to do with those words. For example, if you're wanting them to do practical work, you'll need to give them less reading to do. Likewise if you want them to study from an audiotape or draft an assignment to send to a tutor. Remember also that if you want your learners to read from some **other** book or printed materials, you will need to subtract the required number of words from what you might otherwise have reckoned to write yourself.

Even when the materials have been completed, it is sometimes quite difficult to predict how long the average learner will take over them. Your ability to predict will improve with practice, of course. Meanwhile, the best way to ensure you don't make unreasonable demands is to try out an early draft of your lesson on some typical learners. If they take too long, prune it ruthlessly! Early drafts often need to be reduced by 50% or more as a result of such tryouts.

It is easy for the self-instructional author to get carried away and generate far more work than learners can cope with in the time available. This can cause them much distress -- and they may even drop out of the course. After all, unlike classroom learners, they cannot easily confirm with their teacher (or even with one another) that some of the material (and which?) can safely be skimmed or ignored altogether. I have many times seen evidence that courses are overloaded -- but never the reverse.

How Long to Write?

This is another much-asked question for which there are no cut-and-dried answers. How much time you'll need to develop a given set of self-instructional materials will depend on so many factors -- like, for instance, on:

- How much new thinking/learning you need to do about the subject-matter.

- How much you need to find out about the needs of your learners.

- Whether your materials are meant to be truly self-instructional or just a prelude or follow-up to other teaching.

- The extent to which you can get your learners to work from already-published material.

- How easy it is to think up appropriate and effective teaching strategies.

- What kinds of activity you are setting your learners.

- What media you are using.

- How many drafts you need to go through -- and how many learners you need to try them out on -- in order to get a version that produces satisfactory learning and is acceptable to colleagues.

For example, if you base your lesson on having your learners read a chapter in an existing textbook, it will clearly take you less time than if you had to write the chapter yourself. And very much less than if you had to produce computer software or a piece of interactive video.

Similarly, if the subject-content is clearly defined and well known to you, you should be able to produce your material faster than if the subject is new to you and/or has to be "created" in debate with colleagues -- as often happens in interdisciplinary courses with titles like *Health and Environment, Images of Women, Science in Society*. On the other hand, you may know so much about the subject that you take an inordinate amount of time deciding what to **leave out** -- or else write it all down and then lose time later by having to rewrite (and rethink) it more succinctly.

All the same, one needs **some** idea of how long it's all going to take (even if it usually takes longer). Various estimates are to be heard among self-instructional writers -- from one day per hour of learning time to several weeks per hour. I would suggest you'll need to allow, on average, **at least 50 hours** of development time per hour of learning time. Some lessons may need less -- but some may need twice as much (and maybe more, especially if they involve computers).

As with most things in life, you get what you pay for. Quality learning materials need thoughtful planning, writing, testing and rewriting until they **work**. This takes time. Inferior materials (the "quick and dirty") can be produced more cheaply -- by skimping on or omitting some of those stages. This is what happened with programmed learning in the 1960s, when bad (but cheap) material drove out the good (but expensive) -- leading to the discrediting and collapse of programmed learning. I hope we can ensure that history does not repeat itself with open or distance learning in the 1990s.

WHY NOT USE EXISTING MATERIALS?

Instead of writing your own lessons, why not make up the learning package from existing texts and/or tapes, together with some specially written notes on how to study them? (I am not talking here of taking over a complete **course**, which is an option I discussed in Chapter 2.)

This can seem like an attractive way of saving time. And, in theory, it might provide your learners with more authoritative teaching materials than you could produce from your resources alone. Material of quality does exist, and some of it you may be able to turn to the needs of your learners.

However, in view of the essential features of self-instruction I listed earlier, we must demand answers to a number of searching questions. These are set out in Figure 5.1 overleaf.

We certainly cannot rely on authors' and publishers' claims that their materials will substitute for a teacher. Nor can we base our trust on titles like *Lion-taming Made Easy, Learn Hypnotism in Your Sleep,* or *Teach Yourself Brain Surgery.* Too often they are simply jazzed-up textbooks.

A more promising way to track down usable materials (at least in Britain) would be to consult the *Open Learning Directory* (published by the Training Agency) or MARIS (a computer data base, telephone: 0353-61284). Look also at the materials catalogues of the Open University, the Open College and the National Extension College.

N.B. IT MAY BE WORTH YOUR WHILE ENLISTING THE HELP OF PROSPECTIVE LEARNERS IN VETTING SUCH MATERIALS.

Figure 5.1: **Questions to Ask About Books or Other Potential Learning Materials**

Audience For whom is it written? Is its target audience (so far as we can identify it) sufficiently like our prospective learners?

Objectives Are the learning objectives sufficiently similar to those of our learners?

Starting point What prior knowledge and skills (e.g. numerical, technical or social) are required of its audience?

Coverage Is the subject-matter appropriate for our learners? Is it broad enough? Deep enough? Accurate? Up to date? Any serious omissions? What proportion is irrelevant to our needs?

Teaching approach Does it teach -- or merely act as a reference or as a reminder of what has been learned elsewhere? Is it geared to learners working without other help? Does it require learners simply to read and remember? Or must they apply and practice the material through self-testing exercises and activities? Are they given useful feedback? Are they given guidance in using the material and finding their way around in it?

Style Is the style of the material suitable to our learners, e.g. vocabulary, sentence length and structure, use of pictorial material? Is it interesting?

Physical format	Is it attractive in appearance? Durable enough to survive likely use? Easily carried about, if necessary? Usable anywhere it might be needed?
Reputation	Does the material have a "track record"? Do we know how well it has been received by other teachers/learners?
Costs	How much does it cost to hire or buy? What additional costs might arise (e.g. in equipment or support system)? Is this within our budget and/or that of learners? Is the learning-time it would entail for learners reasonable?
Availability	Can we rely on its being available (e.g. staying in print) throughout the intended life of the course?
Likely benefits	Are learners likely to get what they would expect from using the material? Is the organisation likely to?
Alternatives	How does it compare with other existing material and with what we might produce ourselves?

Supplementing Existing Materials

It is unlikely that any existing material will be completely suitable for your learners. Even so, material may still be usable within your package, e.g. as a "set book". Or you may decide to write your package around the material in such a way as to overcome or compensate for any weaknesses it may have.

A study guide. For instance, you might produce a "study guide" to help your learners get the best out of a not altogether satisfactory text (or tape). Such a study guide might include items like the following:

- Your overviews and/or summaries of the topic.

- Concept maps or other diagrams showing how the main topics and ideas are related.

- Learning objectives.

- An annotated bibliography.

- Guidance as to which chapters/sections to study and which to ignore.

- Specially-written (or audio-taped) alternative explanations -- to be studied instead of sections in the materials that you think are inaccurate, biased, out-of-date, confusing, etc.

- Local examples or case studies -- which you have prepared because they will be more appealing than those (if any) in the existing material.

- Your paragraph-by-paragraph commentary on the argument expressed in the text.

- Questions and activities based on the materials, section by section.

- Model or specimen answers to activities, and/or checklists whereby learners can evaluate their own responses to questions or activities that seem likely to produce unpredictable responses.

- Suggestions for practical work or experimental activity, e.g. guidelines or worksheets.

- A glossary of technical terms.

- A self-assessed test related to the objectives.

- Questions to discuss with fellow learners.

- Instructions for an assignment to be sent to a tutor for comment and/or marking.

Your study guide supplement to the existing materials may be minimal or extensive. At the very least, you must ensure your learners are provided with:

a) guidance on how to approach the materials;

b) a means of assessing what they have learned from the materials; and

c) advice on how to get additional help where necessary.

At some point, you may find yourself not so much supplementing existing materials as writing your own lessons and merely incorporating those materials. At what point? Perhaps at the point where learners must spend more than 50% of their time on "your" material. But no matter. In the following chapter, I assume that the lesson you are producing will be sufficiently "yours" to be called a tutorial-in-print. Even if you are merely supplementing existing materials, however, much of what I have to say will still be relevant.

SAMPLE PAGES FROM SELF-INSTRUCTIONAL TEXTS

Anyone who wants to write -- whether epic poetry, sexsational best-sellers, or self-instructional texts -- would do well to study what others have written in the chosen genre. So, in the remainder of this chapter, we'll look at twelve extracts from tutorials-in-print. They all come from Open University courses, some at under-graduate level, some from post-experience training and vocational updating. I shall be referring back to these examples in later chapters.

N.B.   The sample pages are smaller than the originals (some by more than 50%) and some originals had colour.

4   Changing an organization's culture

In the remainder of the material 'On cultures and structures' Professor Handy points out that changing environments call for organizations to adapt and considers how it might best be done. He identifies three ways of adapting:

- by *deliberation* – improving planning and co-ordination in a role culture by increasing thought, talk and liaison
- by *reproduction* – that is decentralization or divisionalization
- by *differentiation* – by promoting different cultures and different structures in different areas of activity within an organization.

Activity J ▷   Can you anticipate which of these forms of adaptation Professor Handy will prefer?

Read on to find out which and why. Read Sections 4.1 to 4.5 on pp 195–200, ignoring the boxed items.

Clearly, Professor Handy wants an organization to vary its culture from one type of activity to another. He mentions four types of activity.

Activity K ▷   Which of these activities is most typical of your organization as a whole and of your unit within it? Regardless of your answer to those two questions, which type of activity would you personally most prefer to be involved in? Put one tick in each column below.

	My organization	My unit	My own preference
Steady state			
Innovative/developmental			
Breakdown/crises			
Policy/discretion			

Again this exercise may enable you to detect any mismatch between your preferences and what is necessary within your unit and/or organization. For instance, you may have found (though I hope not) that your least preferred activities are the main activities of your unit.

So, differentiation is an approved form of adaptation. But, as we said in Session 9.3, this increases the need for co-ordination, or integration. Charles Handy lists a number of 'integrative devices'.

Activity L ▷   Do any of these remind you of some you read about earlier in the course? Read Section 4.6 on p 201 to find out.

You should have been reminded of Jay Galbraith's mechanisms discussed in Session 9.3. Many of those – rules, routines and procedures, hierarchical referral, improved

◄ **Figure 5.2A**

This extract comes from a "post-experience" course for managers (P670). It illustrates a low cost approach --a "wrap-around" workbook based on a previously published textbook, *Understanding Organizations* by Charles Handy.

Not all of the textbook is appropriate to the objectives of the course. Nor was it written with self-instruction in mind. So, in a separate workbook from which this sample page is taken, learners are asked to read a couple of pages of the textbook at a time. Each time, they are given one or more questions and are asked to write their answers in the wide margin of the workbook.

After each of these "activities", there is a line across the page -- a "reader stopper", reminding learners not to read on until they have answered the questions. There then follows the course author's answers or comments, to help learners check out their understanding or interpretation of the text.

This fairly basic approach can be applied to **any** existing material -- from the blurb on a packet of breakfast food to a full length feature film. Essentially, you are asking the learner "What are they saying?" and/or "What do you make of it?". Thus, you can get your learner to engage with you in the detailed analysis of published materials.

B

Units 2B and 9   Uses and Abuses of Argument

Recently a friend wrote to me that he had been reading Solzhenitsyn's account of conditions in Soviet Russia. 'It's incredible,' he commented. Well, so it is. But just a minute. Did my friend mean that he couldn't (i.e. didn't) believe what Solzhenitsyn had written? That is what 'incredible' (like 'unbelievable') means, strictly speaking. It means that it is not possible to believe. But perhaps my friend was using 'incredible' in a devalued sense; perhaps he merely meant 'hard to believe' or 'very surprising'. The word is often used in this way, and mostly – but not always – the meaning is clear enough and no harm is done. However, on this occasion I really was uncertain: did my friend believe it or didn't he? Did he mean *literally* incredible? That is what I found myself asking in my letter to him. But then it struck me that 'literally' too is used in a devalued way! Thus if my friend had said that he found it 'literally incredible', I might have had to ask: But do you mean 'literally' *literally*? And so on.

Sometimes the desire for hyperbole leads one to choose an expression which is not simply an exaggerated version of the truth, but which actually means something different. I suppose that the writer of A meant to use 'slave' by way of hyperbole. It is stronger, more dramatic, than such words as 'badly off', 'underpaid', or 'exploited by the employer'. The trouble is that 'slave' is *not* just an extreme version of these; it means something rather different. (Of course there are also resemblances, which make it plausible to use that word.)

The word 'claustrophobia' in C is a more subtle case. It is, again, an impressive word: and again there is a certain satisfaction, a feeling of 'speaking out', in declaring that 'all city-dwellers' suffer from claustrophobia. Still, isn't it true at least of some city-dwellers? (Let's not argue here about 'all' and 'some'.) Take those people crowding into a tube-train at rush-hour. They are, literally, like sardines. (Well, perhaps not *literally* . . .) Do you mean to tell me they are not suffering from claustrophobia?

What should we say? Is it correct to use the word 'claustrophobia' of these people? If not, why not? (If necessary, consult your dictionary.)

No doubt conditions in a rush-hour train can be very unpleasant. And the same may be said of certain other aspects of city life today. We may feel quite strongly that people living in these conditions are suffering harm, that they are losing something very important. And no doubt 'claustrophobia' may seem to carry the right sort of punch to drive this home. But it would be driving in the wrong direction. For the point of a word like 'claustrophobia' (as with other 'phobias' and 'manias', for example agoraphobia, kleptomania) is that it refers to an *abnormal* response. And there is nothing abnormal in feeling frustrated, irritated and sometimes enraged, if you travel in rush-hour trains, get stuck in traffic jams and dwell in crowded conditions. If we are going to use the word 'claustrophobia' for this sort of thing, what will we use for cases of claustrophobia?

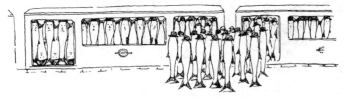

They are, literally, like sardines

22

◀ **Figure 5.2B**

This extract comes from an undergraduate humanities course (A101). But for the box in the middle of the page (and perhaps the cartoon), this might appear, at first glance, like an extract from an "ordinary" book. It presents a sequence of paragraphs in which the author tells of his experience, analyses it, and draws conclusions from it -- all in a quite informal yet closely-reasoned style.

Where it differs from an ordinary book is in what it expects of the reader. The reader is not treated as a passive sponge -- one who will merely "read, learn and inwardly digest". Rather, the reader is seen as an **active** partner in a **dialogue** or conversation. This is revealed by the question in the middle of the page. It is not rhetorical -- not just a stylistic device. The reader really is expected to think out a personal response to the author's question -- and write it in the box provided. Having paused for the reader to make a contribution, the author then goes on to comment on the question.

A couple of technical points: Notice that the "activity" -- the question about the use of the word "claustrophobia" -- is not labelled as such. However, the box will immediately signal to readers that have an activity to tackle. Below the box, you will notice that there is a double line across the page to act as a "reader stopper" -- though we may feel that the box itself is adequate for this purpose.

C

The governors' roles and responsibilities

You can find out about your role with regard to curriculum by looking at your Articles of Government. Here are extracts from three sets of Articles:

Model Articles
8. (a) The Local Education Authority shall determine the general educational character of the school and its place in the local educational system. Subject thereto the Governors shall have the general direction of the conduct and curriculum of the school.

8. (c) (ii) All proposals and reports from the Head affecting the curriculum and conduct of the school shall be submitted formally to the Governors....

Liverpool's Articles
The headteacher in consultation with the Authority and the Governors shall be responsible for the direction of the conduct and curriculum of the school.

Birmingham's Articles
...the Governing Body in consultation with the Head Teacher shall be responsible to the Authority for exercising general oversight of the conduct and curriculum of the School.

◪Which of the three extracts above seems to give governors most responsibility for curriculum and which of the Articles is most like yours?

It seems to us that the Model Articles give governors greatest responsibility for curriculum: they are to be responsible for its *general direction*. Liverpool's Articles, however, see the head exercising the direction, and only needing to *consult the governors* (and the local education authority). Birmingham's Articles are almost the reverse – this time the governors *consult the head*, but general 'oversight' sounds like rather less responsibility than general 'direction'.

As for the Articles which are most like yours – the chances are that the Model Articles come closest. Most governors will find their Articles expect them to exercise general direction (or general oversight) of the conduct and curriculum of the school.

General direction/oversight

Many local education authorities (LEAs) issue 'Notes of Guidance for Governors' which indicate what general direction/oversight actually means.

◪Look at the extracts from two sets of 'Notes' that follow (one from East Sussex and one from Walsall). Underline all the words and phrases that indicate what governors should be doing about the curriculum.

East Sussex
The Governors must therefore be kept well informed by the Head about the curriculum and in particular about any new developments.

It is important that Governors should take an active interest in this key aspect of the school's work. They should not hesitate to ask questions and should ensure that these questions are fully and properly answered.

Walsall
The Governors usually exercise their influence in three ways:
(i) by seeking information
(ii) by requiring to be consulted, and
(iii) by giving advice.
The Governors have a right to be informed about all matters concerning the life of the school. The Head and other teaching staff are trained and expert professionals but this need not cause the Governors to hesitate to ask questions: indeed, if they ask questions enough and listen carefully to the answers they will be in a fair way to becoming experts themselves.

In the East Sussex 'Notes' we underlined 'well informed', 'active interest', 'ask questions' and 'ensure that these questions are properly answered'. In the Walsall notes, we underlined points (i), (ii) and (iii), and again noticed also 'ask questions'.

Exercising your role

Perhaps we can sum it up by saying you can exercise your general direction or oversight of the curriculum by:
- Expecting to be consulted
- Seeking information (asking questions)
- Offering comments or advice
- Taking any necessary action.

Consultation It is perhaps when *changes* are in the offing that you are most likely to get involved. To be usefully involved it is essential for you to *know about* the proposed change.

◪Suppose there *is* to be an important curriculum change in your school, maybe a new method of teaching reading is to be introduced, or maybe the teaching of separate science subjects is to be dropped in the first three years in favour of combined science.
(a) At what stage do you think the governors *should* first hear about such a change?
(b) At what stage do you think the governors of *your* school actually *would* hear for the first time?
Tick the appropriate boxes in the (a) and (b) columns below.

The head first consults governors	(a) Should?	(b) Would?
1 Before consulting staff	☐	☐
2 After consulting staff but before making decisions	☐	☐
3 After decisions but before letter informing parents	☐	☐
4 At same time as parents by sending them copy of letter to parents	☐	☐
5 At next governors' meeting by a reference in his report	☐	☐
6 The head never mentions the change to the governors	☐	☐

◀ Figure 5.2C

This extract comes from a course for school governors (P970), helping them come to grips with their new roles and responsibilities. The most obvious feature of the page is its two-column layout (and the narrow margins).

Perhaps the next things to strike the eye are the three symbols (a white letter "A" on a dark square) that indicate activities. The first two activities get the readers to analyse extracts from other governors' documentation (and, in the first case, compare these with their own). The third activity gets them to relate the general principles expressed in the documentation to how things are actually handled in their own schools.

Notice the variety of the question asked. The first activity is, in effect, a multiple-choice question -- requiring readers to notice the key words in three brief texts and make a couple of overall comparisons. Readers are not told whether merely to think their answers or to mark them somewhere on the page.

In the second activity, readers are given a couple of brief texts and are asked to pick out all the words and phrases that touch on a certain matter. They are to record their answers by underlining.

The third activity is two-fold. Readers are asked what they think should happen and what they think would happen. The question is multiple-choice, and readers are asked to indicate their two answers by ticking boxes.

Notice that the authors' answers are given immediately after each activity. Notice also that there are no "reader stoppers" on this page. On the original, however, the activity material was printed in red, and this might have reminded learners not to read further.

D

Overall, nearly two-thirds expected a prescription. On being asked what they expected the doctor to do for them, they might reply:

> 'More than he did last time. Last time he just gave me paracetamol under another name.'

or   'I've been coming for my blood pressure, and he'll ask me how I've been in the last month. I'll tell him I've been feeling weak in the legs and he'll take my blood pressure. I expect he'll give me the usual pills but he might change the dose.'

or   'What I've come for now is more tablets. Well, the doctor might examine me a bit, have a chat and I'll leave feeling better, feeling the doctor is doing me good.'

Once the patient comes into your surgery, your prescribing is likely to be influenced, not just by the physical signs and symptoms, but also by the *social interaction* between you and the patient. In particular, you are liable to be influenced by the patient's expectations and by your estimates of how he is likely to respond to various forms of treatment.

Here is a consultation (quoted by Byrne and Long, 1976, page 12) with an elderly man who has recently had varicose veins removed from his leg. The doctor seems to be reacting to the patient's concern about his pills.

But is there anything you feel he is missing? Underline any of the patient's statements that you feel should have been pursued further by the doctor before he wrote what was, in fact, a repeat prescription.

Doctor: 'Well now, here you are again. How are things?'
Patient: 'Oh, doctor, I have not been taking all those pills you gave me. They didn't seem to agree with me.'
Doctor: 'Ah ha. Have you been getting your exercise every day?'
Patient: 'Oh, yes, doctor. Every morning I walk to work and I walk home at night. That's nearly four miles a day.'
Doctor: 'Mmm. Now then, how about this leg?'
Patient: 'Oh, that's much better now. The scar is still there though. I expect it will go in time.'
Doctor: 'How about the wife? Is she getting about all right?'
Patient: 'Yes. She gets out of a morning and goes down to the shops. She takes the bus down to the station, you know, and walks from there.'
Doctor: 'You're sleeping all right, aren't you?'
Patient: 'Well, I still take those tablets, doctor.'
Doctor: 'Good. Well now. Take this to Mr Green and get it made up. There are some different pills. Different colour, you know. Let me know how things are getting on. Don't forget your umbrella. 'Bye-bye.'

We have underlined 'I have not been taking all those pills you gave me. They didn't seem to agree with me' and (referring to his ability to sleep) 'Well, I still take those tablets, doctor'. The doctor does not investigate what happened to the patient that made him stop following the prescribed medication. Furthermore, he seems to have completely ignored or misinterpreted the patient's admission that he is not sleeping all right – and with it the implied expectation, perhaps, that the doctor should be doing something about it. The patient may also be seeking praise and reassurance, both on his own account (e.g. the scar) and on that of his wife, but he does not get it. We can only speculate as to why this doctor was either ignoring or not noticing the patient's 'social' messages (tiredness, boredom, irritation?) – whatever the reason, it resulted in less than optimum treatment.

◀ **Figure 5.2D**

This extract comes from an in-service course for family doctors, aimed at improving their prescribing habits (P550). Its most striking feature is its use of quotations from "real world" patients and the activity based on a mini case study.

Notice that the presentation is not academic and detached. It is job-related, specific in its examples, and it clearly expects the reader to relate its ideas to his or her own practice. Notice also that the text is not merely presenting knowledge but is also working on the reader's attitudes.

The "activity" is signalled by bold, indented print (on a coloured background in the original). Readers are asked to analyse the situation presented and to indicate their responses by underlining appropriate statements. The authors then go on to say which statements they regard as significant, and why.

E

2.3   Extraction

The amount of a substance that dissolves in a particular solvent is a function of the solubility of that substance. Solubility is a physical property; its value depends on the nature of the substance being dissolved, on the nature of the solvent and on the temperature. So different substances will have different solubilities in the same solvent (at the same temperature). We can make use of this property in the technique of extraction.

If we take a liquid mixture of substances which we want to separate and add to it a solvent which is fairly insoluble in the mixture then, after shaking the container, we will find that some components of the mixture will have been preferentially extracted into the solvent phase.

For example, pentane-1,5-dioic acid is prepared from pentane-1,5-dinitrile according to the following reaction:

$$NC(CH_2)_3CN \xrightarrow[H_2O]{H_2SO_4} HOOC(CH_2)_3COOH$$

(Don't worry about the chemicals involved in the reaction — all we are interested in is the extraction procedure.)

At the start of the reaction there are two liquid layers present; an aqueous layer containing the sulphuric acid and an organic layer consisting of the dinitrile, as shown in Figure 4. The product, pentane-1,5-dioic acid, is soluble in water in the presence of H_2SO_4 so the reaction is continued until the organic layer disappears. At the end of the reaction there are several substances present in the aqueous layer.

> Can you think of a way of extracting the organic acid from this solution?

In Unit 1 you were told that 'like dissolves like'. This organic acid has both polar and non-polar parts to the molecule, neither of which dominates the other, so the acid should dissolve in both polar and non-polar solvents. Therefore if we add a non-polar solvent to the mixture the organic acid should be extracted, to some extent, into this solvent leaving the sulphuric acid, water and other polar substances in the aqueous layer. Non-polar solvents commonly used are diethyl ether, toluene and trichloromethane (chloroform).

The procedure adopted for this particular reaction reads as follows:

> *Reflux* (i.e. continuously boil, returning the condensate to the reaction flask) the mixture for 10 hours and allow to cool. Extract with diethyl ether (four 150 cm³ portions); dry the ethereal extracts with anhydrous sodium sulphate. Distil off the ether.

So the organic solvent chosen in this example is diethyl ether. The aqueous solution is transferred to a separatory funnel like that shown in Figure 4. A 150 cm³ volume of diethyl ether is then added and, after shaking, the two liquids are allowed to settle. As diethyl ether is insoluble in water, a distinct boundary will be observed between the water and the ether. By running off the lower, aqueous, layer into a separate container until the boundary approaches the tap, we achieve a partial separation.

> Why, in this example, do we extract four times with 150 cm³ portions of the ether rather than extract once with 600 cm³ of ether?

Extracting with four lots of 150 cm³ of solvent is much more effective than extracting with one lot of 600 cm³. We know this from everyday experience; to quote one example, if we were extracting paint from paint brushes, much cleaner brushes would result from washing with five lots of 20 cm³ of white spirit than with one lot of 100 cm³ of white spirit.

After extracting four times with 150 cm³ of diethyl ether, the ether extracts are combined. Water is not completely insoluble in diethyl ether and so the water is removed from the ether by shaking with a solid drying agent (anhydrous sodium sulphate). Finally the solvent is removed from the required organic substance by distillation over a hot water bath. The resulting residue is fairly pure pentane-1,5-dioic acid.

10 hours under reflux

two liquid layers — start of reaction

one liquid layer — end of reaction

transfer liquid to separatory funnel

add 150 cm³ of ether and shake

two liquid layers

running off lower layer

aqueous layer   ethereal layer

transfer aqueous layer to separatory funnel. add 150 cm³ of ether and shake

aqueous layer   ethereal layer

extract twice more with ether

distil off ether

ethereal layer

collect residue

product

FIGURE 4   The preparation of pentane-1,5-dioic acid.

◀ **Figure 5.2E**

This extract is from an undergraduate course on chemistry (S246). The layout is very striking, with the wide right-hand margin entirely occupied by a sequence of diagrams. These diagrams illustrate an "extraction procedure" described in the text alongside.

Within the text, there are two "activities" -- about one-third and three-quarters of the way down the page. They are indented and have more space above and below them than there is between normal paragraphs. The first asks learners to suggest a method of extraction, while the second asks them to explain a step in the procedure. The author's comments follow directly, after a space.

The activities do not exactly leap to the eye on this page. Partly this is because they are not followed by "stoppers". Partly it is because their layout is not distinctive enough; they have exactly the same appearance as the item that begins with the word "Reflux" and much the same appearance as the reaction equation near the top of the page. Might it have been better to print the activities in bold type or a second colour?

Incidentally, the extraction procedure illustrated in the diagrams is the kind of sequence that some course developers might expect to demonstrate with **moving** pictures -- using video. A series of still pictures (together with text or audiotape commentary) can sometimes provide an acceptably effective low cost alternative.

F

eighteenth-century music whereby two bars of $\frac{3}{4}$ become one of $\frac{3}{2}$.[1] afford a welcome relief from the prevailing rhythmic pattern and also yield an apparent extension of the phrase. Examples of hemiola cadences may be found in this air at bars 36–7 and 65–6; less obviously perhaps at 46–7.

At first sight the B section (bar 47), while continuing the dotted accompanimental rhythms, appears to have a new vocal line. However, after two bars the familiar melodic contour with its dotted rhythms recurs:

Ex. 10

Seeks she the groves,   or bathes   in   crys – tal   foun – tains?

(cf. bars 35–8)

showing that Handel regarded this as a continuation of the same, rather than a calculated contrast as one might expect to find in a B section of a *da capo* movement.

EXERCISE
Play the air now. Observe the points I've made (basic 'affect', dotted rhythms, hemiolas) and ask yourself whether the tonal scheme is conventional. The movement is in C minor, so we would expect the following keys to be reached and probably clinched by substantial cadences: E♭ major (relative), G minor (dominant minor), B♭ major (one degree sharp), F minor or A♭ major (flat side). Does this happen? If so, where?

ANSWER
I identify the following principal cadences: E♭ major (relative) 17–18; F minor (subdominant) 23–4; C minor (tonic) 37–8 and, following the ritornello, again at 46–7. The B section begins on the sharp side, B♭ major, and cadences in that key 50–51; in E♭, 54–5; and moves to the dominant minor (G minor), where it cadences (no third in the chord, incidentally) at 66–7.

DISCUSSION
The A section has a tonal scheme of tonic–relative–subdominant–tonic; the sharp side, G minor or B♭ major, is entirely absent. I assume this is because Handel is reserving both these keys for the B section.

3.5 No. 6, Recitative: 'Stay, shepherd, stay!'
No. 7, Air: 'Shepherd, what art thou pursuing?' (Damon)

The delightfully brief and pertinent recitative leads to an Italianate ritornello-based *da capo* air which could serve as the archetype for the hundreds of such movements found in works by Handel and his contemporaries. 'Shepherd, what art thou pursuing?' seems to me first class in every respect: form, tonal movement, melody, accompaniment and deftness of orchestration, all of which are persuasively realized by the St Martin's Academy/Marriner performance we have chosen, especially in the tasteful but thoroughly characteristic embellishments, vocal and orchestral, found in the repeat of the A section. **Listen to the movement now**.

Fairly obviously, the piano accompaniment to the vocal score lacks the finesse of Handel's scoring which is, incidentally, for first and second violins in unison,

---

[1]That is, $\frac{3}{4}$ ♩♩♩♩♩♩ |becomes in effect $\frac{3}{2}$ ♩♩♩♩♩♩ |. You will remember from Unit 3, Section 4.2, that this is a characteristic and prevailing feature of the courante in the French suite.

◀ **Figure 5.2F**

This extract is from an undergraduate course on music (A314). The page bristles with terminology that may be unfamiliar to most of us -- "hemiola cadences", "dotted rhythms", "ritornello", etc. -- though this "jargon" is clearly presumed to be familiar to learners who have got this far through the course. (Notice the footnote referring readers back to an earlier lesson.) Despite its technical vocabulary, the prose is energetic and personal.

The discussion centres around listening to recorded music. In this section of the course, learners are listening to a commercially-produced gramophone record. A pair of symbols appears in the margin at two points on the page -- signalling to readers, the moment they turn to this page, that they will be needing their gramophone record and (the symbol on the right) their printed score. An additional prompt is given by printing the instruction to play the record in bold type.

The first use of the gramophone record and score relates to an activity (or "exercise" as it is labelled here). Readers are asked whether the tonal scheme is conventional in the piece they are listening to -- and to locate the expected cadences in their score. The author's answer follows immediately, the heading "Answer" perhaps acting as a "reader stopper". A paragraph headed "Discussion" follows the answer, and the whole activity block is preceded and followed by a line across the page.

The second "listening" has no exercise associated with it. Readers are given information and judgements about the piece but are not asked questions about it. We can no doubt think of reasons why the course author might choose sometimes to direct the learner's listening and sometimes not, but we cannot confirm them from this extract alone.

G

B4:1.3   11

and is noticeably less spread out. There appears to be a marked peak just below 60 in the sampling distribution whereas it is difficult to identify a peak in the population distribution.

You may also have commented on the fact that the heights of the vertical lines in the sampling distribution are smaller than those in the population distribution. This is due to the fact that the vertical lines measure proportion and in each case the sum of the heights of *all* the vertical lines is equal to one. Because there are many more lines in the sampling distribution, the heights of the individual lines are correspondingly smaller. (This is rather like what happened in Section 3 of Unit B1 when we looked at various probability distributions. Recall that the greater the number of possible outcomes, the smaller the corresponding probabilities.) ■

In fact we are really interested in what happens to the sampling distribution as the sample size increases. So we shall now look at the sampling distribution of the mean for samples of size 5.

Notice that there are about 10^{17} possible samples of size 5.

Activity 1.5   Find the sample mean of each of the following samples of size 5

(a)   10, 20, 45, 62, 91
(b)   82, 24, 33, 33, 60
(c)   52, 61, 73, 61, 43
(d)   79, 64, 46, 59, 91.

Solution

(a)   sample mean $= \dfrac{10 + 20 + 45 + 62 + 91}{5} = \dfrac{228}{5} = 45.6$

(b)   sample mean $= \dfrac{232}{5} = 46.4$

(c)   sample mean $= \dfrac{290}{5} = 58$

(d)   sample mean $= \dfrac{339}{5} = 67.8$. ■

This activity demonstrates that there are many more possible values of the sample mean for samples of size 5 than there are for samples of size 2. This means that the vertical lines in the sampling distribution will be *extremely* close together, in fact so close that it is impossible for us to differentiate between them. For this reason we just concentrate on the *shape* of the distribution as indicated by the *tops* of the lines and we obtain the following picture of the sampling distribution, Figure 1.8.

Figure 1.8   *Sampling distribution of the mean for samples of size 5*

Compare with Figure 1.7. Here we have changed the scale on the vertical axis in order to make the picture as clear as possible.

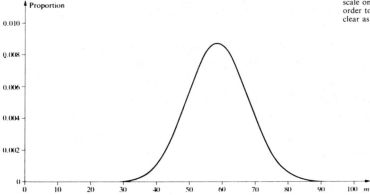

◀ Figure 5.2G

This extract is from an undergraduate course on Statistics (MDST 242). It begins part of the way through the "feedback" to an "activity" in which learners have been asked to comment on a graph. (The black square signals the end of the feedback.) A brief paragraph links this with the next labelled activity -- a set of calculations. Notice that there is no "reader stopper". However, as in Extract F, the next heading, "Solution", may be enough to remind learners not to read on.

With numerical answers of this kind, however, it is quite easy for readers to glimpse them inadvertently before having attempted the calculations themselves. You may or may not consider this worth worrying about. If you do, you may ask learners to guard against it by covering the page below each activity with a sheet of paper. Alternatively, you can print the answers elsewhere in the book.

After the worked solutions have been presented in the extract opposite, the black square again signals the end of the feedback. Then follows the author's comments on the results, leading on to the next step in the argument which is illustrated with a new diagram.

Notice how the wide margin is used both to show a calculator-symbol (signalling to readers that they are about to be asked to do some computation) and to offer comments on the main text and the diagram. Compare this with Extract F in which review material is given as a footnote. The use of footnotes and marginal comments needs thinking about in writing self-instructional texts. Are they optional reading? Or are they meant to be looked at as soon as they are referred to in the main text? If the latter, why not incorporate them into the body of the text? How can they best help the reader?

H

Section 8A:2

METALLURGICAL EXAMINATION OF THE BRAKE ROD

A metallurgical examination of the brake rod was performed at the Safety in Mines Research Establishment (SMRE), Sheffield. This examination included: visual inspection, non-destructive inspection, chemical analysis, metallographic examination and mechanical testing. We shall proceed in a similar fashion with our examination.

8A:2.1   Visual examination

Before we consider the observations made at SMRE, cast yourself in the role of a metallurgical Sherlock Holmes and carry out a visual inspection of the material evidence.

Take Replica 6 (not labelled) from your Home Experiment Kit. It is moulded from the fracture surface of the larger piece of brake rod. Spend at least three or four minutes examining it under a table lamp both with your naked eye and using the magnifier. Pay particular attention to the texture of the fracture surface and to any features on the perimeter of the cross-section. Try to find answers to the following questions (I suggest you cover up the answers in the margin).

How many areas of distinguishable surface texture can you see?

> You should be able to see at least two with the naked eye. The circular fracture surface consists of two segments; the larger one (seen in the lower part of Stereoslide 7) is rather smooth, dull and flat, whereas the smaller segment is rougher and more reflecting. Both segments lie approximately perpendicular to the axis of the rod.

Compare the fracture of the brake rod to the fractures of Replicas 1–4 (the Charpy impact specimens). What conclusion can you draw?

> Replicas 1, 3 and 4 have shear lips and are not similar to Replica 6. The brake rod fracture is similar to that of Replica 2 in that the fracture is flat and lies perpendicular to the side surfaces. In texture, the Replica 2 fracture is similar to the smaller segment of the brake rod fracture. Since you know that Replica 2 is a brittle fracture (Section 6A:1.1), this suggests that the smaller segment of the brake rod surface is a brittle fracture too. This is consistent with it being reflecting.

What is the significance of the path taken by the perimeter of the rod's fracture surface?

> The perimeter follows the root of a screw thread; since this follows a helical path there is a step on the perimeter of the fracture surface (at the top of Stereoslide 7). Clearly the larger fracture segment has followed the screw thread.

14

◀ **Figure 5.2H**

This extract is from an undergraduate course on materials (T351). The layout of the page is striking. After three introductory paragraphs, the learner is presented with a sequence of three "activities" -- indented and underlined. Each activity has its own feedback in the margin (also underlined). Notice that readers are asked to cover up the answers.

Notice also that this extract includes practical work. The activities call for the learner to examine replicas of fractured materials from a "Home Experiment Kit". Among other things, this kit contains a magnifier which learners are expected to use in this "visual inspection". The Kit also includes a simple device for viewing pairs of slides that give a stereoscopic (3-D) image. (These slides are referred to in the feedback to the first and third activities.)

The questions require learners to identify features on one specimen, compare it with other specimens, and make deductions from the evidence. The feedback takes the learners through what they ought to be seeing. Sometimes, to save the learners needing to flip their focus back and forth between a specimen (or slides, filmstrip, etc.) and the explanatory text, it can be worthwhile putting such commentary on audiotape -- thus leaving the learners' eyes free to concentrate on the objects.

I

2   THE MANSFIELD THEATRICALS

(Chapters 13–18, see Introduction pp. 26–31).

At the bottom of page 147 Jane Austen makes the observation that 'a love of the theatre is so general, an itch for acting so strong among young people that he [Mr Yates] could hardly out-talk the interest of his hearers'. But Edmund and Fanny hold out against this general enthusiasm. What are their reasons?

We are told Edmund's reasons first. He is worried by the scale of the upheaval that is threatened, and feels it to be particularly improper while his father is absent (and possibly in some danger) and Maria is in a state of semi-official engagement. Sir Thomas, Edmund is convinced, would 'totally disapprove' (p. 152). Fanny 'had . . . borne Edmund company in every feeling throughout the whole' (p. 153). So does she disapprove simply because Edmund does? I don't think Jane Austen puts this explanation entirely out of the question. She exalts the values of Fanny's love for Edmund (see Chapter 4) but this does not put her above being slightly amused by her devotion. However, Fanny has been considering the situation independently, and has come to the conclusion that if scruples about Sir Thomas won't stop the actors, their own egocentricities may. Edmund's words are very fine, but quiet Fanny is the more down-to-earth, perhaps.

Edmund's resistance begins to crack very quickly. Where do you first see signs of him weakening, and what do you think Jane Austen intended us to understand by it?

When Mary Crawford announces her desire to be useful, Edmund is 'obliged to acknowledge that the charm of acting might well carry fascination to the mind of genius' (p. 154). I'm not sure whether his tone here is meant to suggest stilted pomposity, or ironic overstatement; but it certainly conveys his embarrassment. I don't think this indicates that we are called on to condemn Edmund downright as a hypocrite; what Jane Austen is doing is establishing with masterly care the mixture of his motives. Look at the exchange with Fanny on page 175 where he finally capitulates. Are we meant to praise or blame him? Or is a more complex assessment required of us?

Surely, what we are asked for is richer than simple praise or blame: Jane Austen wants us to see all the irony of the situation. Poor Edmund, not only forced out of his opposition, but made to take one of the leading, and most improper, parts! And his motives hopelessly divided between preserving the sanctity of his father's household, and pleasing Mary Crawford!

◀ Figure 5.2I

This extract is from an undergraduate course on the nineteenth century novel (A302). In a way, it is similar to extract A in that it is guiding learners through their reading of a separate, already-published book. In this case, however, the book (Jane Austen's *Mansfield Park*) is not the source of the teaching (as was Charles Handy's *Understanding Organizations*) but rather the **subject** of the teaching.

Learners are here being involved in a detailed analysis of a chapter they have already read through on their own. The author of the lesson proceeds by asking readers to say what they see in the chapter (e.g. "Where do you first see signs of him weakening?") but also to interpret Jane Austen's intentions (e.g. "Are we meant to praise or blame him?").

The author's feedback to these activity-questions is careful in giving the facts (complete with page-references); but she also states her own opinions. These latter are often questing and tentative (e.g. "I don't think...". "perhaps...", "I'm not sure...") as befits a teacher who is helping learners respond to irony and ambiguity -- rather than memorize some received view of what Jane Austen is all about.

Visually, the page is dominated by the prominent and elaborate "stoppers". Together with the decorated initial letter, they perhaps lend a period flavour to the design of the page; but they are heavier than they need be to remind learners not to read on -- and, in fact, they were reduced in size in later editions of the course.

J

Activity 4.6   Allow 5 minutes

Active listening

This activity, like the last one, uses photographs and is quick and easy to do. These photographs are intended to make you more consciously aware of the non-verbal messages associated with listening.

As you look at the following two photographs, imagine that *you* are the patient. State, in each case, whether you think that the nurse is listening to you in a way that really makes you feel she is concerned to hear what you have to say. Write down what it is about the nurse that tells you whether or not she is listening.

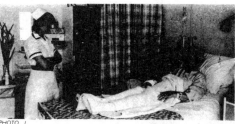

PHOTO 1

PHOTO 2

Authors' comment

PHOTO 1 *this nurse appears to be paying attention to what the patient is saying, for she is looking directly at her. However, the nurse is standing up and has placed herself further away from the patient than is usual for someone who is genuinely interested in developing a conversation. The nurse also has her arms folded so that she is unconsciously creating a physical barrier between herself and the patient. The message which the patient receives from the nurse is to keep her conversation brief and superficial.*

PHOTO 2 *this patient is being listened to. The nurse has positioned herself close to the woman and at her eye level. She shows no sign of hurrying*

away. *She is looking directly at her patient and her face shows that she is concentrating on what is being said. The way the nurse is leaning slightly towards the woman suggests genuine interest, and her touch shows warm concern. The patient should be aware that the nurse wishes to hear what she has to say and indeed, she appears to be quite relaxed and comfortable in the conversation.*

Communication is a two-way process. Once you have perceived what your patient is telling you, you need to respond in a way that shows you understand.

You can convey empathy in your words and your actions. For example, you can use words which simply reflect an understanding of what is being said:

"I can see that is very painful for you to talk about."
"You are really very worried about going home."

You can avoid words that imply an opinion or judgment and thereby focus attention away from the patient and onto yourself.

"That's good", "That's wrong", "I think you should . . ."

Touch can convey a great deal of warmth and understanding, but needs to be used sensitively. Inappropriate invasion of personal space can be discomfiting and irritating and will not be received as an empathetic gesture. However, holding the hand of a woman in labour or a patient undergoing a painful procedure, cuddling an unhappy child or literally providing a shoulder for a distressed patient or relative to cry on are examples of ways in which touch can be used to give comfort. Touch can also be invaluable in conveying empathy when there are major communication barriers, as with a blind person, a patient being artificially ventilated, or a patient who cannot understand English.

Allowing the patient to cry, or to express anger or any other emotion is important. "There, there don't cry", or "try to calm down" imply that you don't think that the emotions being expressed are appropriate, or at least that the person shouldn't be sharing them with you.

Of course, empathy isn't something which you deliberately set out to create — it evolves within a relationship; but a deeper understanding of the elements of communication involved and a heightened self-awareness can make you a much more effective partner to your patient. If this material is new to you, further study in the field is strongly recommended (see *Further Reading* at the end of the module).

Activity 4.7   Allow 10 minutes

Getting involved with your patients

This activity aims to help you think about the practicalities of forming close relationships with your own patients and their families.

List any practical difficulties or personal anxieties which you think may occur if you get more closely involved with your patients and their families.

◀ **Figure　5.2J**

This extract is from a professional updating course for nurses (P553).　As in Extract D, the discussion is clearly job-related and concerns human relationships　It seeks to influence the reader's attitudes and behaviour (as well as understanding) in attaining empathy with patients.

There are two activities -- each labelled "Activity" and numbered.　The presentation of the activities has three features that do not appear in any of our other extracts:

• readers are told about how long to spend on each activity;
• each activity is given a descriptive heading; and
• readers are told what they are meant to get out of it.

In the first activity, readers are asked to identify with the patients in two "micro case studies" and pick out significant aspects of the nurses' behaviour.　(Such an activity might suggest a moving picture treatment, on videotape; but obviously much is possible using still pictures only.)　The second activity asks readers to anticipate likely difficulties in applying the approaches being discussed to **their own** situation. Notice the kind of feedback the author gives.

The two-column format is neither "portrait" nor "landscape" -- for the text area is as broad as it is high. Notice the variety of typestyle.　Apart from the main text, different typefaces are used for headings to the two activities (bold), for the statement of purpose for each activity and for "speech" within the main text (italics), and for the feedback to activities (light italic). Notice also that all these typefaces, unlike those in our other extracts, are "san serif" (no little tails on the letters).

K

2 PERSON TO PERSON

Asserting yourself

Relationships are a matter of give and take. You tell people what you want. You try to understand what they want.

How can you do it without falling into the traps we talk about in the earlier topics? Look at the cartoons on these two pages and decide which is most typical of you when you try to stick up for yourself.

Passive, hostile or assertive?

The first cartoon shows a passive exchange. Mabel approaches Bill timidly. She is apologetic. She is vague about what she wants. Bill hardly bothers to listen. He doesn't even register that there is a problem.

The second cartoon shows a hostile exchange. Mabel is really steamed up. She attacks Bill but she doesn't really say what she wants him to do. The conversation escalates. They exchange insults. Bill slams out of the house.

In the third cartoon strip, Mabel gets what she wants. Bill agrees to 'talk about the problem'. Why? What has happened that is different? Mabel has asserted herself. She has worked out beforehand what she wants to say. She is concrete about exactly what she wants Bill to do. She persists. She is not put off.

Asserting yourself or asserting your rights is part of good, clear communication. People sometimes think that being assertive means being pushy, selfish or manipulative. It doesn't.

You are more likely to be manipulative if you adopt a passive role like Mabel in the first cartoon. This Mabel will probably get back at Bill by sulking, crying or secret acts of revenge. She might 'forget' to wash his socks.

You are more likely to be selfish and pushy if you adopt the hostile approach. The hostile approach assumes that no compromise is possible. The only gains will be those won by force. Blaming, anger and making others feel guilty are the weapons in both cases.

Asserting yourself means first working out what you want, then saying it clearly and negotiating with others. If you are assertive, you retain your dignity and leave others the chance to retain theirs.

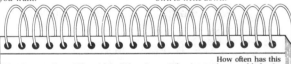

What do you do?

Most people have times when they find it difficult to assert themselves. Someone puts you down. Someone takes advantage of you. You get bad service in a shop. You can't stand up to someone in authority. You feel timid, anxious, or shy. You find a 'good reason' for not making a fuss. And you don't get what you want.

Think of some occasions where this sort of thing has happened to you recently. Write them down, on a separate piece of paper, like the example from Mabel below. For each one make sure you write down what happened, who you were with, where you were, when it happened, how often this has happened before.

Think of at least four events of your own to write down.

What happened?	Who with?	Where?	When?	How often has this happened before?
When I made a comment about politics to Jane, Bill said 'Oh Mabel, you don't know what you're talking about'	Bill	At a party	Last week	Every time we meet his friends

56

For the four events you have written down, tick any of the following feelings you experienced at the time:

	1	2	3	4
sad				
hostile				
bewildered				
frightened				
shy				
resigned				
inadequate				
self-conscious				
stupid				
inferior				

Tick any of the following bodily reactions you felt:

	1	2	3	4
'butterflies in the stomach'				
blushing				
going weak at the knees				
dry mouth				
increased pulse				
heart thumping				
shallow breathing				
hot flushes				
sweating				

And any of the following rationalisations you made to yourself:

	1	2	3	4
it's not worth making a fuss about				
perhaps I'm being selfish				
it's only once				
no-one else is complaining				
it won't make any difference				
I don't want to make a scene				

You now have the information you need to start changing your behaviour to become more assertive. Look through your list of situations. Decide which was the most threatening to you.

Decide which was the least threatening. And which came in between. The more ticks you made on the three checklists above the more threatening or upsetting the situation probably was. Use this as a rough guide to help you judge.

Now pick one of your medium-threat situations. This is the situation you are going to work on for the rest of this topic. If you choose a very threatening situation to work on it is likely to be too upsetting for you to do much about at first. If you pick one with very little threat it will be such a pushover that you won't learn anything.

57

Comments overleaf →

◀ **Figure 5.2K**

The previous extract is a "double page spread" from a continuing education course called *Health Choices* (P921).

The format is similar to that of many popular magazines and "part publications" -- three-column layout, prominent titles and subtitle "trailers", "human interest", illustrations that cut across several columns, questions and quizzes and checklists to tick, and resolutely reader-directed language (look how frequently the word "you" appears). Unlike many popular publications, however, the emphasis is clearly not on entertainment or even on giving information: it is on helping readers to understand themselves better and to act more effectively.

There are two activities in this extract. The first asks readers to identify four events in their own lives of the kind being discussed. As an example, they are shown how Mabel (who appears in the cartoon) might have answered. The second activity asks readers to analyse their responses to the four events, using checklists.

No feedback is provided for the first activity (though Mabel's answer can be seen as a kind of "feed-forward", against which readers can assess the appropriateness of their own answers). Feedback on the second activity is a comment helping readers to interpret their responses.

Incidentally, these pages illustrate the impediments to smooth reading that can result if we abandon single-column layout. Did you ever find yourself reading material out of the sequence intended by the authors (e.g. in the right-hand cartoons or in the text below them)? If so, how might the design have been modified to prevent this?

Figure 5.2L ▶

The following and final extract consists of two consecutive pages from an undergraduate course on biology (SDT286). It concerns the analysis of two experiments about the role of learning in influencing simple behaviour. The course author presents the facts, but the activities require learners to do the analysing.

The first activity asks learners to formulate a suitable hypothesis for the first experiment. The second activity asks them to interpret the results of that experiment as displayed in a bar chart. The third activity invites readers to formulate a new hypothesis about a related experiment. Finally, in the fourth activity (SAQ7), readers are asked to compare the two experiments and come to a conclusion about the underlying principle.

The layout of the first three activities is similar to that in Extract H. The fourth activity is treated differently. In addition to "ordinary" activities, this course contains what are labelled as "self assessment questions" (or SAQs) and prints the answers or feedback all together at the end of each lesson. The activities labelled "SAQ" are those that test attainment of major objectives. In SAQ7, learners are reminded (by reference to a number in an earlier list) that the objective here is "to evaluate experimental evidence concerning the ontogeny of simple behaviour".

The feedback to the SAQs is given at the end of a section. Should the graphs (because they are so eye-catching) also have been kept well away from the activities?

Notice in this extract (as in Extract J) that the pictures are **essential** to the teaching. They alone present the key information on which the activities are based.

L

relative of our own sea gull. When newly hatched, the young Laughing Gulls are fed by their parents, who regurgitate food in response to the young birds pecking at their beaks; the parents then pick up some of the food and present it to the young. Hailman presented juvenile Laughing Gull chicks with several different models of gull heads, to investigate their stimulus preferences.

In the first part of the experiment, Hailman presented newly-hatched naïve Laughing Gull chicks with the cardboard models shown in Figure 8.

Figure 8   The gull-head models used by Hailman (see text for details).

Model A closely resembles the parent Laughing Gull.

Model B has the standard red beak but with an irregular head shape.

Model C is a standard red beak shape with only a fragment of the head.

Model D is the standard red beak shape alone.

Model E is the standard Laughing Gull head without a beak.

Hailman measured the number of pecking responses given to each model in thirty seconds; each chick was, however, only presented with one model and was tested only once.

On the assumption that the instinctive behaviour enables a 'biologically appropriate response' to be made, which model do you expect the young birds to prefer?

Clearly a 'biologically appropriate response' would be one made to the model that most closely resembles the parent's head. The results of this experiment are given in Figure 9.

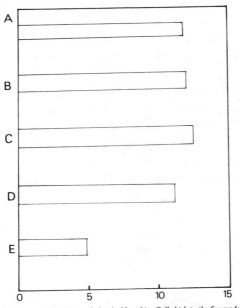

Figure 9   The responses of the newly hatched Laughing Gull chick to the five model heads (see text for details.)

←Comments overleaf

The results of these experiments indicate that the chicks did not discriminate between models A to D, but showed a marked preference for these four models in comparison with model E.

> On the basis of these results, which features of the models appear to be important in eliciting the naïve chicks' begging responses?

The differences between the group of models A to D and model E indicate that some feature of models A to D is the important determinant for this begging response. Further, since models A to D all have the head and beak, but E does not have the beak, it seems that the important common feature is the beak itself.

From Hailman's first experiment we can isolate the parent bird's beak as being the important stimulus in eliciting the naïve juvenile birds' begging responses. As a second part of this experiment, Hailman presented the same model to experienced, older Laughing Gull chicks which had been wild-reared.

> On the assumption that the begging behaviour is 'instinctively determined,' which of the models do you predict will elicit the most begging responses from the wild-reared chicks?

Since, in the first part of the experiment, the naïve chicks all gave similar responses to models A to D, if the food begging behaviour is truly instinctively determined, you might expect experienced birds also to show a preference for models A to D— because they all contain the standard red bill shape. The results of this experiment are shown in Figure 10, together with the results of the previous experiment.

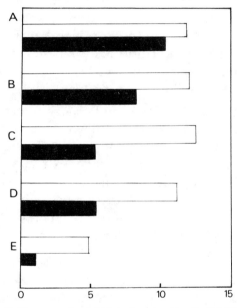

Figure 10 *The responses of newly hatched and experienced Laughing Gull chicks to the five model heads (see text for details).*

SAQ 7 (*Objective 8*)

> Are there any differences between the responsiveness of the newly hatched chicks and that of the older experienced chicks? If so what implication does this have for the idea that the chicks' behaviour is instinctively determined?

This experiment, then, has demonstrated how learning can influence the course of development of stereotyped, species-typical behaviour, such as the food-begging response, that is thought to be instinctively determined. This, of course, is just one example of the modification of stereotyped behaviour, but there are many other such examples and one will be discussed in Unit 14. In general, it is

role of learning

In Conclusion

In this chapter, I have asked you to consider some of the issues involved in writing for self-instruction and, in particular, to look with me at some sample pages from self-instructional texts.

The sample pages we looked at were all from Open University texts but, nevertheless, we were able to see considerable variety in subject-matter, in types of objective and/or learner being aimed at, in layout and typography, in teaching approach, in integration with other media, and (a subject we explore further in Chapter 6) in the forms of "activity" -- from simple questions of the "What do you see?" or "Is this an example?" type up to those requiring the learners to evaluate, interpret or relate what is being discussed to their own lives or work.

It may be that none of the sample pages comes very close to your own subject area. This, however, should not have prevented you from picking up useful insights. Again, you might have liked to see longer extracts from some of the courses; but it is instructive to notice just how much of interest one can glean from a single page. All the same, it is obvious that these pages represent only a tiny sample of the world's (or even the Open University's) self-instructional materials. So:

> START MAKING YOUR OWN COLLECTION OF
> SELF-INSTRUCTIONAL TEXTS (OR EXTRACTS) THAT
> HAVE IDEAS OR APPROACHES YOU MIGHT SOME DAY
> USE IN WRITING YOUR OWN LESSONS.

6. PROMOTING ACTIVE LEARNING

Active learning? This is the most distinctive feature of the kind of self-instruction we are thinking about in this book. As I indicated in Chapter 5, we should not treat the writing of a self-instructional lesson as an opportunity to lecture at our readers -- pouring out a stream of information for them to register and commit to memory. Instead, we should aim to draw responses out of our readers and to get them to learn by DOING.

> OUR AIM SHOULD BE TO PRODUCE THE WRITTEN
> EQUIVALENT OF A ONE-TO-ONE TUTORIAL.

Imagine how you might operate as a tutor or a coach, working with just one learner. You would not expect to ramble on at length about your subject (as you might in a lecture). You would make sure your learner was working with you. You would perhaps present some provocative ideas or give a demonstration -- but every so often you would stop and encourage your learner to contribute something. For instance:

- You might simply check that the learner understood what you had been getting at.

- You might ask the learner to suggest examples from his or her own experience.

- You might get the learner to apply the ideas being discussed to a new situation or example.

- You might invite the learner to carry out a practical task involving the new ideas. And so on.

As a tutor or coach, you would be drawing active responses from your learner. You would then **comment** on each response. You would give your learner **feedback** as to the strengths/weaknesses of his or her response -- or at least say what you found interesting about it. Perhaps also you might mention other possible responses that could have been made to the same question or task. You might then build upon your learner's response in moving on to the next substantive stage in the teaching.

TEACHING THROUGH ACTIVITIES

In short, such a tutorial is an **interaction** between tutor and learner. This is what we are trying to simulate in the tutorial-in-print. Learners are kept more alert and involved -- and learn better -- when they are required to **use** ideas rather than merely reading (or hearing) about them. Bear in mind the old Chinese proverb:

> *I hear, and I forget;*
> *I see, and I remember;*
> *I do, and I understand.*

This is why **activities** -- questions, tasks, exercises -- are a vital feature of self-instructional material (see Figure 5.2/A-L on pages 92-117). They are meant to keep learners purposefully engaged with the material. Without them, our learners would be denied a benefit that "face-to-face" learners take for granted -- the opportunity to do things with their new learning and get comments on their efforts. Without such activities, our learners might assume that the only objective was to memorize the information we set before them.

Frequency of Activities

So, just like a face-to-face tutor, we structure our discussion around getting the learner to **do** something. We build in frequent activities. These must be built in throughout the text, to help the learner learn. It is not enough to stick them on at the end, where their only role would be to check whether or not he or she **has** learned.

Some writers of self-instruction distinguish between what they call:

- SAQs (Self-assessment questions) -- which may appear, perhaps several together, testing major objectives, at the end of perhaps an hour or so's reading; and

- ITQs (In-text questions) -- which may be used at frequent intervals in the text **between** SAQs, generating the running dialogue between author and reader.

This terminology may not seem very helpful -- since **both** types of activity are really "in-text" and "self-assessed" (and they may take forms other than questions). Nevertheless, the distinction between these two uses of activities is worth bearing in mind.

Of course, there are no rules about how frequently to insert an activity. You may have noticed, however, that some of the examples shown in Figure 5.2 A-L (pages 92-117) had several activities to a page. Some topics may lend themselves to more activities per hour of reading than others do. But I would be surprised if you could present more than three pages of reading without mentioning something worth asking learners about before they read on. And if more than four or five pages went by without your requiring the learners to do anything but read, then I'd suggest you'd forgotten about them. And I'd expect them to have dozed off!

Varieties of Activity

There are many ways we might categorize activities in a self-instructional text. Three key aspects are:

- How much time are learners expected to spend on each activity?

- What do they have to do to arrive at a response?

- How are they to record their response (if at all)?

Some activities require the reader to do little more than "stop and think". These may require a pause of but a few seconds. Other activities may demand a few minutes' calculation or a brief written answer. Yet others may send the reader away from the text for quarter of an hour or more to carry out some kind of practical work.

What do readers have to do to arrive at their response to the question or instruction? Readers may be required, for example, to:

- Reflect on what they have read or on their experience of the world.

- Read a new piece of text -- or view a video, listen to a tape, etc. -- in the light of such reflection.

- Engage in an interview or discussion with other learners or with workmates, family members, etc.

- Carry out practical work with equipment and materials -- either at home or "in the field" -- and record their results.

- Keep a diary or log of work done or observations made over some period of time in preparation for a subsequent lesson.

- Develop a workable proposal -- e.g. for a device or procedure to help handicapped colleagues.

- Imagine what they would think/feel/do as one or more of the participants sketched out in the text -- e.g. as a farmer faced with a change in the government's agricultural policy.

Some ways in which they might be asked to record their responses -- rather than just thinking them -- are:

- Ticking boxes to indicate agreement or disagreement with a number of statements.

- Answering a multiple-choice question, perhaps again by ticking boxes.

- Matching items in one list with items in another, by drawing lines from one list to the other.

- Underlining relevant phrases in a piece of text.

- Completing a form or questionnaire.

- Providing the missing word/phrase/number(s) to fill the blank(s) left in a sentence.

- Writing a word/phrase/number in the margin or in a box provided within the body of the text.

- Writing a longer answer, on the page of the text or in a separate notebook (perhaps for showing to a tutor or for discussion with a colleague or mentor).

- Making additions to a printed diagram, chart, graph, etc.

- Drawing a graph, map, flow-diagram, etc.

- Making a tape-recording -- perhaps for the benefit of other learners or a tutor/mentor.

- Producing some artefact -- e.g. a video-recording.

Such possibilities as those listed above are but a few of the many ways in which we might engage the learner's active participation. (I leave you to check which of them are represented among the sample pages shown in Figure 5.2 and elsewhere in this book.) You will need to decide on ways that are appropriate to your subject, your objectives, and your learners.

Levels of Difficulty

You may also like to consider how difficult or demanding your activities should be. Different types of activity will engage the learner's mind (and heart?) at different levels -- making varying demands on his or her ability to apply the ideas that you are discussing.

The list below shows five types of activity I have noticed in self-instructional material. To me, each of the later ones seems likely to be more demanding than those that precede it in the list. What do you think?:

So, the learner might be expected to:

1. Report his or her observations or experience **in everyday terms** -- usually as a first step towards learning new ways of seeing them:

    e.g. *"Who carries out these procedures in your Department and how often are you involved?"*

2. Pick out, restate, or remember important facts, concepts or principles that you have presented:

    e.g. *"What is meant to be the chief purpose of the new system?"*

3. Distinguish between **given** examples and non-examples of the new concepts and principles that you have presented:

    e.g. *"Which of the following procedures would be acceptable under the new system...?"*

4. Provide his or her **own** examples and non-examples -- perhaps by reporting his or her observations and experience in terms of the new concepts and principles:

    e.g. *"Which of your Department's present procedures will be acceptable under the new system and which will not?"*

5. Apply the new concepts/principles (plus native wit and personal experience) to analyse, interpret or plan a new situation (one that has not been discussed) -- perhaps in the process arriving at a new, personal perspective on the subject:

    e.g. *"What advice would you offer to staff in the Department described below if their procedures are to fit in with the new system?"*

    e.g. *"What snags do you foresee in implementing the new system in your Department, and how would you suggest trying to overcome them?"*

All these types of activity could play a useful part within a single lesson. Type 1 activities might be used where you are about to begin on a new concept or principle. Your readers will not yet have considered the new ways of looking at things. Indeed, Type 1 activities can be used as a basis for the "egrul" or "discovery" learning I discuss in Chapter 7.

Activities of Types 2 and 3 may serve the function of "comprehension questions". They can draw your readers' attention to important points in the text and enable them to check that they understand what you are saying.

Type 4 activities go beyond this -- by asking learners to relate their existing knowledge to what you have taught them. You are inviting them to rethink their experience in your terms.

Type 5 activities can make the ultimate demand on the learners' learning -- by inviting them to analyse, plan and create in the new terms. They may even be faced with situations or problems that are not so cut-and-dried as those they have considered previously. This may require them to **extend** their learning. Like Type 1 activities, those of Type 5 can push the learners towards new knowledge, enabling them to **anticipate** or "discover" ideas, connections and relationships for themselves. If the activity is one (perhaps at the end of a lesson or sequence of lessons) where you don't tell the learner which of the several ideas you've discussed are most relevant to the problem -- leaving the learners to decide this for themselves (alone or with other learners) -- then the activity can be extremely demanding.

I do not claim that my five types cover every possible activity you might think of. Nor do I believe they form a perfect progression of difficulty. You may be able to think up some Type 1 or 2 activities that would be more demanding than some of Type 4 and 5. All the same, even if my list does not seem to relate too closely to the topics you'll be teaching, I hope it will stimulate you in thinking about how **you** might use different kinds of activity to make the appropriate levels of demand on your own learners at different stages in your lessons

> WHICH OF THE ABOVE (OR OTHER) TYPES OF ACTIVITY CAN YOU FIND AMONG THE SAMPLE PAGES (92-117) OF FIGURE 5.2?

HOW TO DEVELOP ACTIVITIES

Before we talk about developing activities, let me remind you of the teaching context in which they appear:

1. You introduce or explain a particular aspect of your topic -- one or more teaching points.

2. You ask your learners to make a response on the basis of:

   - what you can assume they have already learned or experienced elsewhere; and/or

   - what you have told them; and/or

   - what they can anticipate, or else find out somewhere other than in your text.

3. You tell them what response you'd have expected and why. If there is no one correct answer, mention several possible answers that would have been acceptable -- e.g. what other learners may have said; and mention criteria against which they can judge the validity of their own responses.

4. You carry on to the next step in your sequence or the next teaching point you wish to introduce (as in 1. above).

See Figure 6.1 for a visual reminder of this sequence.

Figure 6.1: The Sequence in a Tutorial-in-Print

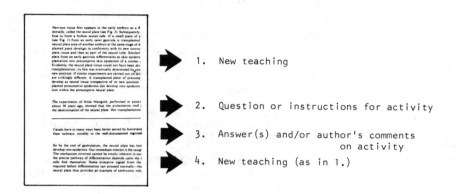

1. New teaching

2. Question or instructions for activity

3. Answer(s) and/or author's comments on activity

4. New teaching (as in 1.)

When to Think about Activities

Some writers are able to think up likely activities even **before** they begin on their text. They can then weave these activities together with suitable exposition. Other writers prefer to launch into the text -- perhaps working through their teaching point outline -- thinking up appropriate activities whenever they reach a critical point in the build-up of their argument.

Yet other authors produce a "straight" version of the text first, and insert activities later -- literally as an after-thought. I used to say that this was about as difficult as inserting currants into a cake that has already been baked. However, my subsequent experience as a "transformer" of less experienced authors' first drafts has changed my opinion. I now believe it is possible to insert worthwhile activities and "study questions" into existing material -- even into material that was not designed for self-instruction. Though I still generally feel that the materials would have been differently (and better) structured if their authors had been thinking in terms of activities at the time they wrote.

Other people's texts. You may need to develop activities in this way yourself, if you ever base a lesson on previously-published texts -- especially if certain passages are not as clear as you would wish. At intervals in their reading of the texts, you could ask your learners to consider questions such as these:

- "The writer mentioned this theory under another name on page 34. What was it?"

- "In the paragraphs above, the writer suggests three exceptions to the general rule. Which of them seems most and which least convincing?."

- "Discuss the viewpoint raised in this section with two or three colleagues and see how their reactions compare with yours."

You will see that one such study question has been added to the "Introduction" shown in Figure 8.2 (on page 169). And Figures 5.2A and I (on pages 92 and 108) show study questions or activities being used to guide learners' reading of a separate text. Clearly, such questions could equally well be applied to audio or video source materials.

Your own texts. However, let's get back to developing your own self-instructional materials. The kinds of activity that are easiest to think up before or after writing the material are SAQs -- questions testing the learners' competence with the main objectives of the lesson.

If you do think up questions in advance, or if you leave it until you have a first draft, do be alert for any that might occur to you **while** you are writing it. If you really are thinking about the learner you are "talking with", such tutorial-type ITQs are bound to come to mind as a means of focussing the interaction -- especially if you apply some of the following advice:

Ways of Generating Activities

Here is a selection of hints and tips to guide you in thinking up activities:

- Keep your objectives in mind while you write. As a rule, your activities should either lead the learner towards an objective through a number of contributory exercises (e.g. ITQs) or else give **guided** practice with that objective (e.g. SAQs).

- Consider what **mis**conceptions about the topic your learners are likely to be starting out with -- and develop an activity that will flush them out for discussion.

- Try to recall the experiences you went through yourself in coming to understand the ideas or procedures under discussion. Try to re-create comparable experiences for the learners; involve them in activities that will help them find their own way through similar routes to understanding.

- Think of group exercises you have used in face-to-face teaching and consider whether any of them might be translated into useful activities for learners working on their own (with or without help from their friends).

- Take a general or abstract point you have made in the text -- e.g. about how people with different values can come into conflict -- and develop a case study in which the learner can be asked to play a certain role.

- If you are bringing graphs or tables or illustrations into your exposition, consider asking the **learners** to read and interpret them -- rather than merely giving your comments on the exhibits. Learners can then go on to read your comments as "feedback" after they have attempted the activity.

- Try not to hand your learners important principles/ generalizations/interpretations "on a plate". Where you can do so without using up a disproportionate amount of their time, enable learners to arrive at the idea themselves -- through an activity. Whenever you find yourself writing phrases like:

  "It therefore follows that..." or
  "From this we can clearly deduce..." or
  "Here is a summary of the argument so far..."

  you perhaps should ask a question instead, e.g.

  "What would you expect to happen as a result?";
  "What can you deduce from this?";
  "What are the four main points raised so far?".

  Again, your deductions or summaries can then be provided as feedback against which the learners can compare their own efforts.

- If you are introducing a steam of important ideas and you want your learner to be able to use them all, make sure they are **all** made the subject of an activity. If they are connected, you may be able to have your learner deal with all of them at once within one activity. Otherwise, group them, or give each idea a separate activity.

- Most important of all: keep thinking about the learner you are tutoring, and keep asking yourself -- page by page -- what would you like your reader to be **doing** with the material you are presenting?

And now three important DON'Ts:

- Don't set vague, pseudo-activities, e.g. "Think about/jot down a few ideas of your own about X". The learner would probably -- and quite rightly -- ignore such half-baked suggestions. Better to say "Tick any of the following comments that are similar to your own ideas about X".

- Don't set an activity unless you are confident your learners should be able to make a reasonably satisfying attempt at it -- satisfying to them, that is. Will they have the necessary knowledge, skills or attitudes -- whether gained from previous learning or from other experience? For instance: Don't base exercises on the assumption that all your readers are male (unless you are sure they are). And don't demand lengthy written answers from readers whose verbal skills are weak.

- Don't set an activity at all unless you are sure it will seem **relevant** to your readers and worth their spending time on. Learners soon learn to skip "trivial" or "busy work" activities. Unfortunately, they may extend the habit to activities that really are crucial.

Technical Issues

Finally, a few technical points about setting activities:

- Right from the start -- e.g. in a "study guide" to the course -- make sure your learners know why you have built the material around activities. What are they meant to do for the learners, and how are they to use them?

- You may also need to tell the learner why certain specific activities -- especially the longer ones -- are worth doing, e.g. "Completing this activity will give you practice in the important skill of ...".

- Be clear about how long you expect the typical learner to spend on each activity. If it is more than a minute or two -- or if it is not obvious from the form of the question -- tell your learners explicitly, e.g. "This exercise should take you between five and ten minutes" or "Spend no more than half an hour...".

- Similarly, if it is not clear from the form of the activity, tell your learners how lengthy an "answer" you require and where you want them to write it. Perhaps you can provide a box or space of appropriate size in the text. If you can't afford the space, however -- or if you wish certain responses to be available for a tutor or mentor to look at -- you may need to ask your learners to write in a separate notebook. In which case, you might say: "Write no more than a sentence" or "In not more than 200 words...", and so on.

- To avoid monotony, watch the balance between, e.g.:
  - brief activities and lengthy ones;
  - those requiring written answers and those merely requiring thought; and
  - closed questions (where there is only one correct answer) and open-ended questions (e.g. "In your experience, what are the most common causes of...?"), where a variety of equally acceptable answers may be forthcoming.

- Use some kind of **"reader-stopper"** to help your readers from accidentally "cheating" by glancing ahead to see your feedback before they have attempted the activity. There are many ways of signalling to readers that here is a place they must stop and do something before reading on, e.g.:
  - a rule across the page;
  - a row of asterisks;
  - an answer box;
  - indented text;
  - a change of typeface;
  - some standard symbol in the margin, e.g., ★

Devices like the above may be used on their own or in combination. (Look back at the reader-stoppers used in the pages shown in Figure 5.2.) You may also provide readers with a **masking card**, of the same width as your page -- to shield those areas of the text they do not yet wish to read.

• As a general rule, place your feedback -- e.g. the answers and your discussion of them -- **immediately** after the reader-stopper. If your readers really wish to, they will use their masking card (or just will-power) to avoid taking a peek. If they do want to "cheat", then attempts to hide the answers -- e.g. by printing them upside-down or on another page -- will merely irritate them. Perhaps to the point where they skip the activities altogether. However, if you can use smaller type or indenting, or even italics or colour, this may be worth considering as a means of "warning off" the reader who is not yet ready to see the feedback.

The only obvious exception to this advice about printing the feedback directly after the stopper is when the answer is a graph or diagram so eye-catching that readers can scarcely avoid registering its salient features as soon as they see the page.

• When the questions you ask are open-ended (e.g. "What do you believe are the reasons why...?"), you will not be able to predict exactly what response your reader will make. However, your feedback should be able to discuss two or three **possible** answers. These you may be able to imagine from previous work with learners on this topic. Alternatively, you may sometimes need to obtain them later -- from the learners on whom you try out your materials in draft form. (For an example, see Figure 6.2 overleaf.)

Figure 6.2: Activity Feedback Provided by Earlier Readers (from *How to Tutor in an Open Learning Scheme* by R. Lewis, CET Publications, 1983)

How to tutor in an open-learning scheme

To meet student expectations by giving 'lectures' can lead to all kinds of problems:

(i) duplication of the course materials

(ii) waste of valuable opportunities for group interaction

(iii) a simple inability to 'cover the syllabus' in the infrequent tutorial time

(iv) the production of dependent rather than autonomous learners.

Q3 How will you (do you) deal with the problems of student expectations discussed above?

132

Face-to-face sessions

Here are some tutor responses.

'By careful structuring of the situation – setting tasks to individuals, getting pairs to work on a problem, syndicates and pyramiding.'

'By concentrating in early sessions on building up a strong sense of "self-help" in the group. This breaks down the shyness and wish to stay separate that often lead to students putting the lecturer in the role of total dominance. When students relax they don't mind admitting to weaknesses, etc.'

'By getting them to meet occasionally between tutorials. Or to ring one another up. This gets round one major problem – the long gaps between tutorials.'

Getting students to work flexibly, and together, can be difficult, especially in early tutorials and when the student population may also be tired after a day's work and reluctant to make the effort to mix and to exchange views. They may feel that it is easier to stay strangers and to be talked at by the tutor. The tutorial may also be very short, say an hour, and you may not feel there's enough time to warm the student up.

A teacher of accounting comments:

'These problems are very real, especially if we want to avoid forcing students into a regular pattern of attendance. I'd look seriously at (artificial) methods of altering expectations, eg,

- name badges (with identifying course details)

- "induction" meetings in which the sole aim was to break the ice and inculcate new expectations

- perhaps a short warm-up period before the session starts, based on a series of "Please find out from your friends" questions: in an English course: find out which poem they like best and why; in an Accounts course: whether

133

At the very least, you should be able to suggest criteria -- e.g. a checklist of points that should have been mentioned in an answer -- by which your learners can evaluate their own responses. If this seems impossible, re-think the activity.

- Be ample with your feedback. For learners working alone, it may be their only way of assessing their own progress. But if your answers are lengthier or more considered than you'd have expected from them in the time implied for the activity, do let your learners know. The relevance and helpfulness of your feedback can make all the difference to how satisfying the learners find your activities and how likely they are to keep doing them.

Look again at the activities included in the pages shown in Figure 5.2 (pages 92-117). Look also at any other self-instructional texts you can find. To what extent do they reflect or contradict the advice given in the previous few pages? What other DOs and DON'Ts would you wish to add to the lists? What decisions do you arrive at about using activities in your own self-instructional teaching?

N.B. If this book were designed as a self-instructional text, I would have inserted a "reader-stopper" at this point. As feedback, I could then have followed up with some comments on the lists of DOs and DON'Ts, provided by people like yourself who had worked through an earlier "tryout version" of the text.

LATER ON, WHEN YOU TRY OUT YOUR LESSON ON SOME LEARNERS, TAKE PARTICULAR NOTE OF HOW THEY TACKLE YOUR VARIOUS KINDS OF ACTIVITY -- AND OF WHAT THEY SAY ABOUT THEM.

7. STRUCTURING YOUR LESSON

How are you to structure your lesson so as to help the learner learn? Chapter 5 discusses one essential structuring device -- the activities. But more is needed -- the **teaching** in which those activities are embedded. How is this to be structured?

As a writer of self-instructional materials -- teaching at a distance -- you will lack the feedback you would get as a classroom teacher. You won't be seeing the puzzled frowns or hearing the exasperated curses of learners who are having difficulty understanding you. You will need to think about all their possible difficulties while you sit at your writing. You will need to structure your lesson in such a way as to help learners avoid, or at least, overcome, them.

To aid you in this task, here is what I am going to talk about in this chapter:

- the importance of your teaching point outline;
- the teaching of concepts and principles;
- two basic teaching strategies; and
- the need for variety of stimulus in your lesson.

REMEMBER YOUR OUTLINE

Keep your "teaching point outline" by your side as you write. If you diverge from it, do so only by conscious decision. Once you have started writing, you will see ways of developing your lesson that could not have occurred to you before you began to clothe general ideas in specific detail. Lessons tend to grow organically, like any creative writing. You may not know exactly what you mean to say until you see what you have already said. But be critical about every diversion and change of emphasis. Don't just wander.

You may find it helpful to stick to the basic rule of **one main idea per paragraph**. This you may state as a teaching point in one sentence -- usually the first in the paragraph. The main idea can then be illustrated, supported, or built upon in the subsequent sentences.

Sometimes, however, you may prefer to lead up to your main idea, rather than starting out with it. In that case, you may hold back your teaching point until the final sentence of the paragraph.

Incidentally, when you finish a lesson, it's worth checking how logically you've sequenced your ideas. Do they hang together, without missing steps? You can check this by noting down the sequence of main ideas you've expressed in each of your paragraphs.

TEACHING CONCEPTS AND PRINCIPLES

In self-instructional teaching, as in other kinds, we are concerned with concepts and principles. Even when we teach techniques and procedures -- like servicing a piece of equipment or filling in a form -- they usually depend on the learner understanding certain concepts and principles. These are our "main ideas".

In the next few paragraphs, I'll mention eight "tasks" that seem to be necessary in teaching concepts and principles. In essence, these amount to the need to provide:

- appropriate and effective examples;
- learner activity or practice; and
- feedback on activities.

Task 1: Analyse Your Main Ideas

This you may have begun at the planning stage. (See Chapter 4.) In the case of each principle you want to teach, what kind of statement is it? Does it define, evaluate, offer an empirical observation, or what? How will different kinds of statement need to be presented?

And what concepts does each principle involve? What are their essential features? Now is the time to put your concept analysis to the test (see page 48). You may even want your learner to work through the concept analysis with you during the lesson.

Let's say the principle we want to teach is the "simple" one -- Area = Length x Width. More precisely, we should say: the area of a rectangular figure = length x width. or, even more precisely: **one** way of finding the area of a rectangle figure is to multiply its length by its width. (Unless it is a square, of course, in which case we could multiply any two adjacent sides.)

Maybe the principle is not quite so simple after all. However, even sticking to the basic computational statement, we see that it involves the concepts of (a) multiplication, (b) length, (c) width, and (d) rectangularity. Each of these, in turn, depends on the learner having acquired certain **prior** concepts. If we feel that the learner may be weak on any of these prior understandings, we shall need to review them, or teach them, within the lesson (see Task 3).

Task 2: Tell Learners what they may Learn to DO

Let the learners know what they should be able to do -- or do better -- as a result of understanding the concepts or principles. Help them see the purpose of the learning. Tell them they'll learn to analyse a Beethoven sonata or a company balance sheet; or to prepare a computer programme or take a statement from a witness. With our area principle, tell them they'll learn to calculate the size of rectangles, and where this ability may prove useful. Learners need this information in order to direct their own learning and monitor their own progress.

Task 3: Ensure Learners have all Pre-requisites

Learners can grasp new ideas only by relating them to ideas they are familiar with already. Your analysis in Task 1 may have revealed concepts a learner must already possess in order to grasp the new concept or principle. These will need teaching first if the learner does not already have them. To acquire even a basic grasp of a concept like, say, "immigrant", the learners would already need to have concepts like "birthplace", "place of domicile" and "travel". In order to distinguish immigrants from emigrants, tourists, travelling business-people, etc., they would need further concepts like "intention", "direction", and "duration of stay".

In the case of our "area = length x width" principle, learners clearly need the notion of rectangularity. Without rectangularity, the calculation would be inappropriate. Learners must also be able to distinguish long sides from wide ones -- or at least recognize that these are two adjacent sides. and they must know what multiplying involves.

Furthermore, if they are to understand the principle -- as opposed to merely being able to apply it (i.e. perform a calculation) -- they must possess some intuitive concept of areas. This latter they may have acquired, for example, by grading rectangles in order of "size" -- or by comparing the number of, say, coins that can fit on surfaces they recognize as being bigger or smaller than one another.

You may need to include some kind of **diagnostic tests** in your lessons -- to establish which of the pre-requisite concepts your learners already possess. Any they do not have already, they will need to learn. Maybe you can provide the necessary teaching within your lessons -- perhaps as an optional sequence which many or most learners will by-pass. Other learners will need to be directed to some other source of instruction, like an earlier lesson or a better-informed colleague.

Anyway, this much is certain: lack of attention to pre-requisite learning -- either not thinking about it at all (assuming that learners will know whatever is necessary) or hoping that they can somehow struggle through without it -- can be the kiss of death to effective self-instructional teaching.

Task 4:   Give Examples and Non-examples of the New Idea

Here you should be able to draw on your earlier concept analysis (Task 1). There are several more detailed points to be made about Task 4:

Provide SEVERAL clear examples. Obvious as this may seem, it is often neglected. If learners are to register all the features of a new idea, they will usually need more than one example. But that is often all they get -- e.g. one photograph of a river's meanders, one specimen of a metal fracture, the recorded sound of one major chord, and so on. If they are to appreciate the variety of situations in which the new idea applies, they need a variety of examples.

Provide several clear NON-examples. Equally, to test the limits of the criteria for using the idea, learners will need several non-examples -- e.g. photographs of non-meandering rivers, specimens of metal that have been cut, recordings of minor chords, and so on. In the case of our "area = length x width" principle, learners will need to recognize that it cannot be applied to shapes that do not have four sides.

Provide BORDER-LINE examples/non-examples. Once our learners can distinguish between clear-cut examples and non-examples of the new idea, they can be exposed to finer discriminations. Present them with border-line examples -- examples they might be tempted to regard as non-examples. For instance, they might not recognize an eel or a sea-horse as "fish".

Examining such border-line examples will help learners to avoid **under**-generalizing the idea -- being too restrictive in its use. With our "area = length x width" principle, a border-line example would be provided by showing how the principle applied to a square.

Conversely, learners may need to avoid **over**-generalizing the idea. Thus, they will need to see some border-line **non**-examples. These are cases to which learners might think the idea applies when in fact it does not. Thus, with the concept of "fish", they might need to be shown that it does not apply to whales or tadpoles or sea-snakes, even though all live in water. These creatures have some of the attributes of the idea in question; but they do not have all that are necessary to qualify as "fish".

Likewise, in learning about "area", our learners may need to be persuaded that the "length x width" principle will not work even on shapes with four straight sides if the shapes do not contain four right angles.

Go from simple to complex, concrete to abstract. (But notice the warning about psychological v. logical order on page 66.) In a way, I have already touched on the simple-to-complex approach in suggesting clear examples before border-line examples. But it is worth singling out for special mention.

Make sure that your first examples of a concept or principle are not cluttered up with inessential elements. For example, in teaching the concept "immigrant", you'd do better to start with a person who has just arrived in your country intending to spend the rest of his or her life there -- rather than with people who were born in your country but whose parents had immediately taken them abroad where they had remained for the last sixty years, returning now to spend their final years in the homeland (if they can adjust to it)! In the case of "area = length x width", an example of simple-to-complex would be to deal with rectangles having sides of, say, 3 x 2 before dealing with sides of, say, 3.42 x 0.07. Clearly, we would not wish arithmetic to obscure the principle.

What about concrete-to-abstract? Generally speaking, it is better to offer concrete examples (and non-examples) before abstract ones. A real fish is more concrete than a picture of a fish. A picture is more concrete than a verbal description. A verbal description is more concrete than the name of the concept.

If learners start off on examples that are too abstract, they may learn only a pallid, verbal ghost of the concept. Conceivably, for example, they might be able to recognize "trout", "herring" and "shark" as the names of fish -- yet not be able to recognize any of these creatures as fish if they were shown unlabelled specimens. Unless they had seen specimens, or at least pictures, while supposedly learning the concept, they would be unable to link the name with the object.

How would concrete-to-abstract apply in teaching "area = length x width"? Well, perhaps we'd have our learners begin by cutting out cardboard rectangles and covering them with cut-out squares. Then we might have them draw squares on rectangles. Next they might do the calculation after merely measuring the sides. Finally, they would apply the principle to rectangles they never see at all, being merely told the lengths of the sides.

Task 5: Link New Idea to Learners' Experience

Whether you are giving examples to convey a new idea, or trying to explain it by use of analogy, do ask yourself whether your learners will know what you are talking about. Do your examples or analogies touch on the learners' experience? For instance, if you wanted an example of "cash flow", you might need to remind some learners about their household accounts -- rather than delve immediately into the possibly remote, and certainly more complex, world of high finance.

Analogy can be a potent means of clarifying a new idea. That is, we can point out all the ways in which the new idea is similar to one that learners are already familiar with. For example, we might tell them that "isobars are like the lines on a contour map". For this to be illuminating, of course, we have to be sure that they **already** understand contour maps.

Unfortunately, it is all too easy to find oneself trying to explain something the learners don't understand by relating it to something else they don't understand! In the last couple of weeks I have watched two television programmes in a series about computers. The first tried to explain how computers work by analogy with a Jacquard loom. The next programme -- as if in recognition that the previous analogy may not have been totally transparent to all viewers -- tried again, this time comparing the computer with a steam organ. In both cases, however, the object of the analogy -- the loom and the steam organ -- seemed too much in need of explanation itself to contribute anything to my understanding of computers.

That last example reminds me of another common pitfall, especially when the analogy you are using is rich or exotic. Your learner may incorrectly assume that the thing you are trying to explain (e.g. the working of the computer) shares certain characteristics with the object of the analogy (e.g the steam organ) **in addition** to those you were identifying. Such errors, which might easily be corrected in face-to-face teaching, can be troublesome when the learner is learning at a distance. Be careful to indicate the limitations of your analogies.

Task 6: Get your Learners to Apply the Idea

At the beginning of the lesson, you may identify all the examples and non-examples of the new idea for your learners. But, as the lesson develops, you may want them to make such identifications -- increasingly subtle ones --

Figure 7.1:   A Sequence of Double-page Spreads
(from Open University course P912, Book 4)

for themselves. If the concept or principle has several aspects which you are teaching one at a time, get the learners to demonstrate that they can apply those you have taught so far before you go on to teach more.

For instance, taking "fish" again, suppose you are beginning with the fact of their living in water. You may start with examples like salmon and sharks, and non-examples like dogs and birds. Before going on to attributes like "cold blood" or "scales" or "no legs", or whatever is essential, you might well present the learners with a set of creatures, only one of which (say a carp) lives in water, and ask them to pick out the fish. Your next exercise might involve them in selecting the fish, using new attributes, from a group of creatures all of which live in water.

Furthermore, once your learners' basic grasp of a concept or principle is established, you will want them to use it, along with others learned earlier. You may get them to apply it, for example, in analysing a case study, carrying out some practical procedure, or exploring a theory. Thus, the concept of "fish" might be used in developing the idea of an evolutionary progression of life-forms from water to the land.

Here I must briefly mention one other way of using examples which I'll be describing more fully in the next section (pages 148-151). That is, you may sometimes want your learners to work out the principles for themselves -- rather than merely apply them once you have pointed them out. For instance, you could provide the learners with a set of examples and ask them to pick out the features they have in common. If they were learning about area in this way, they might be given a series of exercises requiring them to cover rectangles with cut-out squares. These exercises would culminate in their making the "discovery" that the total number of squares on any rectangle was the product of the two sides. Such "discovery learning" can be very effective, although it may be unduly time-consuming in some cases.

However you get your learners to apply the ideas of your lesson, appropriate **activity** is essential. This is discussed at length in Chapter 6.

Task 7: Give Learners Feedback on their Activity

This also sounds almost too obvious to mention. But it is often not done, even in books that include questions and exercises. Sometimes the answers are not printed at all. Sometimes only bare answers are printed, with no indication as to the criteria by which they are justified. So learners who get the same answer as that shown in the book may be ignorant as to whether they reached it by the "best" route. And those with different answers are not told how far they were working on the right lines or where their mistakes occurred.

Feedback is also discussed in Chapter 6. There we are considering pre-planned feedback, the same for all readers, printed in the lesson. However, it is worth remembering that learners working with self-instruction will occasionally need **individual** feedback. They may not be able to monitor their progress satisfactorily by relying solely on your pre-printed specimen answers and comments. You may need to provide a means whereby, from time to time, they can get their work inspected and commented upon -- by colleagues, by other learners or by tutors/mentors. I discuss this kind of feedback at length in Chapter 11 and 13. It can play a vital part in helping your learners learn.

Task 8: Give Your Learners Practice with the Idea

Practice will occur almost automatically in a sequential or hierarchical subject like mathematics or science. Later parts of a lesson -- or later lessons in a course -- will build on earlier parts. In tackling new ideas, the learners will constantly be using those they acquired earlier.

With less hierarchical subjects, you may need to make a special effort to help your learners keep earlier ideas alive in their minds. One way of doing so is to include them in your occasional summaries of the course (or lesson) so far. Another is to refer back to them by way of contrast or analogy with concepts and principles you are discussing in a later section. A third way to encourage practice is to include questions relating to those earlier ideas in your periodic tests and assignments.

> ONE OVERALL POINT ABOUT EXAMPLES, ANALOGIES
> AND ACTIVITIES -- DON'T ALWAYS BE SATISFIED
> WITH THE FIRST ONE THAT COMES TO MIND.

TWO BASIC TEACHING STRATEGIES

How are you to get your main ideas across? Here I assume that your purpose is not simply to have your learners read those ideas, or even to read and remember. Rather it is to have your learners read and **understand** them -- in such a way that they can relate them to what they know already and apply them in new situations. That is, you are not telling -- you are teaching.

I suggest there are two basic strategies for teaching the concepts and principles that are our main ideas:

- We can give the learners a "rule" (e.g. a definition); then illustrate with an example of the rule being applied; and finally offer the learners an example to which they must apply the rule themselves; OR

- We can show the learners a number of examples and non-examples of the idea we are trying to develop; then encourage them to notice the similarities and differences among these examples; and finally help them to come up with the "rule" that distinguishes examples from non-examples.

The first strategy is sometimes called the RUL-EG strategy -- rule followed by example. Conversely, the second is the EG-RUL strategy -- examples lead up to the rule.

Let me give you a simple example. (Here I'm following the ruleg strategy). Suppose we wanted to teach the meaning of "triangle". We could start by saying "A triangle is a three-sided figure. Here are some figures. Which of them are triangles? Now you draw some triangles". With (ruleg) practice, we'd drive the definition home.

Alternatively, we might begin by showing our learners a set of shapes, all of which have four sides, except for one that has three. We then ask the learners to tell us which shape stands out from the others. We could then give them the name "triangle" and ask them to pick out the only triangle from a new set of shapes, all but one of which have four or five sides. Then we might show our learners a number of different triangles mixed together with other shapes and again ask them to pick out the triangles. Next we ask them to draw a triangle. To do this they must actively see what attribute distinguishes a triangle from other shapes. Finally, we can ask them to put into words what makes a triangle different. So we'll have taken our learners through four stages of discovery:

1. recognition;

2. naming;

3. reconstruction; and

4. definition.

In this egrul strategy, experience comes before verbal definition.

Below, you will see a couple of examples of how the two alternative strategies might be applied in a tutorial-in-print. (As it happens, these examples also deal with triangles, of a sort.) Of the two extracts on the left, dealing with spherical triangles, the first one tells the secret and then asks learners to apply it (ruleg); while the second encourages them to observe it for themselves. Similarly, the first of the two alternative approaches to Pascal's Triangle is ruleg, while the second is egrul.

In a spherical triangle, the sum of the angles is *greater than* 180°.

So, if two angles in one particular spherical triangle are 80° and 60°, the third angle must be greater than ... *(how many degrees ?)*

PASCAL'S TRIANGLE

This arrangement of numbers is known as Pascal's triangle:

```
              1
            1   1
          1   2   1
        1   3   3   1
      1   4   6   4   1
    1   5  10  10   5   1
  1   6  15  20  15   6   1
```

It has many interesting properties. One of the most interesting is the rule by which rows can be added to the base of the triangle indefinitely. Notice that any number in the triangle is the SUM of the two numbers directly to the left and right in the row above.

Suppose we added another row to the triangle. The numbers would be: 1 7 21 ? ? 21 7 1. What are the two numbers in the middle of the row?

              28 and 28
              30 and 30
              35 and 35
              42 and 42

You are correct. This was the only diagram showing a spherical triangle. Every side of the triangle is an arc of a 'great circle'.

One side of this particular spherical triangle is part of the 'equator' of the sphere. The other two sides are part of two 'lines of longitude'.

From this particular spherical triangle, we can learn something that is true for *all* spherical triangles:

Remembering that lines of longitude meet a sphere's equator at *right-angles*, what is the *sum of* the angles (A + B + C) in this particular spherical triangle ? Is it:

    (a) Exactly 180°
or (b) More than 180°
or (c) Less than 180° ?

PASCAL'S TRIANGLE

This arrangement of numbers is known as Pascal's triangle:

```
              1
            1   1
          1   2   1
        1   3   3   1
      1   4   6   4   1
    1   5  10  10   5   1
  1   6  15  20  15   6   1
```

It has many interesting properties. One of the most interesting is the rule by which rows can be added to the base of the triangle indefinitely. See if you can work out this rule for yourself. Look at any number in the triangle; then look at the two numbers to the left and right of it in the row above. How are these three numbers related?

Write down your answer, then turn to the next page to check.

The general idea behind the egrul (discovery) strategy is that we try to enable the learners to formulate the rule (or principle, or definition) for themselves. We aim to present whatever information or experience the learners need in order to be able to tell **us** that, e.g.:

- A is an example of B; or
- P must be bigger than O; or
- N must result from M; or
- X is the reason for Y; or
- F must happen before G; or
- R is the reverse of S; or
- D is part of B...and so on.

Once we've led our learners to notice the key point, we can elaborate upon it just as if we'd stated it openly for them in the first place. We'll be hoping, however, that they will have understood it better -- because they will have contributed more thought in arriving at it.

Sometimes this will be too time-consuming, of course, both for us and for our learners. Besides, we can't always arrange for the learners to have all the necessary information and experience from which to derive the rule themselves. Sometimes we have no choice but to give them the definition or principle first and then help them practise with examples.

The important thing, though, is to keep these two possible strategies in mind while writing your tutorial-in-print. Be aware of which you are using from section to section, and why. Choose whichever seems most appropriate and practicable. You may be particularly interested to find out which of the strategies is preferred by (and works best with) your learners.

> BOTH STRATEGIES ARE WORTH USING -- NEITHER IS SUPERIOR TO THE OTHER FOR ALL PURPOSES.

VARIETY OF STIMULUS

Learning at a distance can be boring. Learners working on their own, deprived of the stimulus of interacting with other people, may well think print a cold and dreary substitute. To some extent, your use of **activities** (see Chapter 6) should help avoid the tedium of "one damn paragraph after another". But you can do more. Bear in mind the potential loneliness of the long-distance learner. Build variety into your lessons.

Vary the Physical Format

Try to avoid offering page after page of solid print. Think of your text as a number of "double-page spreads". Aim to make each one visually distinct from others. Vary your format. This will refresh your learners with a new image each time they turn the page. The visual uniqueness of each spread will itself help many readers to learn and remember. See Figure 7.1 (page 145) which shows a sequence of double-page spreads from a tutorial-in-print; note the variety.

Illustrations. One way of varying the format, and making your pages more interesting, is to use illustrations. You could use maps, diagrams, graphs, old etchings and engravings, drawings, cartoons, and photographs. Practically every lesson might benefit from one or more of these. Some lessons can usefully be presented almost entirely as sequences of illustrations with captions. Figure 7.2 shows a double-page spread from such an approach to Einstein's theory of relativity.

Layout. Be prepared to vary the layout of your printed page. If your lesson is to be printed in two columns, for instance, go to a single column occasionally -- perhaps to get a wide margin for pictures, or for readers to add their own data. Alternatively, switch from single to double column, if and when it makes sense.

Figure 7.2: A Double-page Spread from *Einstein for Beginners* by Schwartz & McGuiness (published by Writers and Readers Co-operative, London, 1979)

Don't feel bound to the traditional prose paragraph. At times, you may wish to use alternatives like:

- Lists -- perhaps with each item numbered (if you intend referring back to them) or simply marked with a "bullet" as I have done here.

- Material enclosed in a box (see below) in order to give it special emphasis.

- Blocks of print whose
shape reflects the subject being
discussed. For example, the block of
print in which you discuss
nuclear power
accidents
might be
mush-
room
shaped

- Blocks of print arranged around an illustration with arrows leading to those parts of the illustration they are commenting on.

- **A sentence or two (no more) printed in white on a dark background, for special emphasis.**

- Material printed sideways OR umop-əpᴉsdn OR *in a different typeface.*

WARNING: DON'T OVER-DO IT! THESE

DEVICES ARE FOR OCCASIONAL USE ONLY.

Vary Your Voice

In general, you will do well to write as if you are a sympathetic coach or tutor explaining your subject to an individual learner. The extent to which your learner will find you stimulating as well as informative may depend on the extent to which you can **vary** your tutorial voice. How might you do this? Here are three suggestions:

Lightness of touch. So much "educational" prose is heavy, stuffy and indigestible. The exposition rolls endlessly on, talking to no-one in particular -- solemn, pedantic and remote. It seems to have been produced by a computer for consumption by a committee (or possibly vice versa). The tone is uniformly dreary and impersonal.

Such prose is best kept out of your tutorial-in-print. The American writer, E.B. White, spoke of writing as "the self escaping into the open". So let your personal voice emerge in your prose. Cultivate a lightness of touch. Remember that both you and the learner have interests other than the subject you are writing about. Imagine you are talking to such a learner, and write what you might say. (More about this in Chapter 10.)

You should thus find yourself varying your voice from one section of your lesson to the next. Sometimes you will be exhorting your learners, at other times provoking or sympathizing with them. Sometimes you will be painstakingly explaining the intricacies of an idea; at other times you will be reminiscing about your own experiences in learning about it or using it.

You may even feel sufficiently at ease to introduce humorous "asides" or even jokes if they really do illuminate the subject rather than distract from it. Unfortunately, one person's joke is often another person's wisecrack.

Note, however, that a lesson can still be human, light of touch and **good-humoured** without any efforts after humour as such. Be friendly, be conversational, but talk to your learners with respect both for them and for the subject of your discussion. Take care to avoid the flippant chit-chat which authors sometimes inject in a misguided attempt to be matey -- and which they would never dream of using face to face with a learner.

One of the best safeguards against monotony in your writing is to READ IT ALOUD. If it sounds dull, it probably is. Re-write it. With a bit of practice, you may find that you can "hear" your prose in your head, without actually needing to speak it.

Dramatize your teaching. Where appropriate, try to get a bit of human drama into your writing. Rather than simply reading about abstract ideas, most of us like to hear about how those ideas impinge on **people**. Where it is relevant, develop your subject-matter in terms of people's problems, discoveries and activities. Tell what happened to them or what they made happen.

Sometimes you will be referring to actual people, whether living or dead. For instance, you may be reporting a debate between Darwin and Huxley -- or showing how a film-star's latest divorce case illustrates a new legal rule. At other times, you may need to invent people to illustrate your argument. Either way, you may be able to dramatize your teaching by including, for example:

- quoted remarks
- complete conversations
- narrative sequences; and
- case studies.

These can stimulate interest and help your readers relate your subject-matter to everyday life. Very often you can involve your reader as one of the "characters" in the dramatization. You can ask what the reader would say or do in the situation you describe. For examples, see Figures 7.3 and 7.4 (and also Figure 5.2D on page 98).

Figure 7.3: **Teaching with Conversation** -- adapted from *Educational Technology in Curriculum Development* by D. Rowntree (Harper & Row, 1982)

they can 'get by' without developing their methods. What I'm suggesting, really, is that the educational technology approach involves not just using scientific *knowledge*. . . .

T: Which may be pretty thin on the ground?

E: All right. . . but also using scientific *method*. By that I mean a hyp-othesis-testing method.

T: Now how would you explain that?

E: Well, educational technology would want the teacher – the 'professional' teacher, as you called him – to think of himself as a tester of hypotheses about teaching and learning. That is, he'd start with hypotheses, insights, about what purposes might be worthwhile, or about possible ways of achieving the purposes. . .

T: From science?

How would **you** answer T's question about the source of the teacher's hypotheses ?

. . . .

. . . .

. . . .

Now read on to see how E answered it.

E: Maybe from science, maybe from philosophy, maybe from his experience or from that of his colleagues, very often from the suggestions of his students. But quite often his hypotheses would seem to come right out of the blue. After all, there's nothing in science itself to generate new hypotheses. Even Einstein once said they came from 'intuition, resting on sympathetic experience'.

T: So you do allow for inspiration.

E: But of course. Inspiration, intuition, wisdom, good judgement. These underlie all innovation and growth in education. Science itself doesn't produce the new ideas.

T: Anyway, once you've got them . . .?

E: Yes, though scientific method doesn't produce the hypotheses, it does enable you to evaluate them and elaborate on them once you've got them.

T: I'm not sure I know what you mean by scientific method here.

How would you reply, as E, to T's remark ?

. . . .

. . . .

. . . .

Now read E's reply.

E: Simply that you regard your hypotheses experimentally. You try them out with learners, expecting to find that they work with some and not with others, and to different degrees. You'll be trying to account for these differences, using whatever scientific or practical knowledge seems relevant. And you'll expect to modify your

Figure 7.4:   Part of a Case Study
(from Open University course P970)

---

32   PUPILS

What do you do?

Your conscience as a governor is jolted. The school has always been a pleasant community and discipline has never been thought of as a problem. Yet here are signs of disruption. You must do something about it, you feel. But what?

▲Which of the following actions seem sensible at this stage?
- ○ Contact the girl's parents?
- ○ Contact the headteacher?
- ○ Contact the chairman of governors?
- ○ Contact the welfare services?

Contacting either the head or the chairman of governors would seem like a sensible first step. As a governor you should not contact the parents on your own initiative, or the welfare services.

As it happens, you decide to call on the chairman, who lives in the next street from you. It appears she has already heard about Rachel and shows you the following note she had from the head a couple of weeks ago:

> I think you ought to know we have a
> child here I really don't think we're
> going to be able to keep. Her father
> came to work on Blunt's farm in
> October. She is 8 years old and has
> been to six different schools already.
> She's in Mr Dean's class and is quite
> uncontrollable. I have taken her into
> my class for some of the time and she's
> been rude and insolent to me. Some of
> the other children are starting to
> copy her and parents have been
> complaining about bad language. The
> primary adviser came in to see
> Mr Dean (you remember he's a
> probationer) and she thinks Rachel
> does need special help. I've only
> three mornings' teaching help so I
> can't have Rachel on her own. I went
> to see her parents and they started
> rowing between themselves. They say
> that she's not badly behaved at home
> and that it's my job to deal with her.
> I'm going to ask if the educational
> psychologist will see her.

(Head to chairman of governors)

The chairman tells you that she has since been in touch both with the head and with the assistant education officer (AEO) at the education office. The head told her that Rachel has now been seen by the educational psychologist. The primary schools adviser has also seen Rachel in action and, according to the AEO, said:

> I don't think Rachel should be in Mr Dean's class. He hasn't the experience to deal with a child like that. I would suggest an additional part-time remedial teacher, but is there anyone available? And could anyone get out to that school? I don't suppose there are many buses. It would have to be someone with a car.

(Primary adviser to AEO)

The AEO has also given your chairman the gist of the educational psychologist's initial report, which is as follows:

> I've been to see Rachel. She showed signs of disturbance and she needs a lot of help. I am reluctant to suggest a change of school. She ought to have the chance to settle in one school and be helped to make progress. I have discussed a programme of remedial work with the head and I think Rachel could also be fitted in a couple of mornings a week at the special unit in Newton. If that fails, she may have to be considered for special education. I've seen the parents. There seem to be problems there. They were very aggressive and critical of the head. I will be sending you and the head a copy of my full report as soon as it is typed.
> *(Educational psychologist to AEO)*

Problems and treatment

So, Rachel appears to be presenting the school with problems.

▲Consider these two questions before reading on.
1 How would you sum up these problems from what you have heard so far?
2 What solutions (treatments) have been suggested by the three people whose reports you have read?

1 **The problems?**   Rachel is rude and uncontrollable, uses bad language and is influencing other children to their parents' displeasure and is not making satisfactory progress in her schoolwork.
2 **Solutions and treatments?**   The head is thinking of getting her moved elsewhere. The primary adviser suggests putting her in the class of a more experienced teacher and getting an additional part-time teacher to come in to give her remedial help. The educational psychologist is resisting the head's desire to get her moved, believing that she should be given a chance to settle in (after all, she's been at six schools already) and make some progress. To this end he has suggested a programme of remedial work and is also trying to get her a couple of mornings a week at Newton's special unit. However, he does consider, as a last resort, the possibility that, if she doesn't respond, she may need to be considered for transfer to a special school.

So, it seems that things are happening and, from what you know of the head, you have every confidence that he will be doing his best for Rachel – even if she is upsetting the peace and productivity of his hitherto trouble-free school.

Other Voices. Another means of giving the learner a rest from the sound of your voice, now and again, is to bring in the voices of other people. This can be done by quoting conversation, of course, as in Figure 7.3. The most generally applicable way, however, is to bring in quotations from other writers on your subject -- or spoken comments from practitioners. These may consist simply of a few words or they may run to several paragraphs.

If you are quoting another writer's words, don't take more than you need. Sometimes you may want your learners to read a whole journal or newspaper article or a chapter from a book. But often you will do better to select from it -- perhaps interspersing paragraphs of your own between the paragraphs you quote. More than a couple of hundred words and the tonic effect of a change in voice will begin to wane. In addition, you may be running into copyright problems. Remember that all quotations must be credited to their authors; and copyright permission must be sought (and perhaps be paid for) if the amount quoted exceeds what is normally accepted as reasonable (see page 367-371).

Another way of bringing in some other expert's voice is to get a colleague to comment on an early draft of your material -- and then print his or her remarks in the margins of your text or as footnotes. You could then do the same for your colleague's lesson, if appropriate. Figure 7.5 shows an extract from a management lesson -- in which the author presents her argument in the body of the text but prints her colleagues' comments in the margins. (The comments of learners on whom you try out your draft materials can be used in a similar way -- or in providing feedback on activities, as in Figure 6.2.)

Finally, and most substantially, you may be able to vary your voice in the literal sense -- from written voice to **spoken** voice -- by recording some part of your lesson

Figure 7.5: Colleagues' Comments in the Margin of a Text (An example from Open University course T243, Block 5)

Mechanistic attitudes to the design of work organizations had already had a long history before the popularization of the idea of scientific management in the United States at the beginning of this century. Scientific management embodied a refinement of the mechanistic view of the workforce which had flourished since the Industrial Revolution. It saw individuals as basically predictable, controllable and largely independent components. It advocated such practices as the division of work into small, easily-learnt tasks, which made workers more interchangeable and increased the scope for managerial control. It used the measurement of time and motion to high levels of precision to establish efficient work patterns which led to setting targets, measuring performance and comparing it with the targets set; it was a simple step to the linking of pay rates to the amount produced as a means of correcting the 'error-signal'.

> During the Industrial Revolution employers and others put a lot of time into attempts to structure attitudes – the obedient thrifty, and pious servant of the firm, and so on. *ER*

Scientific management has long since given way to succeeding managerial rationalities, but the kind of mechanistic thinking behind it did not die with the advent of new fashions in management. As Unit 5 points out, many years after Taylor, similar principles are still being used in the design of jobs on assembly lines. Some of these are the concentration of control functions, and setting of targets, in the hands of a single control unit; the division of tasks; and the attempt to correct deviations or error signals by means of remunerative controls.

> Not really. As a single coherent theory of management certainly, but people still talk a lot about scientific management in the West, USSR and China! *ML*
>
> But not just assembly lines – such principles have spread to all areas of work, including much white collar work through the use of various performance assessment or measurement techniques. *ER*

Control is more or less consciously embodied in the design of many production systems, but job designers have increasingly recognized that a variety of controls may be necessary to persuade the workforce to adopt the goals of management. For the greater variety of human behaviour, compared to the behaviour of machines, necessitates a greater variety of control mechanisms in people management systems than in mechanical ones. Managerial control strategies include not only remunerative control but coercive control (for example, by the mechanical pacing of the assembly line) and normative control (that is, control exercised through the granting or withholding of status, appreciation or respect). Each of these control strategies is perfectly compatible with the analogy of the control model, which specifies a particular *what* (the sequence of control procedures) not a particular *how*. But although managers may try to build an organization in which they *match* their control strategy to the expectations of type of involvement of the workforce (an interactive process, involving considerations such as the level of technology involved), this is a much more difficult process than in even quite complicated engineering systems. Not only do

> I'm not sure the slant of this passage is fair. A complicated process requires a very high degree of coordination. Achieving this requires a degree of uniformity (not all of which is necessarily unacceptable to the people involved). *JH*
>
> No. Normative control is essentially about trust relations and is therefore *much* more akin to open-loop control. *RP* (For a description of open- and closed-loop control, see Units 1/2.)

on audio-cassette. Audiotape opens up a whole new world of learning which I discuss in Chapter 11.

Vary the Activities

In Chapter 6, I suggest how learner-activities might be varied. You can vary them in:

- *Level of difficulty* -- e.g. you can begin with easy activities to build up the learner's confidence, but gradually make them more demanding.

- *Type of activity* -- e.g. reading, drawing, calculating, observing, discussing, making, etc.

- *Manner of recording responses* -- e.g. ticking boxes, providing a missing word or two, writing a sentence or more, drawing a chart, etc.

Within one lesson, and certainly from one lesson to another, you should find need to give your readers variety in all three ways. Sometimes, partly to encourage your readers to get other people's reactions to what they are studying, you may think it worth saying something like: "Why don't you try this question on some friends, and see if they take a different line from you?"

Activities may be varied even further if you can bring in other media, other ways of learning -- practical work, audio-visual material, interaction with tutors and other learners. (More about other media in Chapter 11.)

* * *

In this chapter, I have offered some basic ideas about teaching at a distance. Clearly, this is in many ways more demanding, than is teaching face to face. In a written lesson, your teaching has to be right first time.

> BEING A DISTANCE TEACHER IS
>
> NEVER BEING ABLE TO SAY: "I'M SORRY
>
> -- LET ME TRY TO PUT THAT ANOTHER WAY."

8. EASING YOUR READER'S ACCESS

If your teaching is well-structured, readers stand a fair chance of learning from it. But their chances will be much improved if they can see what that structure is. If learners are to use your lesson intelligently, they'll need to get some idea of how it all hangs together. Otherwise, they will be reduced to hacking through it, page after page, in the hope that some grand design will eventually emerge. Unfortunately,they may get so bogged down in detail that they never see the wood for the trees.

ACCESS DEVICES

Happily, there are several means by which you can make clear the structure of your teaching. These are often called "access devices" They will help your readers to **access** your material -- that is, to find their way **into** the text and to find their way **about** in it.

In the list below, I have grouped these access devices according to whether you would insert them before, during, or after the main body of your lesson:

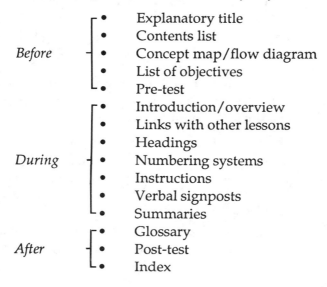

Before	• Explanatory title
	• Contents list
	• Concept map/flow diagram
	• List of objectives
	• Pre-test
During	• Introduction/overview
	• Links with other lessons
	• Headings
	• Numbering systems
	• Instructions
	• Verbal signposts
	• Summaries
After	• Glossary
	• Post-test
	• Index

Now let us look at each of these devices in turn. Not every lesson will need all of them. Some of them you may choose to use for **groups** of lessons rather than for individual lessons.

BEFORE THE LESSON

There are five access devices that might usefully appear before the body of the lesson itself:

Explanatory Title

An obvious point, but one that's often neglected -- give your lesson a title that tells the reader what it's about. Don't call it simply *Botany: Lesson 12* if it might, more explicitly, be called *The Morphology of Flowering Plants.* Similarly, *The Use and Abuse of Chisels* gives learners more idea what to expect than would *Hand Tools: Module 4.*

Contents List

Present the learner with a list of the main topics in your lesson, arranged in order of occurrence, with page numbers. Show this right at the beginning. If you are including more than half a dozen topics in your list, indicate which are the most important ones. You can do this by underlining, indenting, using bolder type, and so on.

Such a structured list can provide a useful overview of the lesson. One way of producing it is to list the headings and sub-headings you have used in your text.

If several lessons are being bound together as a book, you'll need to decide where is the best place for the contents lists. You could print them all together at the beginning of the book. Or you could print each one at the beginning of the appropriate lesson. Or you could compromise -- putting a brief contents list, covering just the main ideas in each lesson, at the beginning of the book, and the full, detailed contents list in front of each lesson. Remember, however, that wherever you put them, their purpose is to help your readers. They should help them get a broad overview of the territory you are covering in the lesson and, if only some areas are relevant to their present needs, to locate them quickly.

Concept Maps/Flow Diagrams

A contents list can make clear the topics that are to be dealt with -- but may reveal little or nothing about the relationships between them. A concept map or flow diagram, however, can show up the inter-connections. This can help learners in their approach to the subject-matter. Chapters 3 and 4 contain several examples of concept maps and flow diagrams.

Figure 8.1 is an example from a course on systems management, revealing to students how most of the sixteen units of the course can each be classified in two different ways. Each unit concerns either goals, information or implementation and behaviour AND either operational, people-management or socio-economic aspects. Thus, whatever the learners are working on within this course, they can relate it to this map of the main themes.

In fact, the diagram shown in Figure 8.1 is rather generalized. It is typical of the kind you might want to present at the beginning of a **series** of lessons. It shows the relationships between the main topics only. Lesson by lesson, however, you might wish to offer more detailed diagrams, like Figure 8.2 (and some in Chapters 3 and 4) -- showing the relationships within each topic.

List of Objectives

Learners can find it helpful to be told what they might expect to be able to do (or do better) as a result of reading the lesson. A list of objectives near the beginning may help them adopt a suitable approach to it.

Figure 8.1: A Course Structure
(from Open University course T242, *Study Guide*)

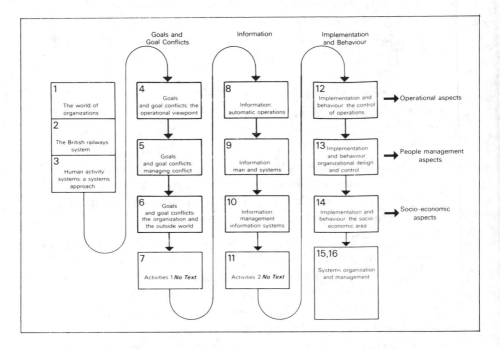

Figure 8.2: A Topic Structure
(from Open University course T101, Block 1)

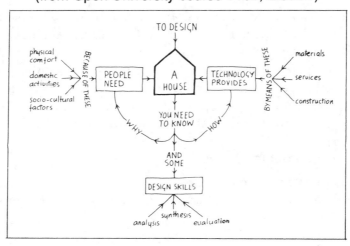

However, a couple of reservations:

- Don't include so many objectives that your learners are overwhelmed by the apparent enormity of the learning task ahead. Select the most important.

- Don't couch the objectives in technical language that will mean nothing to learners until they have completed the lesson. Find more familiar terms, even if you have to be less precise. For instance, "You will learn how to ungrunge the fedroonix" may need to be expressed, more generally, as "You will learn how to overcome the fault that occurs most often in the equipment."

If the objectives can't be expressed non-technically, you may like to put them at the end of the lesson rather than at the beginning. In any case, you may wish to restate your objectives at the end of the lesson. Instead of saying, for example: "You will learn to distinguish between...", say "Can you now distinguish between...?" Thus you can provide a checklist against which your readers can review what they have learned.

Whether you begin or end with the objectives (or both), it can be helpful to mention the pages or sections where each is dealt with in the text.

Pre-test

Tell your learners what skills or knowledge you expect them to have before they can benefit from your lesson. You may deal with this by stipulating some previous lesson as a pre-requisite. Alternatively, you may ask your readers whether they can already define certain concepts, simplify certain equations, or whatever it is you wish to assume they can do already. You may even set them a pre-test -- some sort of exercise which they'll need to be able to carry out satisfactorily if they are to cope with the work in the lesson ahead.

DURING THE LESSON

Now for the access devices that belong in the body of the lesson:

Introduction/Overview

An introduction can be very helpful, even if it takes only a paragraph or two. It can fulfil any combination of the following functions (and others):

- Providing an overview of what is to come.
- Whetting the readers' appetites and convincing them that the lesson is worth spending time on.
- Dispelling any false expectations as to what the lesson might be about.
- Forging links between what readers know already and what you are expecting them to learn.
- Pointing out links with other lessons (or courses).
- Giving guidance on how to learn from the lesson.

You may sometimes find it appropriate to include in your introduction a discussion of the concept map and/or objectives. See Figure 8.3 for a sample introduction: how many of the above functions does it embody?

Links With Other Lessons

Links with other lessons may have been pointed out in your introduction, but they may be worth mentioning later as well. Don't assume that readers will necessarily notice such links for themselves. If your lesson aims to:

- extend some ideas dealt with in earlier lessons; or
- blaze the trail for a later one; or
- offer a counterpoint to some other lesson,

then let readers know, whenever and however often it seems appropriate.

Figure 8.3: An Introduction
(from Open University course T101, Block 1)

Part Two What is a house?

4 Introduction

Imagine yourself going to view a house that your are considering buying. You would try consciously to 'view' the house from different viewpoints. Are the rooms large enough? Are they conveniently planned? Does the structure look sound? Is the house easy to keep warm? Is there noise from neighbours? Can you afford it? And so on. You try quite deliberately to make yourself very critical towards the house, so that you won't overlook any of its potential shortcomings.

However, back in your own old house (or once you have bought the new one) you quickly let your level of critical awareness drop. You learn to live with the house's shortcomings because they are outweighed by its advantages, or you adjust your patterns of living so as to manage within the house as it is, not as it ideally might be. Few of us ever manage to find, or to afford, our ideal dream house.

In Part Two of this block my aim is to help you to develop your critical awareness of a house from many different viewpoints. This is not simply to help you if you are buying a new house. Rather, it is to try to develop in you an awareness of a house as a designed artefact. I shall be trying to get you to develop a designer's view of a house, and this is a view that sees the house simultaneously in many separate ways and also *as a whole*, because the designer of any artefact sees his design as a combination, or synthesis, of many separate factors.

What better example of a house could I choose on which to base my teaching than your own house? Throughout this part of the block you will be asked to carry out study activities that are based on your own house. The purpose of these activities is not only to reinforce your learning from the text by applying the theoretical knowledge to a practical example, but also to provide you with practice in the design skills of analysing and evaluating. You will learn how to 'model' your house from different viewpoints and in ways that encourage and enable you to 'see' it more clearly from these various viewpoints.

Obviously, I am assuming that you do, in fact, have a house of your own that you can use as the example in the activities. In some cases, the activities also assume that this house is a fairly conventional one: terraced, detached or ..emi-detached; probably two-storeyed, and so on. If you don't live in such a conventional house, then I'm afraid some of the activities will be impossible or irrelevant for you. The relevance of the activities will depend on what kind of 'house' you actually live in. If it's a family-sized flat, then most of them will still be relevant, but if it's only a small bed-sitter, then most of them probably won't be. If you find that you are stuck in this way, then you might consider using as your example someone else's house that you know well, such as your parents' or that of a friend.

In all the activities you will see that I have carried out the instructions myself, using my own house as the example, so that you can see exactly what the instructions mean, and what you have to do.

Exercise

What do you think was the purpose of the 'Introduction' you have just read? Look back over it and underline one sentence that seems to you to convey the purpose of the 'Introduction' most clearly. Write down in your own words what you think the purpose of the 'Introduction' was.

Discussion

The purposes of the 'Introduction' seem to have been to convey the author's main aims for Part Two of the block, and to give you some idea of what you will be doing in working through it. The first sentence of the third paragraph is a clear statement of an aim. You may have underlined another sentence, but check back to satisfy yourself that the sentence you chose

Headings

In theory, headings should be invaluable as an aid to learning from a text. They should help learners to:

- Find the parts of the text they wish to read.

- Recognize where one topic ends and the next begins.

- Appreciate which topics are grouped together as aspects of some larger topic.

- Estimate (by noticing the number of pages devoted to each) which topics the author considers more important and which less.

I say invaluable "in theory" because I am not convinced that learners always know how to "read" the headings. Many scarcely even notice them. It is true, also, that many authors don't know how to handle headings helpfully. If you suspect your learners might not otherwise be able to make good use of your headings, perhaps you'll think it worth **explaining** your system in the introduction to your lesson(s).

In planning your headings, you may like to keep in mind a hierarchical pattern such as the following:

Lesson title

Section headings

Sub-section.

Sub-sub-sections.

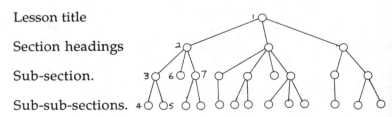

Such a hierarchy of headings should reflect the structure of ideas you are developing in your lesson. In fact, thinking about the headings may help you sort out the structure for your own benefit while writing.

Certainly your learners may need to appreciate the hierarchy in order to grasp your structure. This may or may not be easy, since they will be meeting the headings one by one, in the order indicated by the numbers in the example above. You may consider revealing such a structure to your learners by presenting your contents list in hierarchical form. Alternatively, a separate concept map or flow diagram might serve the purpose.

Notice that the diagram above suggests three grades or levels of heading below the main title. Try not to use more than two or, at most, three grades. Otherwise, learners will find the system difficult to follow. Whether your text is to be typed or set in print, you'll have trouble making the headings visually distinct from one another if you use more than three grades. In this book, you'll notice, I have used three grades and have distinguished between them as follows:

*   **VARIETY OF STIMULUS**
*   **Vary the Physical Format**
*   ***Illustrations.*** (Text continues on the same line)

To use headings logically, follow this simple rule:

> A HEADING SHOULD REFER TO ALL THE
> TEXT THAT OCCURS BETWEEN IT AND THE
> NEXT HEADING OF THE **SAME** GRADE.

So far, I have been speaking about what are often called "cross-headings" -- headings in the main body of the text. There are two other types worth mentioning: running headings and side-headings.

Running head(ing)s are so called because they run along the top (as in this book), or sometimes the bottom, of every page in the main text. With books, it is traditional for the running head on the left-hand page to mention the book-title while that on the right-hand page gives the chapter title. Since most readers actually do know what book they are reading, I would suggest that the running heads might more usefully state the chapter (or lesson) titles and **section** headings. This can help your readers both in locating the start of a particular section and -- when they are following the discussion in a lengthy section -- it keeps them aware of the heading that still covers what they are reading.

Keeping readers aware

Now, what about side-headings? Unlike cross-headings, which break into the discussion, announcing a change of topic, side-headings simply comment on it, allowing it to flow on. They are written in the **margins** -- (see the examples on this page and the next). They are used less often, nowadays, than they might be. They can be useful in highlighting issues and in picking out the main points of the argument for readers who want to skim through quickly in order to preview or review. Of course their use needs to be planned. Use them too sporadically and readers are likely to overlook them. Use them too abundantly and there'll be little space left in the margins for diagrams or for readers to write notes.

Side headings -- in margins

Numbering Systems

Some writers number the sections and paragraphs within their lessons. The first section would be 1.0; the first sub-section within it, 1.1; the first paragraph within that would be 1.1.1; and so on. Such systems can be cumbersome, and difficult to keep logical. Hence they do not tell readers much about the structure of your lesson. They are best avoided unless you have a frequent need to refer readers to particular paragraphs by number.

Numbering best avoided?

Instructions

Remember that your readers are studying on their own. They need to know what you expect of them. They cannot read your mind, and there is no-one else to tell them. All your expectations must be clearly written down -- or spoken if you are providing an audio-cassette..

Say what you expect

*What to
tell them?*

If you want your readers to memorize something or write it down in their notebooks, tell them so. If you want them to think up examples of their own or relate a point to their family or working lives, say so. Let them know which bits of the text are vital and which they can skip if they run short of time. Make sure they know whether they are supposed to read the text/listen to tapes/ perform experiments, and so on, in a certain order, or whether this doesn't matter. With activities, make clear that some are meant to take only a few seconds while others may occupy half an hour or more.

*Keeping
readers
informed*

In general, keep your learners informed as to what they are supposed to be doing. They may still choose to do otherwise, but at least they shouldn't be able to say they haven't been told.

*Specific
v general
instructions*

Notice that these are specific instructions, inserted in the text wherever you think them relevant. They are additional to whatever more general instructions you may have given in your introduction (about how to tackle this lesson) or in a separate Study Guide (about learning from all the lessons in the series).

Verbal Signposts

*Where are
you going?*

Try to keep your learners informed as to what **you** are doing. Let them know where the argument is going. Don't just tell them what you are telling them; tell them **why** you are telling it. As you write, you should be able to help your readers with "verbal signposts" like these:

"On the other hand..."
"In much the same way..."
"Another example..."
"But that's not the only way..."
"Now we come to an aspect that may surprise you..."
"Let us turn aside for a moment to examine..."
"Now we come to the really tough part of the argument..."
"What this all adds up to is..."
"But this no longer holds true when we look at..."

Such phrases -- and countless others will occur to you while you write -- seem to lay bare the structure of an argument. They can give your readers a glimpse into how your mind is working, and help them read with a sense of intelligent anticipation.

Visual Signposts

You will further help your reader if you can use visual as well as verbal signposting. Where possible, let the structure of your teaching be apparent at a glance.

For instance, suppose you are learning from a text and have just turned to the two pages shown in miniature below:

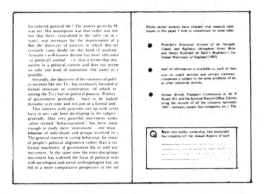

The left-hand page tells you nothing about the structure. It is just a slab of prose. But the right-hand page tells you -- at a glance -- that there are three main points and a question to answer about them. Your mind has begun to engage with the learning task before you've read a single word of the page.

Several of the layout features I mention in Chapter 7 (page 154) can help with visual signposting. So too can some of the graphic devices I mention in Chapter 9. Different coloured paper for distinguishing between different sections (e.g. main text, project notes, tests, etc.) would be another way to reveal structure at a glance.

Symbols in the margin are often a useful means of alerting readers to the kind of material that lies ahead. The symbols alongside might be used next to paragraphs that describe, or refer the reader to (in order):

- an activity (a question or exercise);
- practical work;
- video material;
- audio material;
- reading from another book;
- follow-up work; and
- an assignment to be sent to a tutor.

Some examples of such visual signposts can be seen in Figure 5.2F and G (on pages 102 and 104). Obviously, it doesn't matter what symbols you use so long as they are visually distinct from one another and are understood by your reader. As always, however, discretion is called for. If more than three or four kinds of material were being visually signposted within one text, the signals would be liable to shout each other down.

Summaries

A summary reviews the main points that have been covered so far. The most obvious need for this device is at the end of a lesson. But you may sometimes want to summarize also at the end of sections within it.

Keep each summary as brief as possible. A common error (bringing confusion to the learner) is to introduce material that has not been previously discussed.

It can be worthwhile, as an activity, to ask your learners to attempt **their own** summaries, with or without guidance from you. Then, as feedback, you can show them your version. Such an activity can form a **post-test**, or part of one, as shown in "SAQ 13" in Figure 8.4.

AFTER THE LESSON

There are three access devices you may want to deploy after the body of the lesson:

Glossary

At the end of some lessons -- and even more certainly after a **series** of lessons -- you may need a glossary. This should contain working definitions of all the new concepts that have been introduced. These will normally be definitions that refresh your readers' minds about what they have learned -- rather than being so extensive that they don't need to read the lesson at all.

Your glossary might usefully give references to the pages in the text where each idea is discussed. Again, compiling a glossary may seem to you an activity worth setting your readers after some lessons. It could be one way of helping them summarize what has been taught.

Post-test

This would consist of one or more exercises that learners should be able to carry out successfully **after** having worked through the lesson. Be careful not to over-do it. I have seen people set post-tests that take longer to work through than the lesson. This can be justified if the test is a learning experience in its own right. For example, the activity required may be one that learners find satisfying for its own sake (e.g. building a working model), or it may be one that brings them personal feedback from a tutor.

But, with the majority of lessons -- where all you're wanting to do is let learners check their grasp of the main ideas -- I would suggest that a post-test should add no more than, say, 20% to the time your learners have already spent on the lesson. This is not to say, however, that they would not appreciate a rather more extensive post-test after a **series** of lessons.

Figure 8.4: An End-of-lesson Post-test
(from Open University course S101, Units 6-7)

Thus, by 1968, a wide variety of geological and geophysical observations had been integrated into one global theory, that of plate tectonics. In Section 5 of these Units we shall outline in more detail some of the processes that occur where plates are formed, and where they collide.

4.10.1   Objectives of Section 4.10

You should now be able to:

(a) Describe the plate tectonic hypothesis (this will be elaborated in Section 5.1). (SAQ 13)

(b) Describe the evidence that favours the plate tectonic hypothesis (SAQ 14):

(i)   seismic zones and first-motion studies of earthquakes;
(ii) geometry of spreading centres and transform faults;
(iii) poles of plate rotation and spreading.

Before reading on, complete SAQs 13 and 14.

SAQ 13 (*Objective (a)*)   Complete the blanks in the following description of plate tectonics:

Ocean floor is envisaged as continuously accreting to a ..... (a) plate which is ..... (b) inactive, and which interacts with other plates along active zones of ..... (c) and seismicity. The movement of the plates over the surface of a ..... (d) can be described with reference to a ..... (e) of rotation. ..... (f) faults trend along the direction of ..... (g) circles about the ..... (e) of rotation, whereas oceanic ridges between these faults trend along ..... (h) circles passing through the ..... (e). There are three types of plate boundaries:

1 .... (i) (do not worry if you list these in a

2 .... (j) different order to those given in the

3 .... (k) answer)

Along the first type, new ..... (l) is formed by ..... (m). Along the second type, oceanic crust and upper mantle is being ..... (n).

SAQ 14 (*Objective (b)*)   Consider the list of topics we have considered in these Units:

A   Deep-sea drilling results

B   Palaeoclimatic data

C   Palaeomagnetic data

D   Ocean-floor magnetic anomalies

E   Fit of the topography of continental margins

F   Earthquake first-motion studies

G   Magnetic polarity reversal timetable

Match these topics with those of the following concepts to which they contributed in a major way:

1   Continental drift (choose three items)

2   Sea-floor spreading (choose three items)

3   Transform faults (choose three items)

4   Plate tectonics (choose one item only)

A post-test can help your learners read with a sense of purpose. Seeing it ahead, they know what they are working towards. In this respect, it works rather like objectives. Indeed, if you are printing objectives at the end of your lesson, you may follow them with related post-test questions (as shown in Figure 8.4).

By the way, if a prospective reader can carry out your post-test exercises satisfactorily **before** working through the lesson, you might want to consider advising that reader to skip it and go on to the next. (Provided your exercises really have focussed on the essential learning.) You might also consider whether the post-test for one lesson could serve as the pre-test for the next.

Index

As with the glossary, an index may need to relate to a **set** of lessons rather than to each one individually. It can be invaluable to learners -- both to those trying to find out whether your lessons might have anything to say about topics of concern to them and to those who have already worked through your materials and are now trying to check back on a few points.

The index should consist of the key words (terms, names, concepts) that readers are likely to look up. They should be in alphabetical order, with the numbers of the pages on which the associated idea is dealt with.

So far, so obvious. But compiling an index is not a trivial task. For instance, it's no good just reading through your material and writing down only the key words and their page numbers. You need to be alert also for pages where the relevant idea is discussed but the key word is not actually mentioned. There is also the danger of getting lost in detail. List only the most important ideas, or distinguish them from lesser ones by typography -- e.g. print them in **bold type** or CAPITALS.

Your tutorial-in-print may contain several other components -- acknowledgements of help from colleagues, thanks for copyright permissions, a list of sources, suggestions for further reading or practical follow-up, etc. But these do not play a part in revealing the structure of your lesson, so I have not dealt with them above. (Nor have I talked about the kind of Study Guide in which you might inform learners about the structure of a whole course.)

SUMMARY

All the **access devices** mentioned in this chapter have two functions:

- They enable readers to find what they need within the structure of your lesson; and

- They make that structure more apparent to your readers and so help them to learn.

Use access devices where appropriate and, if necessary, tell your readers **how** you are using them.

CHECK TO SEE WHICH OF THE ACCESS DEVICES I HAVE USED (AND HOW) IN THIS BOOK. DO LIKEWISE WITH OTHER MATERIAL AS A GUIDE TO USING THEM YOURSELF.

9. TEACHING WITH PICTURES

Like most writers, and perhaps most teachers, I probably rely too much on words. That is, I no doubt overlook many occasions when pictures would teach better. For instance, one could churn out who knows how many words in an attempt to explain to the less numerate reader why $(a + b)^2$ -- that is, $(a + b)$ multiplied by $(a + b)$ -- gives $a^2 + 2ab + b^2$. But the diagram below, with a side measuring $a + b$, **shows** the truth of it directly:

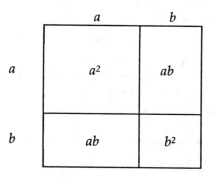

As Alice said, "What's the use of a book without pictures or conversation?". I've suggested elsewhere (page 155) how conversation might usefully be brought into your lesson. Now let us consider the role of pictures -- or, more broadly, the **pictorial approach**.

GETTING AWAY FROM SOLID PROSE

What do I mean by a "pictorial approach"? Obviously, I include the use of such items as diagrams and graphs, drawings and paintings, photographs and maps. But I want to suggest a broader use of the term. I would say we introduce a pictorial element into our teaching as soon as we use the printed page to convey **something that could not be spoken in words**. The "something" may appeal to the reader's intellect, or emotions, or both at the same time.

Very often we launch into prose without even considering that there might be other, perhaps better, ways of conveying what we might be about to say. For instance, Figures 9.1-9.4 show four different ways of talking about soil classification. All use words, but the pictorial element increases from 9.1 through 9.2 to 9.3 to 9.4. In fact, 9.4 reveals the structure of the classification in a way that is entirely hidden in 9.1. However, 9.2 and 9.3 may be quite practicable for the learner who just wants to do quick classifications. Which one do you find easiest to follow?

So 9.2, 9.3 and 9.4 get away from conventional, solid prose. Although they present words, they do not ask readers to begin at the first word of a paragraph and read on until they come to the last word. Instead, the prose is **patterned** so that one reader may use it differently from others. Except with 9.3, all will probably start at the first sentence, but where each goes after that will be up to them. No-one will be expected to read all the words, let alone the same words as every other reader.

The patterned presentations in 9.2-9.4 could be made more obviously pictorial by adding photographs of the various soil types. What might be even more helpful (even essential) in this case, however, would be **specimens** of the soil types against which to check the classification system.

Also, like most pictures used in teaching, all three need some form of introduction or commentary **in words** -- to help the learner get the most out of them.

Figure 9.1: Classifying Soils -- Prose Version

If your soil specimen feels gritty, like sand, and is sticky, then if you can polish it between your fingers, it is a **sandy clay loam**. If it does not polish, then it is a **sandy silt loam**. If it is gritty but NOT sticky, and you can mould it into a ball that holds together, it is a **sandy loam**. If you can't mould it into such a ball, then it is a **sand**. Furthermore, if it leaves a mark when you rub it on a patch of clean skin, it is a **loamy sand**. If your soil is NOT gritty but feels silky (creamy) and you can polish it and change its shape, it is a **silty clay loam**. If you can't change its shape it is a **clay**. If the soil feels gritty and silky, but won't polish, it is a **silt loam** (if clearly silky) or a **silty loam**. If it is neither gritty nor silky, then it is just a **loam**.

Figure 9.2: Classifying Soils --
Directed Prose Version

1. Soil feels **gritty** (like sand)   ...Go to 2
    Soil does **not** feel gritty   ...Go to 4

2. Soil feels **sticky**   ...Go to 3
    Soil does **not** feel sticky   ...Go to 9

3. Soil will **polish** when rubbed
              between fingers   ...**Sandy clay loam**
    Soil will **not** polish   ...**Sandy silt loam**

4. Soil feels **silky** (creamy)   ...Go to 5
    Soil does **not** feel silky   ...**Loam**

5. Soil will **polish** when rubbed
              between fingers   ...Go to 6
    Soil will **not** polish   ...Go to 8

6. Soil's **shape** can be changed   ...Go to 7
    Shape can **not** be changed   ...**Clay**

7. The shape is **easily** changed   ...**Silty clay loam**
    Shape is **not** easily changed   ...**Clay loam**

8. Soil is **clearly** silky   ...**Silt loam**
    Soil is **not** clearly silky   ...**Silty loam**

9. Soil moulds into a **ball**   ...**Sandy loam**
    Soil does **not** mould into a ball ...Go to 10

10. Soil leaves **mark** on clean skin   ...**Loamy sand**
    Soil does **not** leave mark   ...**Sand**

Figure 9.3:   Classifying Soils -- Tabular Version

Ticks (√) indicate the features shown by each soil type:

	Gritty	Sticky	Silky	VERY silky	Polishable	Forms ball	Mouldable	EASILY moulded	Marks skin
Sand	√								
Clay			√	√					
Loam									
Sandy clay loam	√	√			√				
Sandy silt loam	√	√							
Sandy loam	√					√			
Loamy sand	√								√
Clay loam			√	√		√			
Silty clay loam			√	√		√	√		
Silt loam			√	√					
Silty loam			√						

Figure 9.4:   Classifying Soils -- Algorithm Version

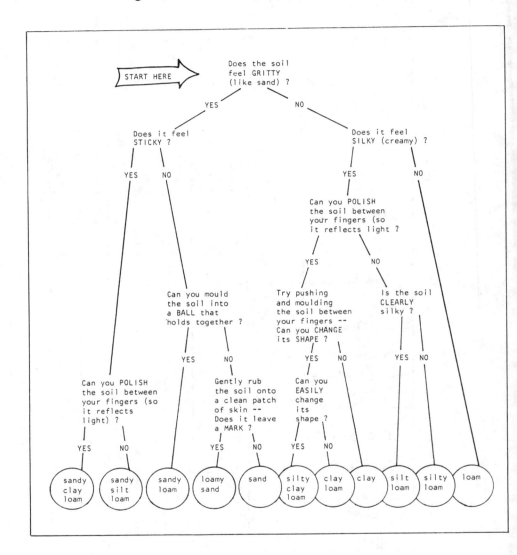

Broadly speaking, there are two ways of making your text more pictorial. You can use graphic devices (special layout, for example, as in Figures 9.1-9.4) or you can use pictures. Let's look at each of these in turn.

Graphic Devices

In this category I would include...

...prose set out in such a way as to emphasize a point or make sure the reader's attention is drawn to what is vital;

e.g. "Illustrations should be relevant, clear, accurate, and easy to use."

OR "Illustrations should be:
- relevant
- clear
- accurate
- easy to use."

...tables of words that highlight the relationships between ideas,

...and charts that do much the same thing,

...and tables that do it with figures;

...decorative symbols, which are also available on rub-down sheets for the do-it-yourselfer;

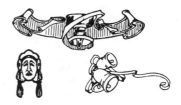

...as are textures and shadings, and

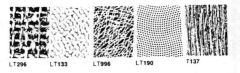

...borders or "rules" (lines of print) which may be used as "stoppers" or as decorative borders or boxes.

Pictures

All of the graphic devices I've mentioned above can be useful in bringing pictorial relief or support to your prose. Notice that none of them requires you to be able to draw. If you **can** draw -- even if only a straight line with help from a ruler -- your pictorial resources will be that much richer. Similarly if you can take usable photographs, or produce computer graphics.

If you can't create your own pictures, you will have to brief someone else to do it for you -- or else make best use you can of pictures that have already been published elsewhere. However:

Almost certainly you will be able to draw your own charts and graphs:

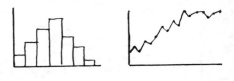

...simple maps;

...perhaps some rough-and-ready cartoons;

...and possibly recognizable objects, provided they don't have to look like any particular specimen.

a flower

And, even if you can't draw, you can perhaps use a camera;

...or assemble illustrations from rub-down sheets;

...or obtain permission to reprint someone else's pictures (giving proper credit);

Reproduced by kind permission of my son

...or adapt materials from the many books of old (and nicely out-of-copyright engravings),

Who would believe she was adapted?

Clearly, there are many ways of being pictorial. I have already suggested how graphic devices can help the reader's comprehension. But what about pictures?

WHY USE PICTURES?

Pictures can have any of several functions in a tutorial-in-print. They may have more than one at the same time. Indeed, you may include a picture for one purpose while your reader uses it for another. Here are ten possible functions for graphs, drawings, photographs , etc:

Decoration

Pictures can be used (as can graphic devices) simply to relieve the monotony of solid print. Almost any kind of picture can serve to give your readers a visual break -- thus helping motivate them to carry on reading.

Amusement

Some pictures, cartoons in particular, can more deliberately motivate the readers by humanizing the subject and showing its lighter side. Here is one of a series of cartoons featuring a troubled dog with which one Open University author lightened the mood of his lessons on curriculum theory.

'The complex nature of social reality only emerges when individuals are forced, through the pressures of interaction with one another, or in attempting to make sense of their world, to dive deeper and deeper for new or modified typifications to account for and make sense of their situation.'

Clearly, cartoons and other light-hearted pictures can also teach. As in the cartoon above -- which presents a far-fetched but thought-provoking example of the principle being discussed -- they can highlight a key point and make it memorable. (Another example of this kind of exaggeration to make a point can be seen in Figure 5.2B on page 94.)

However, cartoon-type drawings do not necessarily have to be "funny". There is a long tradition of using the "strip cartoon" to convey ideas in dramatized form. (Figure 5.2K on pages 112-113 for example.)

Expression

Pictures can be used expressively -- to convey an emotion or feeling. Thus, photographs might be used to suggest the despair of unemployed workers; facsimiles of old documents might be used to express the "actuality" of some historic occasion; a strip cartoon (as in Figure 5.2K on page 112) might be used to involve the reader in some situation of conflict or confrontation.

A "montage" (as in Figure 9.5 on page 192) can be useful in conveying a variety of expressive images simultaneously. In Figure 9.5, the montage is being used as a kind of visual contents list for a tutorial-in-print.

Persuasion

Sometimes a picture may be used not simply to express or provoke feelings, but also to persuade the reader towards a change of attitude. The picture alongside, from a Russian anti-smoking poster, is clearly of this type.

Figure 9.5: A Montage (from Open University course E262)

Block 9
Language and Values

Illustration

This is a superior form of decoration. It involves selecting some aspect of the text that does not absolutely demand to be described pictorially, and picturing it nonetheless -- perhaps with a pen-and-ink sketch or photograph. For example, the learner who is reading about Wordsworth's poetical philosophy may not actually learn much from an eighteenth century print of Grasmere -- but may still appreciate it as an adornment of the page. The notebook shown in Figure 5.2K (page 112) is another example of illustration. See also Figure 7.4 (page 158).

Description

Here the picture is meant to convey a necessary understanding that could not be conveyed in words alone. It shows what something looks like. As Bertrand Russell once said, most of us can recognize a sparrow, but we'd be hard put to describe its characteristics clearly enough for someone else to recognize one. Far more sensible to show them a picture. The pictures in Figures 5.2G and J are of this type (pages 104 and 110).

Pictures can save us, by the way, from a danger I mention in connection with analogies (page 144). That is, it's no good, for example, describing a turtle by reference to a tortoise if the reader has no idea what a tortoise looks like. A picture avoids this problem.

Explanation

Some pictures do more than describe what things look like. They show how they work, or how they can be operated. Such visual explanations are often necessary in the teaching of physical tasks. Imagine the difficulty of trying to teach someone to tie a reef knot or play chords on a guitar if you were denied the use of pictures -- and had to rely on print (or a pre-recorded voice) alone.

Many physical processes, and the operation of much machinery or physical equipment, will also call for visual explanation. (See Figure 5.2E and perhaps even 5.2F -- pages 100 and 102.)

Notice, however, that a full explanation will usually need words **as well** as pictures. Figure 9.6 below shows a combination of:

- a photograph to **describe** what a thing looks like;

- a line drawing to **explain** how it works; and

- several lines of text to make clear what is not apparent in the pictures

Figure 9.6: Two Uses of Pictures
(from Open University course S236, Block 4)

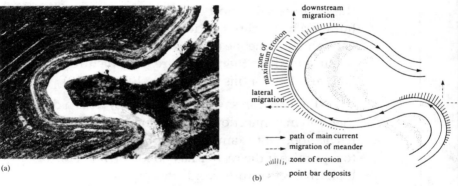

(a)

(b)

path of main current
migration of meander
zone of erosion
point bar deposits

Figure 42   (a) A small meander in the River Ouzel, Bedfordshire. (b) The lateral migration of a meander caused by erosion of the outside bend and point bar accretion on the inside bend. Downstream migration also occurs, because maximum erosion occurs downstream of the mid-point in the meander.

So how does the amplitude of the meander increase? On the outside of a bend, water flows at a faster speed than on the inside. So while the outside bank of a meander is actively eroded, material is deposited on the inside bend of the next meander downstream. The sediment deposited accretes slowly sideways as a *point bar* at the same time as the outside bend is eroded further. The overall result is that lateral erosion is compensated by lateral deposition and the amplitude of the meander increases (Figure 42).

point bar

Simplification

Pictures offer us a means of simplifying reality, of making it more amenable to inspection. After all, reality may be:

- too big -- e.g. the solar system;
- too small -- e.g. the heart of a water-flea;
- too fast -- e.g. the wing movements of a humming bird;
- too inaccessible -- e.g. the four stroke cycle in an internal combustion engine;
- too dangerous -- e.g. defusing a bomb; or
- too cluttered up with confusing detail -- e.g. the dissected body cavity of a frog.

Worse still, the reality may even be:

- invisible -- e.g. the pattern of sound waves from an underwater echo device;
- extinct -- e.g. dinosaurs; or
- not yet come into being -- e.g. a "nuclear winter" scene.

In all such cases, pictures enable us to convey **something** of the reality. But it will be a simplification we convey -- satisfactory perhaps for our immediate purpose, but not to be confused with the real thing. A picture is like a visual analogy -- similar to the reality in some respects, but different in others.

Quantification

Many learners have trouble with numbers. So, when we need to consider quantities, compare sizes, recognize changing proportions, and so on, it often helps the learner if we can present the data pictorially. Figure 9.7 shows some common ways of doing so. Such pictures work by using differences in size between one part of the

picture and another to represent differences in size
between one number or quantity and another.

Figure 9.7: Common Ways of Picturing Quantities

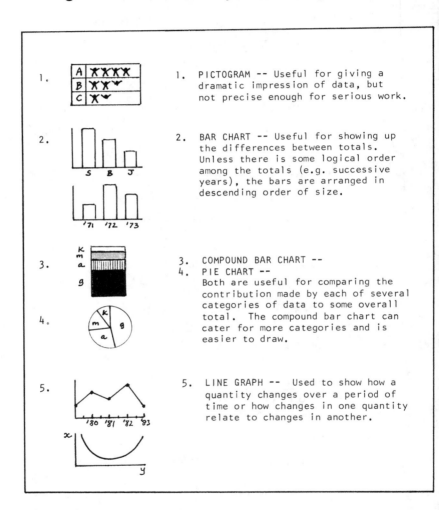

All such pictures of quantities would need an accompanying caption to enable the reader to interpret them. An alternative might be to show your data in a **table**. This is a less pictorial form of presentation -- but still better than burying your figures in a wodge of prose. In a table, there are no size differences to suggest numerical differences -- £9999 occupies no more space than £1000. But at least the figures can be made to stand out clearly.

Problem-posing

A picture can pose a problem or question to your learners. Or it can be the focus of a question you put to them verbally. Look at Figures 5.2J and L (on pages 110 and 116) and at Figure 9.8, for some examples. As you'll appreciate, many topics give rise to important questions that simply cannot be asked **without** using pictures.

At the very least, your learners may be asked what a picture represents. For instance, you might show them a picture of a glaciated valley and ask them to point out evidence of glacial activity. Tables, graphs, charts and maps can be used to involve the learners in quite complex feats of analysis and interpretation.

REMEMBER THAT

- PICTURES CAN SERVE MANY FUNCTIONS
- ONE PICTURE CAN SERVE SEVERAL FUNCTIONS AT THE SAME TIME.

BE SURE YOU KNOW WHAT FUNCTION(S) YOU INTEND EACH OF YOUR PICTURES TO SERVE.

GUIDELINES FOR USING PICTURES

Here are some guidelines to bear in mind when using pictures (including tables and graphs) in your self-instructional materials:

Explain the Function

Consider whether you need to tell the learner why you have included the picture. What function is it meant to serve? This should not be necessary with pictures that are meant to be decorative, expressive or illustrative; but it may be needed, let's say, with explanatory or problem-posing pictures -- if the learner is to be persuaded not to disregard them.

Balance the Functions

Try to make sure that some minor function of a picture does not work against its major function. For example, photographs of battered babies might produce too great an emotional (expressive) effect for the learner to use them easily as evidence of what the injuries actually consist of.

Set Activities

Whenever you regard a certain picture as vital in developing your learner's understanding, base an **activity** upon it. This will require your learners to examine the photograph, interpret the table, compare the graph with those they have drawn themselves, or whatever. Without such activities -- and especially if your text gives the gist of what is in the pictures anyway -- many learners will simply ignore most of your pictures.

Explain Conventions?

Ask yourself whether your learners will all understand the **graphic conventions** you are using in your pictures. For example, do they understand the purpose of shading or hachuring on a map? Do they appreciate the distinction between solid lines and broken lines on a scale drawing of a three-dimensional object? Can they judge the size of the objects shown in the photographs?

If there is any doubt, you will need to provide a key or a caption and/or describe the picture in the text. Again, however, don't tell your readers so much that they feel (correctly or otherwise) that they have no need to consult the picture itself.

Print Picture Close to Text

As a general rule, try to print each picture as close as possible to the piece of text that refers to it. Don't expect your readers to hunt around for it. Any picture on which an activity is based should certainly be on the same page -- or at least on the same "double page spread" -- as the instructions for that activity. You may even need the "feedback" to be on the same page also.

What if the section of text referring to the picture occurs near the bottom of a page, leaving no space for the picture? It might be tempting to fill the remaining space with text relating to the next topic -- and put the picture on the next page instead. Unfortunately, many of your learners will read straight on, and will have lost interest in the subject of the picture by the time they come to it.

It would be better to put both picture and text on the **next** page. This would, of course, leave a sizeable space towards the bottom of the first page -- but there is no law saying all the pages in a teaching text must have the same number of lines. Indeed, some variety in page length may even be a relief to your readers.

If a picture needs to be consulted repeatedly -- say more than three times -- while working through the pages of your text, consider presenting it as a **fold-out sheet.** Readers will then be able to keep it in sight throughout the lesson.

There are exceptions to the general rule discussed above. Some of your pictures -- especially decorations and perhaps some illustrations -- may not relate too closely to any specific piece of text. So you will have much more freedom as to where you insert them. You may use them wherever you think will afford most relief to the reader's eye.

Again, if your subject calls for colour photographs, technical considerations may demand that you print them all together -- and separately from the text commentary. A fold-out sheet might be useful here also.

Graphic Emphasis

People learn best when they can easily see what point you are trying to make. How can you help your learners to identify the important features of your pictures? You may direct their attention verbally, in your text or in a separate caption. In addition, you may do it **graphically**, within the picture itself. For instance:

- You may draw a box around the key area in a photograph, or use arrows or pointing hands to bring the reader's attention to various parts of a diagram.

- You may print certain figures in a table in bold type or even in colour.

- You may number or letter various parts of a diagram to suggest the order in which you would like your reader to examine its parts.

There is an example of such graphic emphasis in a diagram on page 154. Figure 9.8 includes another example (and also shows a question being asked about the picture).

Figure 9.8: An Example of Graphic Emphasis
(Adapted, with permission, from an Olivetti training manual)

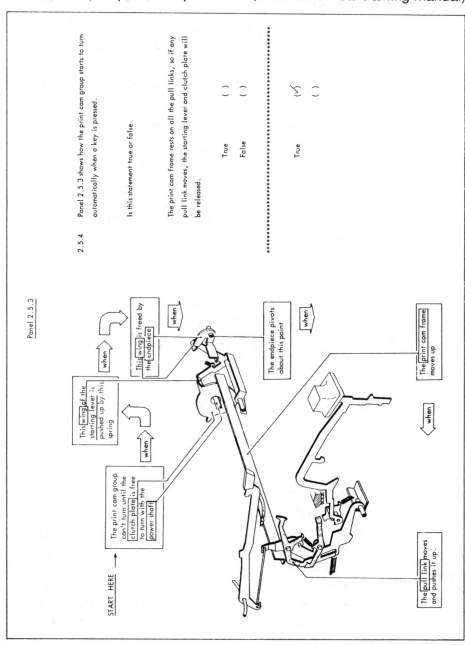

Avoid Information Overload

Don't overload your pictures with information. For example, suppose you have a photograph that contains a good picture of the kind of fossil you are writing about. But many other fossils are in the picture also, and might distract the learners. Here you might consider cutting out the irrelevant parts of the photograph, and printing only the image that concerns your learners.

For another example, compare Charts A and B below. Chart A is readable, but Chart B is too complex.

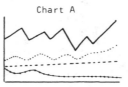

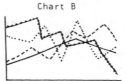

The visual spaghetti in Chart B above might be unravelled by making two or more charts out of it, as shown alongside.

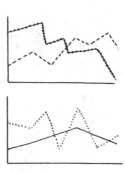

Whenever a picture looks unduly complicated, ask yourself whether you really do need to present **all** the information. Even if you do, ask whether you need to present it all at once. Perhaps you could present a little to start with -- getting your learners to note the main points -- before building up the complexity by offering further pictures, each of which contains further information.

Indeed, you might **build up** to a picture that contained all the information. And you could be confident that readers would understand it because they would have worked on it during its construction.

Tables of figures are often heavily overloaded. Excessive detail, together with unhelpful layout, can make it difficult for readers to pick out the important trends, patterns and relationships. If you are thinking of using tables produced by other people, you may well need to simplify or clarify them for your readers. Figure 9.9 is an example of such a clarification.

Pictures Don't Tell All

Pictures allow us to edit reality and get rid of all kinds of "superfluous detail". For instance, we might present our learners with a photograph or diagram of a fruit they are studying -- rather than a real specimen. Thus we could ensure they concentrated on what we regard as the "essential" features.

But we should not forget to ask whether the learners' concept of the fruit might thereby remain impoverished. Do they **also** need experience of the colour, smell, taste, texture, weight and three-dimensionality of some real specimens? If so, pictures may be necessary, but they will not be enough.

Avoid Racism and Sexism

If you include pictures with people in them, take care to avoid charges of racism and sexism. Don't use picture that present racial or sexual stereotypes. Don't let your pictures suggest that blacks and asians are not encountered in the "developed" countries of the world -- except in low-status or subservient roles. Do not imply that women are essentially housewives and mothers, and

Figure 9.9: Clarifying a Table of Figures
(Adapted from Open University course P670, Book 7)

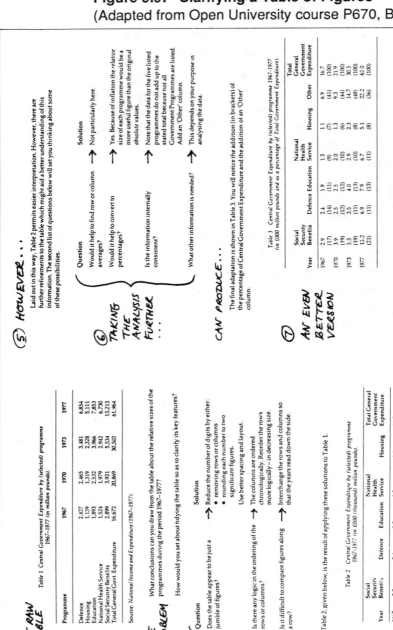

are not to be seen in responsible occupations -- except perhaps in a role clearly subservient to men.

I remember one distance course on child-rearing whose authors were careful to show photographs of black and asian mothers as well as white ones tending their children. But it didn't occur to them to show fathers of any colour sharing in these traditionally "female" concerns. (This oversight was corrected, however, in the second edition.)

Using Other People's Pictures

Sometimes you may wish to use tables, diagrams, photographs, and other pictures that have appeared in other publications. You may want to use the picture exactly as it is. Or you may want to use just part of it. You may want to print a section out of a photograph, or a couple of columns from a table, or just one of several curves from a graph. You may also want to add material -- e.g. verbal captions or graphic emphasis -- to suit the particular needs of **your** learners.

If you intend to print the picture as it is -- or if your alterations will still leave the picture (or part of it) identical with the original -- **make sure you get copyright permission** (see page 367).

If you re-draw the picture (or take a new photograph) so that it looks obviously different, you will not need copyright permission. But it may be appropriate to mention where the original of your picture appeared.

Testing Your Pictures

However careful you are in teaching with pictures, learners may respond to them in unexpected ways. When you developmentally test your lesson on a sample of learners (see pages 338-350), find out how they respond to your pictures.

Learners' responses will show up very clearly where you have based activities on pictures. But other pictures, illustrations for instance, may also be having unexpected effects -- and perhaps ones that you are not too happy about. I remember one photograph showing two children sleeping in each of three beds crammed together in a tiny room. It was meant to describe over-crowding in slum houses. But, when the text was used in parts of the Third World, readers made remarks like; "They're lucky; they've got beds to sleep in" or "Look: only two to a bed".

However handsome a picture may be, learners may seem not to understand it -- or may understand it wrongly. In which case you'll need to replace it with a better one and/or give a better explanation of what the picture is trying to do.

Build Up a Picture Library

All the time you are involved in preparing self-instruction you'll be running across pictures (or ideas for pictures) that may be relevant to one of your topics. Keep a folder or box-file in which to store such materials. They could save you hours of work later on. Remember to note the sources (where the pictures are from other people's work), so you'll know where to apply for copyright, and whom to acknowledge, if you use them.

- NOT EVERYTHING CAN BE SAID IN WORDS
- IF YOU CAN'T FIND THE WORDS TO SAY SOMETHING, TRY PICTURING IT INSTEAD.
- EVEN IF YOU CAN FIND WORDS, CONSIDER PICTURING IT AS WELL

10. MAKING YOUR LESSON READABLE

As I hope you will agree, the tone of your lesson should not be that of a textbook, nor of a lecture. Rather it should be that of an enthusiastic teacher enjoying a discussion of the subject with a responsive learner. Ideally, you should try to create in print the kind of tone you might use in a one-to-one tutorial.

Somehow, in writing your tutorial-in-print, you need to mentally conjure up your learner and imagine you are talking with that individual. If you do this successfully, your writing will be "readable". Your learner will "hear" your voice reaching out from beyond the page.

There are two main components in developing a readable style:

- writing conversationally; and
- writing plainly.

THE CONVERSATIONAL STYLE

The best way of getting across to the learner is to make your writing friendly and informal. (By which I do not mean chummy and careless.) Put down on paper what you might say to the learner if he or she were there in front of you. To help in this, I offer four suggestions:

Use Personal Pronouns

Speak to the learner directly. Call your learner "you" -- never "the reader" or "the learner". Speak of yourself as "I" -- never as "the author" or "the present writer". See what can happen if you ignore this advice:

> "The reader is reminded at this point that algorithms were brought to his or her attention by the author in the preceding chapter."

Those third-party references to "the reader" and "the author" are alienating. The reader may well ask "Are they talking to me?" In fact, such authors are talking to their typewriters rather than to another human being.

Notice the effect if, instead, we use personal pronouns and speak to the reader directly. Not only does the tone become conversational, but the excess verbiage floats away also:

> "You'll remember I mentioned algorithms
> in the previous chapter."

Here are some more examples of this direct approach to the learner:

> "Now try the problem below..."
> "Look at the diagram opposite..."
> "Compare your result with those I have listed below..."
> "If I had been asked the question, I would have said..."
> "You may disagree with me about some of these, but..."

You may, on occasions, feel you need to say "we" instead of "I". If so, make sure that both you and the learner know to whom it refers, e.g.:

> We = the author (royal/pompous plural); or
>   = the author and the reader together; or
>   = the author and his or her colleagues; or
>   = the author and other experts in the subject; or
>   = human beings in general.

Use Contractions

Contractions offer another means of making your writing conversational. Don't feel it necessary, for instance, to write "do not" in full every time you use that idea in a sentence. According to the rhythm of the sentence, and whether you'd have made the contraction in speaking it, you may want to write "don't" -- as I did in the previous sentence above.

Contractions can have a tonic effect. They help keep the stuffiness our of your prose. Here are some that you may want to use:

- I'm - I've - I'll - I'd
- you're - you've - you'll - you'd
- he's - he'll - he'd
- she's - she'll - she'd
- we're - we've - we'll - we'd
- they're - they've - they'll - they'd
- isn't - aren't - wasn't - weren't
- can't - couldn't - mustn't
- here's - where's - how's - what's - who's - that's
- let's - it's (it is)

But remember to use the contraction only if you'd have used it in speech. Thus, you might properly have the same pair of words repeated in one sentence, one pair contracted and the other not. For example:

> "It is important that you should attempt the experiment and you'll find it's not at all time-consuming."

Use Rhetorical Questions

Rhetorical questions can also help your conversational flow. This is the kind of question you might pose without expecting the reader to answer it. Indeed, you will often ask such a question near the beginning of a paragraph -- and then go on to answer it yourself. Here is an example:

> "Now which of these averages is going to be most useful to us? We've already seen that the median depends on the middle-sized observations only and ignores the extremes. The mode, on the other hand,..."

Such an opening aims to grab your readers and engage their interest. It encourages them to anticipate the answer emerging in the rest of the paragraph. As a way of presenting the teaching point, it can certainly be more stimulating than the routine alternative:

> "Now let us consider which of the averages will be most useful to us..."

Of course, you can pose rhetorical questions anywhere in your text. You do not have to confine them to the beginning of paragraphs. For instance, you may sometimes want to use one as a section **heading**. Again, they can be useful in breaking up long and unwieldy sentences. For instance, what can we do to improve the following sentence?:

> "In order to distinguish between constant values and variable values, lower-case letters are assigned to the variables and upper-case letters to the constants."

Instead, we can start with a question:

> "How shall we distinguish between constant values and variable values? Let's use lower-case letters for the variables and upper-case letters for the constants."

But always make clear that the question **is** rhetorical -- and not one that you are putting to the learner as part of an activity. Also, don't over-do it. The focussing effect of rhetorical questions would soon be lost if nearly every paragraph had one.

Use a Light Touch

You may already have come across a mention of this (page 156) -- but it is an aspect of the conversational style, so I'll mention it again here. Be serious in your writing, of course -- but without being solemn. Be precise; be particular; be penetrating -- but don't be pedantic.

Exploit the "human angle" in whatever you are writing about. That is, how does your topic impinge on your reader as a person living in the everyday world -- not just as someone studying your subject? For instance:

> "If you've trundled a trolley round your local supermarket in recent months, you may have noticed the mysterious patterns of parallel lines that have begun to appear on all kinds of items from bottles of ketchup to paperback books..."

If you see a "funny side" to the subject, let your reader in on it. Don't drag in jokes for jokes' sake -- but don't keep them out if they carry useful truths about the subject. For instance, in drawing the distinction between short-term and long-term planning, I might want to mention the man who fell from the top of the Empire State Building and who, as he passed an open window on the 63rd floor, was heard to mutter "So far, so good".

But remember that your writing can still be friendly, human and personal, without any striving after comic effect or attempts to be matey. The suggestions given above should help you avoid the sterile "written for posterity" reference-book style.

Write as if you were **talking** to a learner with whom you are **not too well** acquainted, and you will probably succeed in being conversational without sounding over-familiar. Even computers, nowadays, try to be "user-friendly". Can you afford to do otherwise?

> "He that will write well in any tongue, must follow this counsel of Aristotle: to speak as the common people do, to think as wise men do; and so should every man understand him..."
>
> *Roger Ascham (1515-1568)*

WRITING PLAINLY

Any writer with objectives in mind -- and you have, haven't you? -- should warm to the words of H.G. Wells:

> *"I write as I walk, because I want to get somewhere. And I write as straight as I can just as I walk as straight as I can, because that is the shortest way of getting there."*

So, what is the secret of writing straight, clearly, plainly? I suggest it is a matter of choosing the **right words** and the **right structures** that will effectively carry your message. Let us begin by looking at words. Then we'll consider the structures -- especially the sentences -- in which those words will be carried.

The chief message that will emerge is that plain, readable English depends on **short** sentences made up of **familiar** words. To see what I mean, compare the old nursery rhyme on the left below with the "committee-speak" (or gobbledygook) translation on the right:

Traditional version
Hey diddle diddle!
The cat and the fiddle!
The cow jumped over the moon.
The little dog laughed
To see such sport,
And the dish ran away
        with the spoon.

Gobbledygook version
The amazing feline musicianship demonstrated in connection with a rustic member of the violin family occasioned among spectators a diversity of reactions including, in the case of a female bovine quadruped, translunary saltation; of a diminutive canine, cachination; and of two articles of tableware, collusive flight.

Choosing Your Words

When writing, you will have a **choice of** words. Some will convey your message more plainly than others. Here are some guidelines:

Use words, not phrases. Cut out surplus words. Don't let yourself use several words where one will do. Watch out particularly for elephantine phrases like "in the approximate vicinity of" -- which can be replaced by "about". Such phrases will be a drag on the action, and can usually be replaced by one or two simple words. Here are some examples of phrases to avoid, together with their substitutes:

- a large number of.. many
- a certain amount of... some
- at the present moment in time........................ now
- for the reason that... because
- exhibits a tendency to....................................... tends to
- in the event that... if
- in a satisfactory manner................................... satisfactorily
- having a value of... worth
- in the great majority of cases........................... usually
- of a serious nature... serious
- with a view to.. to
- on the grounds that/owing to the fact that... because

You'll run into many more such phrases -- committee-speak, circumlocution, gobbledygook -- that can be simplified, replaced or omitted altogether. Remember Alexander Pope's telling couplet:

"Words are like leaves and where they most abound
Much fruit of sense beneath is rarely found."

Use familiar words. Use words your reader is likely to understand. I don't know about you but, in that gobbledygook version of the nursery rhyme, there were at least two words I'd have had to look up in a dictionary.

Psychologists have drawn up lists of the most-used 500 words in the English language, the most-used 1,000, and so on. There is no reason for you, as a writer, to know exactly what words are on each list. But the idea behind them is worth bearing in mind. Generally speaking, the more syllables a word has, the less often it is used. So, given a choice between two words, e.g. "count" or "enumerate", you should be able to guess which is likely to be more-used than the other.

Try not to use words like "relinquish", "interment" and "exacerbate" when you might quite properly write "give up", "burial" or "worsen". Always look for the everyday word and, unless one of your objectives is to stretch the reader's vocabulary, use it in preference to the less familiar one. If you need help in finding everyday alternatives, consult a copy of *Roget's Thesaurus.*

Here are more examples: Notice that the less familiar word, usually of Greek or Latin origin, tends to be longer than the more homely alternative:

- reside   =   live
- initiate   =   start
- utilize   =   use
- locate   =   find (or place)
- terminate   =   end

The fancy words are even more of a barrier when they gang up in phrases. For instance:

- endeavour to accelerate   =   try to speed up
- tender assistance   =   offer help
- capable of ambulatory locomotion   =   able to walk
- cardiac arrest   =   heart stopped
- nasal haemorrhage   =   nose-bleed
- disseminate misinformation   =   spread lies
- comprehensive cessation   =   complete stoppage
- employment terminations   =   sackings
- aggravation of the redundancy situation   =   more sackings
- non-animate personal transportation system   =   bike/car

Such pompous gobbledygook just looks silly when you see it isolated like this. But it is not at all amusing when you find whole paragraphs are infested with the stuff. Look at this for instance:

> "The provision of mathematical instruction for post-adolescent persons is a task the difficulty of which is of a considerably larger order of magnitude, by virtue of the fact that their antecedent exposure to mathematics

instruction of less than optimum effectiveness has
resulted in attenuation of confidence. Their personal self-
evaluation implies that mathematics is a field of human
enquiry in which they are destined to suffer perpetual and
irremediable lack of success, and it is a universal human
prediction to exhibit avoidance-behaviour in respect of
pursuits deemed likely to augment the individual's initial
self-perception of intrinsic ineffectualness."

Translated, this seems to mean:

"It's much harder to teach adults about mathematics
since poor teaching has already robbed them of
confidence. They feel doomed to failure in
mathematics -- and we all shrink from trying
something at which we feel likely to fail."

The long-winded phrases were not the only thing wrong
with that paragraph, but you'll see how removing them
has shortened its length and clarified its message. In
general, try to do without multi-syllabled words and
phrases, and your writing will become more emphatic
and your meaning plainer. Don't say "the vegetation
exhibited heliotropic inclination in the direction of the
source of illumination" when you could say "the plants
turned towards the light".

Use precise words. Where possible, avoid using words
that are general, abstract and vague. Any such word will
be open to a variety of interpretations. So some of your
readers will either form no clear understanding or will
misinterpret it. To prevent this, choose words that are
specific, concrete and precise. For instance:

Vague/Abstract	**Precise/Specific**
"Extreme danger is associated with the incorrect operation of this equipment"	"Keep the safety shield down or this machine may kill you."
"Appreciation was expressed in respect of the successful directorial intervention concerning research funding."	"The team clapped and cheered when Dr Jones told them she had obtained the funds they needed to continue their research."

Vague abstractions are responsible for much of the waffle that can clutter up our writing. Let us examine three examples, culled from self-instructional texts I have looked at recently:

Example 1:

- "It has long been recognized that this model is not suitable."

By whom has it been recognized? By the author? By the general public? By specialists? And how long is "long"? A few years or a century or two? This statement says so much less than it appears to that its first six words might just as well be omitted.

Example 2:

- "Society's attitude is still ambivalent to domestic violence."

What is meant "society"? Does the writer mean that some people in society feel one way about domestic violence while others feel differently? Or does he mean that most (all of us?) hold contradictory attitudes at the same time? Or does he take "society's" attitudes to be those expressed in the law courts or the mass media? One may well feel there is some kind of truth behind what he is saying. But what exactly is he saying? Like the first statement we looked at, this one would have been acceptable as an introductory sentence which the author then went on to explain. But neither author did so.

Example 3:

- "There is an inverse relationship between socio-economic status and the importance of physical or functional incapacity as a factor in identifying someone as sick."

Let's assume readers know that "inverse relationship" means that one of two related things will grow as the other shrinks, and vice versa. "Socio-economic status" is abstract and vague; but let's assume readers know it has something to do with how well off a person is, and maybe something to do with the person's social class. This still leaves a yawning vagueness in the phrase "physical or functional incapacity". This shows up as soon as we try to translate -- or rather, interpret -- the sentence, e.g. "Poor people are less likely than those who are better-off to be thought of as sick *{By whom? Doctors/friends/ themselves?}* merely *{This seems to be implied}* because *{Because what? The following is just a guess:}* some limb or organ is not working as well as it normally does or they are no longer able to carry out their normal activities".

The reader should never be put to such trouble in trying to decide which of several possible meanings to assign to a vague statement. Unless you really don't know yourself -- in which case, admit as much to your reader -- then say exactly **who** did **what** to **whom** with **which**, and **where, when how, why**, and with **what** consequences. If your statement really does have several valid interpretations, spell them out.

The advice I've given in this section is related to what I say in Chapter 7 about making plentiful use of examples and case studies. Don't just generalize -- be specific.

Admittedly, it is not always easy to spot the vagueness in our own writing -- especially if it reflects vagueness in our thinking. But our use of certain "weasel-words" and verbal "padding" **may** warn us that we are not being as specific as we ought to be. Here are some expressions to watch out for:

- cases - factors - fields - areas - issues
- considerations - circumstances - respects
- may well - often - for the most part - by and large
- is affected by - tends to be associated with - relates to
- suggests to many people - is widely believed to
- position in regard to - has some connection with

Any one of the above may be enough to obscure the meaning of a sentence. Put several of them together and the result may be total inscrutability:

"The position in regard to the employment situation is widely believed to be affected by balance of payments considerations."

People who write like that either don't know what they are talking about themselves or don't care for their readers to know. Or so it would appear.

Use strong, active verbs. Of all the words in your tutorial-in-print, it is the verbs that carry the weight of the argument. Try to choose full-blooded verbs that really tell what somebody or something **does**. Take an example: "Hamlet killed the King". In that sentence the verb is **active**. It tells what someone did. What happens if we make the verb passive, indicating what was done to someone?: "The King was killed by Hamlet". Because the verb is passive, the punch has gone from the sentence. The tone would be equally drab if the verb were active but weak, e.g. "Hamlet occasioned the death of the King" or "Hamlet was responsible for the death of the King"..

Here are some more examples of the contrast between passive and active verb forms:

Passive	Active
"An experiment was performed."	"We performed an experiment."
"Calculators may be used."	"You may use a calculator."
"Errors in forecasting have been reduced owing to use of the new microcomputer."	"The new microcomputer has reduced errors in forecasting."
"The flask is to be held over a gas flame and heated until a colour change is observed in the liquid."	"Hold the flask over a gas flame and heat it until you see the liquid change colour."

Notice that the passive verbs usually involve roundabout phrases; and the sentences are generally longer than when the more direct, active verb is used. So active verbs usually shorten sentences as well as giving them punch.

Naturally, you'll sometimes choose to use a passive verb. This will happen if you want to put special emphasis on the action rather than on the agent. For example, "Free beer is provided by the management." Here, the fact that beer is provided free seems to be more significant than who makes it available. Otherwise, we might write, "The management provides free beer."

If your writing is to be forceful, your verbs will need to be both active and strong. Too many textbook sentences are merely agglomerations of gerunds and participles, nouns and adjectives, strung together with a few prepositions and bits of the verb "to be". Consider the following example:

> "The typical Equatorial day is of a fixed pattern. In the morning it will be noted that the sky is in a clear, calm condition. But with the daily accumulation of heat, so the ascent of hot-air currents is begun, leading to the formation of towering cumulus clouds and the regular afternoon commencement of downpours of heavy rain."

There is not one strong or active verb in the whole paragraph. Let's see if we can give it a little more zest by putting some action and some strength into the verbs:

> "The typical Equatorial day follows a fixed pattern. In the morning the sky is clear and calm. But, as the earth heats up, currents of hot air begin to rise, causing the towering cumulus clouds to fill the sky. Regularly, every afternoon, these clouds release downpours of heavy rain."

Apart from making it more forceful, the strong, active verbs have reduced the length of the paragraph.

Make a habit of inspecting your own writing. Are weak verbs silting up your prose? Keep an eye on the number of words that end in:

ed   (e.g. "noted")
tion   (e.g. "formation")
ment (e.g. "commencement")
ing   (e.g. "leading")

These examples are from the first of the two passages about the Equatorial day.

Such weak endings as those above usually go hand-in-hand with a weak verb like "to be", "to make" or "to have". The verbs "occur", "become", and "take place" can also rob a sentence of energy. For example:

Weak	Strong
"A decline in enrolment was noted."	"Enrolment declined."
"To study for a higher degree is my intention."	"I intend to study for a higher degree."
"The briefing of new tutors took place last Thursday."	"We briefed new tutors last Thursday."
"Complaints from students become audible when delay in feedback occurs."	"You'll hear students complain if you delay their feedback."

Weak and passive verb forms can easily wrap one's meaning in cotton-wool. This is fine for people who are unwilling to be pinned down to a point of view. But it is no use to the teacher with objectives to reach.

Of course, you will need passive forms some of the time; and there is no need to avoid weak verbs altogether. My advice is simply that you should be aware of what kind of verbs you **are** using from paragraph to paragraph -- and be sensitive to the effect they are having on the tone of your prose.

Use specialist vocabulary -- but with care. So far I have not mentioned the word "jargon". Some people use the term to refer to any abstract language that they find incomprehensible. Others use it for language they think pompous, snobbish, or trendily fashionable, whether they understand it or not. Such language I have discussed already under previous headings. Other people use the word "jargon" to mean specialist vocabulary -- the "in-words" used by experts in a particular subject to talk to one another about their common interests.

Much as I would complain about jargon of the former sorts -- especially abstract long-windedness -- I don't see how we can survive without our specialist vocabularies. For the most part, the new terms we wish to teach the learner relate to new **concepts**. Once the learner has learned to attach meanings to the terms, we have an invaluable shorthand that saves us having to spell out the attributes of a concept each time we want to use it. Imagine the bother, for instance, if we decided that jargon like "triangle", "area" or "degrees" was not to be used in a lesson on geometry.

If the technical terms you introduce into your lessons are to avoid being derided as jargon, you'll need to take care. Here are some basic DOs and DON'Ts:

- Don't use a technical term unless you are convinced that the learner needs it.

- Do explain a new term very carefully when you first introduce it -- e.g. purpose, definition, examples of the concept.

- Do give reminders at appropriate points -- e.g. when the term is being brought in again after not having been used for a while.

- Do give a guide to the pronounciation of new terms that are at all "difficult" -- e.g. "Pronounce it **may-triss-ease**". This will be so much easier, of course, if you intend providing an audiotape as part of your package.

- Do emphasize the introduction of a new term by use of typography -- e.g. <u>underline</u> it, **embolden** it, put it in CAPITALS, or print it in the margin also. This can be helpful to the learner who is reviewing earlier lessons in search of the first mention of key ideas. (The traditional *italics* really don't give the necessary amount of prominence to a word.)

- Do be especially careful in explaining technical terms that have a different meaning:
  - in everyday use, e.g. "significance" in statistics; or
  - in another subject your learners may be familiar with, e.g. "objectives" in education and management.

- Don't use too many new technical terms in the same paragraph. One new idea per paragraph is enough.

- Don't use alternative technical terms for the same concept (e.g. "microcomputer"/"personal computer") unless you are deliberately trying to habituate the learner to a variety of usage and have mentioned this intention earlier in the text. An alternative strategy would be to mention all the variants early on, and then stick to one of them.

- Don't use a different technical term for the same concept in different lessons -- or not unless the reason for doing so is clear and spelled out to the learner, e.g. "Since this lesson is based around a chapter from Bloggs and Moggs in which they use the term "grundlefink" for what we have so far called "skewdop", we too will use their term in our accompanying commentary". Here, you will need to compare usage with any colleagues writing related lessons.

- Don't revert to an everyday term once you have introduced the technical word.

And finally:

- Don't use everyday terms or personal expressions (e.g. "tutorial-in-print") in such a way as to suggest that they are generally-accepted technical terms.

Now for the second aspect of writing plainly. Even well-chosen words can lose their effect if they are embedded in poor structures. So how can you write sentences and paragraphs, and use punctuation, so as to carry your message plainly and readably? Here are my suggestions:

Simplify Your Sentences

One of the underlying suggestions of this chapter is that you should write like you would talk to a learner. If you do so, your sentences will be short and simple; for long, convoluted sentences just don't occur in ordinary conversation -- even among subject-specialists.

In educational and technical prose, however, they occur with depressing frequency. It is all too easy to pick up a textbook or specialist journal most of whose sentences meander over three lines or more. Such sentences tend to be too crammed with ideas, relationships and qualifications to allow of easy reading. You often have to read them two or three times before you can be sure you've understood them. For instance:

> "Pellagra, a slow-developing disease which used to be very widespread among rural dwellers in warm, sunny climates where maize was the staple food, and which is a disease characterized by skin rash, diarrhoea and, in later stages, by deterioration of mental faculties, sometimes to the point of imbecility, is, however, (as proved scientifically by Goldberger and his colleagues who, in 1916, in the United States, studied the incidence of the disease in seven textile mill communities, proving indeed that it can be produced, prevented or cured by changes in diet), a nutritional disorder."

Keep them short. The shorter your sentences, the more vigorous they will be. The fewer the words, the more emphatic. The more often you use the full stop, the more often your readers can pause for thought. And it is during those pauses that your meaning will seep through.

As a general rule, try to prevent your sentences from exceeding 20 words. (That's about two lines of typewriting.) Some must unavoidably be a little longer. A few may even contain 30 or 40 words -- so long as you have a good ear for the rhythms of prose and a firm grasp of the ideas you wish to convey. But if you need several longish sentences in any one paragraph, you'd do well to balance them with some very short ones -- of 10 words or less.

Indeed it is important that you do vary your sentence length. If they were all short, they would make for a choppy, breathless, read. To some extent, the length of a sentence may be influenced by its position in the paragraph. For instance, readers may be able to digest a longish sentence in the middle of a paragraph -- if you have enticed them in with a couple of short, snappy ones. Likewise, you may sometimes want to punch home the point of the paragraph in a brief final sentence.

Whenever you read through a piece of your writing, look for places where you can split the complex sentences. Look out for the "ands", the "buts", the "howevers", the "furthermores", and all such words that introduce phrases and clauses that might practicably be broken off to make separate sentences. See how we might thus re-write the paragraph about pellagra that I showed you earlier:

> "Pellagra is a slow-developing disease characterized by a skin rash, by diarrhoea and, in the later stages, by deterioration of mental faculties, sometimes to the point of imbecility. It used to be very widespread among rural dwellers in warm, sunny climates where maize was the staple food. However, pellagra is a nutritional disorder. It can be produced, prevented, or cured by changes in diet. This was scientifically proved by Goldberger and colleagues who studied the incidence of the disease in seven textile mill communities in the United States in 1916."

Keep the Pattern Simple. Actually, if you keep your sentences short, you'll probably find they stay simple in pattern. That is to say, they will not contain so many clauses and phrases that the learner gets confused by the number of relationships involved. Here is a sentence that is too densely packed to allow easy comprehension:

> "The fact that the molecules in a liquid are closer together and thus the attractive forces between them are very much greater than the very minute forces between the molecules of a gas, is responsible for the greater resistance by a liquid to compression."

But we can make this message easier to read and comprehend if we re-package it into shorter sentences. In doing so, we also simplify the sentence patterns:

> "The molecules in a liquid are closer together than they are in a gas. As a result, the attractive forces between the liquid molecules are much greater than the very minute forces between the gas molecules. Hence, liquids are more resistant to compression than are gases."

Be careful with negatives. Many learners find negative constructions difficult to handle. The very sight of phrases like "not unsuitable" may send them back to the beginning of the sentence to re-read. Do try to avoid double negatives. For one thing, you may say the opposite of what you mean, e.g.:

> "There is no reason to doubt that the evidence is not devoid of significance."

But even if you get it right -- and you really are trying to say that the evidence has some significance -- you give your reader too much trouble in working out what you are saying and in wondering whether that is also what you mean. Usually, such a sentence can be expressed more positively, e.g.:

> "There is no reason to doubt that the evidence is significant."

Or, better still: "The evidence is significant."

Here is a negative construction that gave me trouble recently:

> "The use of force should not be seen to be the prelude to any concession which was not acceptable to the islanders before the occupation."

The sentence is not helped by its use of "which" instead of "that". But the main difficulty comes from its two negatives; this can be eased somewhat by replacing "not acceptable" by "unacceptable".

Watch your word order. Pay some attention to the order of words in your sentences. This advice is sometimes illustrated by showing how the placing of a word like "even" or "only" can totally transform the meaning of a sentence. For example:

- "Only the cat sat on the mat."   *(None of the other creatures present did so.)*

- "The cat only sat on the mat."   *(It didn't stand or lie down.)*

- "The cat sat on the only mat."   *(There was just one mat -- the one the cat sat on.)*

- "The cat sat only on the mat."   *(It sat nowhere else.)*

- "The only cat sat on the mat."   *(Other creatures were present -- at least two from another species; they may or may not have been sitting on the mat also.)*

More generally, however, word-order does make a difference to the rhythm and emphasis of your sentences. Compare these two examples:

"We say a current flows when electrons move in the same general direction for a period of time."	"When electrons move in the same general direction for a period of time we say a current flows."

Usually, the emphasis comes at the end of a sentence. Thus the sentence on the left above might be defining a term ("current") that learners have already met; while the sentence on the right is presenting them with a term to attach to an already familiar concept.

Vary your patterns. Try to avoid a monotonous repetition of sentence structure. Notice the tiring rhythm of the sentences in this next paragraph:

> "Railway lines expand in hot weather. So they are laid in separate lengths. Three is a gap between each length and the next. The lengths are bolted together by fish-plates. The fish-plates are drilled with oval holes. These oval holes allow the bolts to slide when the rail expands."

These sentences look as if they have all been poured from the same mould. They are all virtually the same length -- between six and twelve words; and they all have a similar structure. Furthermore, the flow of the paragraph is so staccato that it is difficult to see how the various ideas link together. To cure the resulting tedium, it's forgivable even to increase the average sentence length:

> "Since railway lines expand in hot weather, they are laid in separate lengths with a gap between one length and the next. Fish-plates are used to bolt the lengths together. Each fish-plate is drilled with oval holes which allow the bolts to slide as the line expands."

This revised version varies the length and pattern of its sentences, and the relationship among the various ideas emerges more clearly. Even though the average sentence length has increased from $8\frac{1}{2}$ words per sentence, none is longer than 22 words and the average is still quite acceptable at 16 words per sentence.

Watch Your Paragraph Length

Remember that each paragraph you write should be elaborating on or leading up to a key sentence. That key sentence contains the main idea of the paragraph. If your paragraphs tend to ramble on indefinitely, there's more than a chance that each contains more than its fair load of main ideas. If so, some of them are likely to get overlooked by your reader.

Inspect each paragraph. If any contains more than one main idea, make each the subject of a separate paragraph -- even if you need to add more words. For instance, the paragraph about pellagra (page 224) should really have been two paragraphs -- the first describing its general characteristics and the second identifying it as a nutritional disorder. Notice the key sentence for the "second" paragraph stuck in the middle of the extract.

In most popular newspapers, the paragraph is just about extinct. In the interests of layout and "white space", practically every sentence is its own paragraph. Yet this risks falling into another trap -- of failing to show how the ideas in separate sentences link up to form a coherent argument. All the same, if your learners are *Daily Tabloid* readers, don't give them many paragraphs that are longer than this one. Too solid a block of print will weary their eyes and confirm all their worst anxieties about learning.

And, remember, the breaks between paragraphs -- just like those between sentences -- provide your readers with "thought pauses". They may or may not want to use every one, but it's wise to make them available .

Remember also, as I mention in Chapters 7 and 9, you can break from paragraphs altogether, where appropriate. You can create breathing space on the page by using, e.g.:

- lists (like this one);
- boxed items;
- tables (of words or figures);
- flow diagrams; and so on.

Punctuating for Meaning

Punctuation does play a part in readability; but if you use short sentences and active verbs, you'll probably have few problems with it. The more frequently you use the full stop, the less use you'll have for any of the other punctuation marks.

The purpose of punctuation is to help the reader grasp your meaning. It substitutes for the pauses and emphasis you would use if you were speaking to the learner. If you ever do have trouble punctuating, try reading your sentences aloud. Notice where you pause briefly; notice where you read as if in amplification of what you've just said; notice where you try to read two consecutive sentences as if they were more closely connected than usual; notice where you want to give particular emphasis to a word or phrase:

- If you want the reader to pause only briefly; insert a comma.

- A full stop gives a longer pause.

- If you want to insert a comment (not too lengthy a one) on what you've just written, enclose it in brackets.

- Alternatively -- perhaps to make your writing more open in texture -- you can set off the comment by a pair of dashes.

- If you want two short sentences to be linked together, use a semi-colon; this gives a longer pause than a comma but shorter than a full-stop.

- If you want to give particular emphasis to a word, underline it or have it printed **bold** or in CAPITALS.

- If you must emphasize a complete statement, use the exclamation mark! (But one only, and not too often!!!)

- Notice the use of "bullets" as a punctuation mark (as on this page) -- to tell your readers they are approaching a list of related items.

MEASURING READABILITY

By this time you should be clear about some of the factors on which readability depends: Friendly, conversational tone. Human interest. Well-chosen words, preferably short ones. Specific, concrete references. Strong, active verbs. Short, simple sentences.

A number of people have used such factors to develop ways of measuring readability. One of the most practical is that described by Robert Gunning in *The Technique of Effective Writing* (1952). He called it the Fog Index. This judges the "fogginess" or heaviness of a piece of writing by the average length of its sentences and the proportion of multi-syllabled words it contains.

The Fog Index

In order to calculate the Fog Index of a piece of writing:

1. Take a random sample of about 100 words.

2. Count the number of complete sentences, stopping your sentence count with whichever sentence ends nearest the 100 word target.

3. Divide the number of words by the number of sentences to arrive at the **average sentence length** in the passage.

4. Count all words that have **three** syllables or more.

5. To get the Fog Index, apply the following formula:

$$\frac{2\left(\begin{array}{ccc}\text{Average} & & \text{Number} \\ \text{sentence} & + & \text{of} \\ \text{length} & & \text{long words}\end{array}\right)}{5}$$

Thus, if the average sentence length in a certain passage were 17 words and the passage contained 8 words of three syllables or more, the Fog Index would be:

$$\frac{2(17 + 8)}{5} = \frac{50}{5} = 10$$

Clearly, the more you use long sentences and long words, the higher will be your Fog Index. Gunning suggests that 12 is the danger point. Of all the successful authors whose prose Gunning tested, none came out with a Fog Index above 11. Of the popular American magazines he tested, *Reader's Digest* had a Fog Index of 9 and *Time* had one of 10. I leave you to calculate the index yourself for some of the publications you believe to be typical of your learners' preferred reading. I doubt if many of them will exceed 12.

The Complexity Quotient

If the Fog Index looks too tedious to calculate, here is a short-cut cousin you might try instead. I call it the Complexity Quotient -- it is simply the **average number of long words per sentence.** To calculate it :

A. Count the number of complete sentences you have on a page.

B. Count the number of "long" words (three or more syllables).

C. Divide B by A.

If your Complexity Quotient exceeds 3, your prose will be more difficult than that of most novelists and, indeed, of most top-selling authors writing for non-specialists. You may like to check this quotient for the kinds of material you know your learners **do** find readable.

Such measures as the Fog Index and Complexity Quotient are rough-and-ready tools. They offer a useful check on material that looks difficult. If you apply one a few times, you'll probably develop an eye for prose that would over-tax your readers -- without even having to do any calculations. You'll see at a glance where you need to cut out long words and break up long sentences.

SUMMARY

To produce effective, readable writing:

- Write in a friendly, conversational style:
  - Use personal pronouns
  - Use contractions
  - Use rhetorical questions
  - Use a light touch
  - Exploit the "human angle"

- Write plainly
  - Cut out surplus words
  - Use short, familiar words
  - Use precise words
  - Use strong, active verbs
  - Take care with specialist vocabulary
  - Write short, simple sentences

And, as a check on how well you have done so:

READ YOUR WORK **ALOUD**.

ANYTHING YOU FIND TEDIOUS OR AWKWARD

TO SPEAK MAY BE EQUALLY SO FOR YOUR

LEARNERS TO READ.

11. INTRODUCING OTHER MEDIA

In Chapter 4 I discussed the issues involved in choosing appropriate teaching media. The chief of these is:

TO WHICH MEDIA DO YOU AND
YOUR LEARNER HAVE ACCESS?

Multi-media Packages

Throughout this book I have assumed that PRINT will be your most accessible medium. That is, your learners will spend **most** of their time, I imagine, considering words and pictures on the printed page.

But it is both possible and desirable that they should use other media as well. For one thing, the additional media may enable certain kinds of understanding that would not otherwise be possible. Furthermore, the variety -- the change of stimulus itself -- may refresh and invigorate the learner.

Hence you might aim to make each course, and to some extent each lesson, a **multi-media** experience -- even if one medium is used more than all the others put together. Which media might **you** be able to use in addition to print? How will you choose and use media?

Basic Requirements

There are seven requirements to be met by a medium if it is to make an effective contribution within a course:

- You must have the necessary know-how to exploit the unique educational potential of that medium.

- Your teaching in that medium should be clearly related to that in the rest of the course material -- i.e. not be "tacked on" as an optional extra.

- Learners should recognize that the medium has something special to teach them.

- They should be able to use the medium conveniently.

- They should have appropriate expectations about the medium -- and the study skills necessary for using it.

- They should have some control over the timing and rate of presentation.

- They should be provided with printed support material.

Consider how these conditions might be met as you read about the five media I discuss in the rest of this chapter:

- Practical work
- Audio material
- Video material
- Computers
- Human media.

PRACTICAL WORK

Practical work is essential for many subjects, especially when our objectives relate to work-related competences as well as knowledge. Even knowledge, however, may sometimes be acquired more easily and with deeper understanding and interest if the learner can carry out suitable practical work. Such work may vary from observing the behaviour of patients in a doctor's waiting room, to interviewing fellow-trainees, to cutting up a sheep's brain, to compiling a weather record, and so on.

Self-instruction does not rule out practical work. In some cases, learners may be able to carry it out without moving from their chairs. (See Figure 11.1 and 5.2H). Certainly, much practical work, especially in the arts and social sciences needs no very special equipment. (See Figure 11.2.) For example, even distance learners could easily carry out an interview or census, make a musical instrument, or collect plant specimens.

Figure 11.1: **Practical Work** (from Open University course S101, Unit 1)

Home Experiment 2   Pendulum

Take a piece of thin string about 1 metre long and make a simple pendulum by tying some small, compact object to one end—a normal-sized key would do. Place a watch with a seconds-hand in front of you so that you can see your pendulum and the watch at the same time. (Alternatively you can, of course, use a stop-watch in one hand while holding the pendulum with the other hand.) Hold the free end of the string, or better still tie it up to a hook or any other suitable support. Count how many times within 10 seconds your pendulum has gone through the complete sequence of one swing. Or, alternatively, measure the time it takes the pendulum to complete 5 or 10 swings. Try to answer the following questions.

ITQ 3   Does it matter whether you count as one swing the sequence of motion from one extreme position to the opposite extreme and back, or the sequence starting from the vertical position to one extreme through to the opposite extreme and back to vertical?

ITQ 4   How does the number of swings completed in 10 seconds (or the time taken to complete 5 or 10 swings) change when you shorten the length of the pendulum by holding or suspending the string at a point nearer to the swinging object?

ITQ 5   Can you find, by trial and error, the lengths at which the pendulum will complete 5, 8 and 10 swings within approximately 10 seconds?

ITQ 6   What are the periods of the swinging for the three cases described in ITQ 5?

Figure 11.2: **Practical Work** (from Open University course TAD292, Unit 3)

7   AN 'OVEN GONG'

Try the following.

Take a metal rack from an oven and attach to each of two adjacent corners a piece of string about three feet long. Wrap the free ends of the pieces of string around the index fingers of your hands, and plug your ears with these fingers, the rack suspended below. Now get a friend gently to play the rack as a metallic gong, with a spoon, a pencil, and perhaps another small object made from a different material. Ask the friend to vary the point of striking, the strength of blow, the density of the sounds, as much as possible. Allow long periods for listening to the resonance. *You have tapped yourself in to a remarkably intricate vibrating structure which previously was virtually inaccessible.* Even your partner can now hardly hear the sounds he is making for you.

Can you find further objects with a virtually self-enclosed vibrating system, that can be tapped in a similar way, to reveal their hidden sound world?

Figure 11.3:   Use of Home Experiment Kit
(from Open University course S101, Unit 14)

Home Experiment 2

To do the experiment you will need the following items from your Home Experiment Kit, Part 2:

Apparatus*	Chemicals
100 cm³ beaker	sodium hydroxide
100 cm³ measuring cylinder	dilute hydrochloric acid (8.9%)
rack of test-tubes	ferric nitrate (iron(III) nitrate)
5 cm³ syringe	potassium thiocyanate
2 dosing pipettes†	
wash-bottle containing distilled water	
spatula	

Part 1

(a) Using your measuring cylinder, measure 50 cm³ of distilled water into a beaker and add five pellets of sodium hydroxide, NaOH. Allow to dissolve.

(b) Add enough ferric nitrate, $Fe(NO_3)_3$, to a test-tube until the rounded bottom is full. Add enough distilled water to half-fill the test-tube, and shake until the solid dissolves.

(c) Add *one* crystal of potassium thiocyanate, KSCN, to a test-tube and add enough distilled water to half-fill it. Again shake to dissolve.

All three solutions are ionic. Note the colour of each solution and try to decide which ions are present: record these in Table 2.

TABLE 2   Observations for part 1 of Home Experiment 2

Solid	Colour of solution	Ions present
sodium hydroxide, NaOH		
ferric nitrate, $Fe(NO_3)_3$		
potassium thiocyanate, KSCN		

Now listen to the first part of the tape.

EXTRACT FROM TAPE:

"*Now that you've prepared the three solutions, check your entries in Table 2. First, the columns: Both the sodium hydroxide and the potassium thiocyanate solutions are colourless. But the ferric nitrate solution should be yellow. If you found any marked difference from these colours, you should make up that solution again, taking care that the test tube or flask is really clean -- wash it well with distilled water before adding the chemical, and don't forget to wash and dry your spatula before using it.*

Now what about the ions in these solutions? Well, you've already met sodium hydroxide, so I expect... "

Making Facilities Available

Sometimes, however, practical work is impossible unless learners can get to use special equipment or materials. In such cases, either the learner must be brought to these facilities, or the facilities must be sent to the learner.

Face-to-face. If learners are studying on-site, then laboratory or workshop facilities can perhaps be scheduled at suitable times. There may well be difficulties, of course -- in that learners studying at their own pace may be ready to carry out a given piece of practical work on quite different days (or even weeks) from one another.

If learners are studying at a distance, it may not be easy to bring them to a centre for practical work at the most opportune time -- if at all. But the possibility is worth exploring -- e.g. as a "one-day school" or a "summer session" in a local college.

Another possibility, with some distance courses, will be to arrange for someone connected with the learner's job (e.g. a manager) to organize practical experience -- perhaps as part of their role as mentor.

Home experiment kits. Otherwise, or maybe additionally, we need to consider the second alternative -- sending the equipment to the learner. Some Open University courses send a treasure chest of equipment to students in the form of a "home experiment kit". Students may be sent chemicals, glassware, microscopes, rock specimens, seeds, and so on -- even extending to an electric reed organ and a helium neon-laser for producing holograms.

At the other end of the scale, I know of one college whose home experiment kit for an elementary physics course includes household items like a duster, a comb, and a reel of cotton thread. You might suppose that such items would be easily obtainable by the learners anyway. But the course developers were presumably unwilling to take the risk that they might not bother. If you suspect that your learners might be at all disinclined to carry out practical work that you believe to be essential, then you will need to anticipate any difficulties or inconveniences they might use as excuses for avoiding it.

With the necessary equipment -- and the guidance and feedback from printed workshops or an audio-cassette (See Figure 11.3) -- learners can obtain a wide variety of experimental experience. Nevertheless, the value of such experience (in terms of attaining the course objectives) must be weighed against potential problems in such areas as the following:

- costs;
- safety;
- warehousing
- insurance;
- distribution and recovery of equipment, and so on.

Models. Sometimes, practical work may be based not on real objects but on **models**. This was essential with one Open University course in which students needed to understand how the Greek astronomer, Ptolemy, contrived to "explain" the seemingly irregular motion of the planets while under the illusion that they revolved around the earth. The course materials provided a "do-it-yourself Ptolemaic universe kit" -- two sheets of card on which were printed various shapes which learners could cut out and manipulate on the turntable of a record player. By this means, the ingenuity of Ptolemy's thinking was made physical for the learners.

Another course, on geology, provided similar sheets of printed card from which the learners could make three-dimensional models of faulted blocks of rock. Figure 11.4 shows the instructions given to learners. By moving the model blocks around in relation to one

Figure 11.4:   Using Cardboard Models
(from Open University course S23, Block 2)

Faults do not simply go up and down, nor are fault surfaces simply vertical planes of movement. The 'downthrow' we have been looking at so far is merely the simplest, most conspicuous effect of a fault movement and serves only to introduce us to the topic. To familiarize yourself with the sort of displacement that can happen on a fault, build Models 8a and b. They represent two blocks separated by a fault plane which is the inclined plane (Fig. 63a). The first thing to notice is that steeply dipping beds are involved, and that the *same* sequence of beds dipping in the *same* direction is represented on both Models. Move the models about to find out how you can bring the beds into concordance on either side of the fault. You should find that you can do this by moving the block either vertically (Fig. 63b), or horizontally (Fig. 63c). Thus a movement straight up and down the fault plane can produce a lateral offset of the beds exposed at the surface (Fig. 63d).

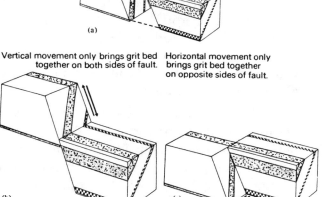

(a)

Vertical movement only brings grit bed together on both sides of fault.   Horizontal movement only brings grit bed together on opposite sides of fault.

(b)   (c)

(d)

Figure 63   Models 8a and 8b which represent two parts of a faulted block (a and d) and can be moved either vertically (b) or laterally (c) to bring the beds on either side into concordance.

This is an important point to grasp and you should study the models until you understand it fully. Maps record the distribution of rocks only at the surface, so faults on maps will only show an *apparent* movement, and much of the terminology of faults is concerned with their apparent movement. The actual amount and direction of movement, however, is much more important, and much more difficult to determine. It is only when one can recognize a particular point on each side of the fault that the true displacement can be measured. On the Models 8a and b, an ancient wash-out channel has been located in a thick grit band on both sides of the fault, to provide a marker point on each side of the fault.

another, learners could come to realize how the surface-distribution of rock types (as shown on a geological map) relates to what might be under the surface.

Such physical manipulations -- e.g of the earth's crust or the solar system -- allow a different route to understanding than would reading about the movements or even watching someone else perform them.

Observed Experiments

All the same, it may be impossible, or inappropriate to provide the learner with facilities for carrying out **all** the practical activities that might conceivably be of interest within your course. Some experiments or manipulations may be too dangerous, too costly, too time-consuming, too demanding of skills irrelevant to the course, and so on. In such cases, you may revert to a method common enough in "conventional" courses, and let the learner **observe** a demonstration.

You, however, are less likely than conventional teachers to have an opportunity to demonstrate "in the flesh". If you were producing videotapes, practical demonstrations could be shown in moving pictures, with accompanying sound track. Without videotape (or film), you would have to make do with "still" pictures, together with either a printed commentary or an audiotape. In some cases, such a series of still photographs or drawings -- like a strip cartoon -- may serve perfectly well to demonstrate successive stages within an experiment or other practical manipulation. See Figure 11.6 (page 254) for an example.

Activate your learners. You will, of course, ensure that your learners are not passive observers. You'll need to engage them in critical and constructive activity. Prior to the experiment or demonstration, you might ask them to suggest how it might be designed. Or you might ask them to point out weaknesses in designs that you have suggested. During the experiment or demonstration you might get them to record their observations, according to some specified criteria. Afterwards, you might get them to explain what they have seen -- or even to come up with hypotheses based on their observations and design a further experiment to test these hypotheses.

Such observed demonstrations need by no means be a waste of time. They are certainly preferable to the "cookbook science" so many of us did at school -- following a recipe like robots and "adjusting" our results to fit what we knew was expected. That was rarely an enlightening activity. Practical work of the "hands on" variety can sometimes inhibit thinking. There are times when learners can learn **more** by observing, so long as we lead them to do so thoughtfully -- anticipating, explaining, and criticizing the demonstrator's actions and results.

Summary

It is clearly quite feasible for self-instructional courses to include practical work -- especially in the arts and social areas where it often takes the form of working with other people or with documents. Even in scientific and technical subjects, much can be done with cheap and easily available materials and equipment, or with models. Where necessary practical work requires more specialized apparatus, ways must be found of getting it to the learners, or them to it -- or of enabling them to observe (and mentally participate in) a demonstration.

> SOME COURSES INCLUDE A **PROJECT**
> -- MAYBE SEVERAL WEEKS OF LARGELY
> SELF-DIRECTED PRACTICAL WORK.

AUDIO MATERIAL

Here we are talking chiefly about **recorded sound**. This can be presented in several different ways:

- Audio-cassettes (audiotape)
- Gramophone records
- Radio broadcasts
- Television (or film) "sound track".

In this section I shall concentrate on audio-cassette and radio. Gramophone records I shall mention in passing when dealing with audio-cassettes; sound tracks I shall assume (but not discuss) in the later section concerned with "video-material".

Radio

When Open University courses began in 1971, each had a half-hour radio programme broadcast twice each week by the BBC. But few courses make much use of radio today. The reasons for this lie among the conditions listed at the beginning of this chapter. Radio has the following drawbacks (as does broadcast television):

- Learners must tune in at a **fixed time**, regardless of whether that time is convenient and whether they have completed any necessary preparatory work.

- Learners **cannot replay** the broadcast at will (unless they have taped it).

- Learners must learn at the **fixed pace** of the broadcast. (No opportunities to pause for thought).

- Learners may not be used to paying attention and **learning** from broadcasts -- as opposed to using them casually for entertainment or news.

The burden of these disadvantages can be judged by comparing listening to a broadcast with reading a book. With a book, the learner has control -- and probably possesses more of the necessary skills and expectations as well. Fortunately, the solution is at hand in the shape of a tape-player. Cheap audio-cassette players are now easily available, and broadcast radio can do little that cannot be done better by an audio-cassette. In the Open University, the use of audio-cassettes has grown as that of radio has declined.

This is not to dismiss radio altogether. If, for example, a local radio station were interested in broadcasting programmes associated with your course, the possibilities might be worth discussing. Such "air time" might be useful for general "familiarization" material, where no great concentration is required from listeners. For example, you might broadcast discussions between tutors and learners, or "phone-ins" with learners quizzing a panel of experts, or even a "magazine" covering a variety of talking points related to the course.

Such programmes would have the advantage over audio-cassettes (pre-recorded before the course begins) of being able to exploit **current** issues. They could even be broadcast "live". You would probably find, however, that learners listened only sporadically to such programmes -- unless they expected the content to be crucial to what they wanted from the course. And you might well feel that any such crucial material would have been better deployed on audiotape or in print.

Audio-cassettes

With audio-cassettes you can avoid the inflexibilities of radio. In particular, they enable your learners to:

- use the material at any time they choose;
- stop and start the sound at will;
- replay a passage as often as they wish; and
- skip over any material they do not need.

In what follows, I discuss three ways of using audio-cassettes:

- for presenting aural source material;
- for lecturing; and
- for tutoring.

Naturally, more than one of these may be used on one cassette -- and even within a single learning session. If you can think of yet other uses, so much the better.

Source material. Clearly, you can use audiotape to present the "raw sounds" of your subject -- e.g. the call of the coot, the grinding of the gears, the magic of Mozart. In that last case, gramophone records might be needed for acceptable sound quality, but they would be very expensive if you had to compile and produce them specially for the course.

Here are some further types of source material that might be presented on audio-cassette:

- Foreign language dialogues.

- Spoken glossaries of "hard-to-pronounce" terms.

- Conversations to be analysed -- e.g. between doctor and patient or sales-staff and customers.

- Discussions or interviews with practitioners of the subject -- e.g. police officers and criminals talking about their way of life.

Some of the above items, e.g. the conversations, could be transcribed into print. But to do so would lose the nuances of speech (and the telling silences) that might be vital to both understanding and empathy. Non-verbal sounds could not be transcribed at all.

Needless to say, a tape of source material would not be much use on its own. Learners would need guidance, either in printed form or on the tape itself, as to how to approach it and how to use it in their learning.

You may sometimes want your learners to listen to source material at intervals while reading a tutorial-in-print. For example:

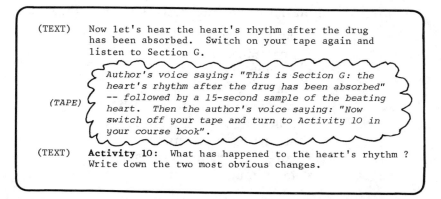

(TEXT)   Now let's hear the heart's rhythm after the drug has been absorbed. Switch on your tape again and listen to Section G.

(TAPE)   *Author's voice saying: "This is Section G: the heart's rhythm after the drug has been absorbed" -- followed by a 15-second sample of the beating heart. Then the author's voice saying: "Now switch off your tape and turn to Activity 10 in your course book".*

(TEXT)   **Activity 10:** What has happened to the heart's rhythm ? Write down the two most obvious changes.

Another example of this way of using source material is to be found in Figure 5.2F (on page 102).

Lecturing. This is an obvious but potentially boring way of using the medium. Some distance learning institutions began by basing their distance courses on recordings of the lectures that were first presented to on-site students. These would be supplemented by printed notes, which might reproduce any chalkboard drawings or slides that the lecturer may have shown.

But the usual lecturing voice is likely to sound too formal, too elevated for easy listening, when it's coming from a plastic box on the learner's bedside table. The most effective audio "lectures" have the more intimate tone of a radio "talk" -- where listeners can feel the speaker is talking to them alone.

Learners often find such informal talks extremely helpful. Apart from adding humanity and variety to the teaching, they do score over print in that learners can follow them while driving their car or doing the ironing.

Tutoring. This approach combines the intimacy of a "talk" with getting the learner to do something else besides listening. You can guide the learner through some task or exercise requiring eyes and hands as well as ears. For instance, you might talk the learner through:

- studying a series of photographs;
- operating a machine;
- assembling a model;
- handling soil specimens;
- completing a form or questionnaire;
- following a sequence of printed calculations;
- setting up an experiment;
- consulting tables of statistics;
- examining a map or blueprint;...and so on.

Giving such guidance by your spoken voice would be particularly beneficial in situations where your learners need to keep their eyes on what they are doing -- and **not** keep turning back to a printed page for instructions.

The most striking example I have come across was in an Open University course in which the learner needs to inspect a number of stereoscopic photographs of geological structures, using a 3-D viewer. In practice, it takes the eyes a few seconds to achieve the full 3-D effect, because one must force oneself to focus "through" the photograph rather than on it. It would be literally nauseating, as well as time-wasting, if one had to keep re-focussing on a printed page (and then back on the photograph again) in order to find out what features to look for next in the photograph. Thanks to the audio-cassette "talk-through", one can maintain the difficult focus without interruption once one has attained it.

Such guidance or talk-through tapes can even be used away from the desk. In many of the world's big art museums it is possible to stroll around looking at exhibits with the recorded voice of an expert burbling into one's ear through headphones. If your learners are willing to wear lightweight headphones out of doors, and carry a cassette-player, your recorded commentary could accompany them on nature trails, town walks, visits to exhibitions and building sites, tours of architectural edifices, or whatever is appropriate to your subject.

Notice that the medium in the examples mentioned so far is not just recorded sound. The learners are not merely listening. They also have to **look** -- at pictures, at real objects, even at print. This mixture of media, a planned combination, is often called "audiovision".

As with audio source material, audio tutoring also can be used within a tutorial-in-print. Figure 11.3 shows an example where the instructions for performing an experiment are given in print, and learners are asked to write their observations in a printed table -- but the author **speaks** her comments on this activity on the audiotape. (This makes it less likely that learners will run across the feedback accidentally before trying the experiment themselves.) Once the author has finished commenting, she asks learners to switch off the tape and perform the next experiment.

You can, of course, shift the balance of your teaching from print towards tape -- and aim for the **spoken** equivalent of a tutorial-in-print. However, learners will still need to look at things as well as use their ears -- so it will be an audiovisual tutorial. In this kind of sequence:

1. You talk to your learners rather than expressing your teaching points in writing.

2. While they listen, you may be getting them to turn the pages of a booklet, which you have laid out with text and pictures.

3. Every so often you will ask them (on the audiotape) to answer a question or carry out some exercise

(like an ITQ or SAQ) -- perhaps writing their answers in the booklet.

4. Each time you set such an activity, you will say "Stop the tape now, and start it again when you have finished..." You may record a few seconds of music at this point, as another signal for the learner to switch off.

5. When learners switch on again, they hear your feedback and comments on the activity. You will talk about the kind of answers they should have come up with. Or, if they're not the kind of answers that can be spoken (e.g. diagrams or complex calculations), you may direct your learners to a page in the booklet where the answers have been printed.

6. Having finished commenting on the previous activity, you go on to the next teaching point you want to talk about, as in 1 and 2 above.

Figure 11.5 shows an extract from an audiovision booklet. It contains a number of "frames" which carry the material that the teacher is discussing and asking questions about on the audio-cassette. The blank boxes are for the learner to write answers before getting feedback from the tape.

Audiovision tapes have become increasingly popular in the Open University -- both with teachers and learners. Teachers comment favourably on the fact that they can speak naturally to the learner, exploiting informal examples and minor asides. They can also use tone of voice to suggest what is important and what is less so, in a way that would not be possible in print. (Everything I say in Chapter 10 about writing **conversationally** applies with even greater urgency when you are writing a script for an audiovision cassette.)

Figure 11.5: Audiovision Notes
(Adapted from Open University course D210)

NOTE 11 SHIFTS IN DEMAND AND SUPPLY CURVES

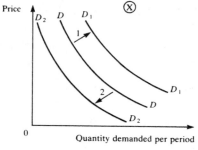
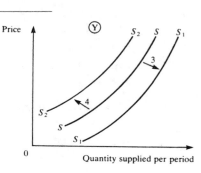

Question
Which of the shifts 1–4 are increases and which are decreases?

	Shift	Increase or decrease
Demand	1	
	2	
Supply	3	
	4	

NOTE 12 WHAT WOULD BE THE INITIAL EFFECT OF THE FOLLOWING CHANGES IN CONDITIONS?

Change in conditions	On demand	On supply	Increase	Decrease
1 A product suddenly becoming fashionable	✓		✓	
2 Frost affecting much of Brazilian coffee crop				
3 Sudden fall in incomes affecting sales of a product				
4 Bumper grain harvest				
5 New and cheaper system for extracting oil/gas				
6 Rise in the costs of transport of a product				

NOTE 13 FOUR BASIC DEMAND AND SUPPLY SEQUENCES

What happens after:
1 An increase in demand?
2 A decrease in demand?
3 An increase in supply?
4 A decrease in supply?

Learners, for their part, speak of the satisfaction of hearing their teacher's voice: "It's just like having your own tutor in the room with you". And if you have any learners who are not too adept at reading, they may be even more appreciative.

Fortunately, audiovision lessons are cheap and easy to prepare. Most teachers can record perfectly usable lessons in their own homes without help (or interference) from professionals. And they are equally cheap and convenient for learners to use.

One final thing to remember: Because the learner carries on working, under the tape's guidance, even when the cassette player is switched off:

> 20 MINUTES OF TAPE TIME MIGHT PROVIDE
> FOR AN HOUR OR MORE OF LEARNING TIME.

VIDEO MATERIAL

Here I am talking about **moving pictures**, with or without accompanying sound. Television is now the most typical means of presenting moving pictures in education and training (though film is far from defunct). It can take three main forms:

1. *Television programmes.* The typical television programme is around half an hour in length and is meant for viewing from beginning to end without a break. It is heavily influenced by professional broadcast standards and formats -- e.g. documentary or drama. Some teachers will use broadcast programmes or "off air" recordings (copyright requirements permitting), while others will make their own.

2. Video segments. Here, the videotape contains a number of separate clips, sequences, segments. Each lasts no longer than six or seven minutes -- some perhaps only a few seconds -- and each is designed to trigger some kind of activity from the learner. Viewers are meant to stop the tape after each segment to answer questions about it (perhaps rewinding to view it again first) -- or, if they are viewing in a group, to discuss it with colleagues. The video viewing may well be interspersed with reading or learning from audio-cassette and there is no need for the video segments to make up a continuous "storyline" as in material of Type 1.

3. Interactive video. Clearly, Type 2 video is already more interactive than is Type 1. But the label has been captured by a form of presentation in which Type 2 video segments (usually on video-disk) are called on to the screen by the learner's interaction with a microcomputer. Such a system allows you to run a tutorial-in-print on the computer screen (interspersed with appropriate moving pictures and sound) -- but in such a way that your teaching really does vary according to the learner's responses, and different learners may be branched into different teaching sequences.

Production Problems

Unlike audio, the production of video material is no do-it-yourself operation for the teacher with a couple of weekends to spare. It demands access to very costly production equipment and considerable amounts of time for planning. Furthermore, if you are to produce video material of respectable quality, you will need the help of professionals. This opens up the possibility of conflict between what they consider "good television" and what you consider "good teaching".

With interactive video, the production costs are particularly horrendous. There you would have to work with computer experts as well as television experts. Current experience suggests that many months of highly expensive professional time are needed to produce material that will keep the learner busy for perhaps half an hour. For this reason, interactive video seems unlikely to be available to most developers of self-instructional courses in the near future. If you do get a chance to explore the medium, compare the costs and benefits compared with those of other media.

Presentation Problems

Presenting video material to self-instructional learners can also be both difficult and costly. On-site learners and distance learners pose different problems:

On-site learners may either be:

- brought together periodically for **group** viewing of material appropriate to the part of the course they are **supposed** to have reached, or

- given **individual** access to a video player whenever each learner is ready to view the material.

Group viewing has the advantage that learners (and tutors if they are present) can **discuss** the video material. It may also economize on equipment. The disadvantage, however, is that some learners may have pushed on further than most. So the single showing of the video might come too early for some, too late for others -- unless it is designed to be independent of the sequence in the rest of the course materials.

Individual viewing offers the learner more control. He or she can choose the most pertinent time at which to work on the video material. And, as with audiovision, the learner can stop it and think about it, and replay bits of it as often as he or she likes -- or as often as the video lesson itself suggests. However, the individual will be one of several; so a number of copies of the video material, and a number of playback machines, may need to be available. Furthermore, there will be the expense of providing accommodation, security, supervision, maintenance and, perhaps, an appointments system.

Distance learners, on the other hand, are impossible to reach with moving pictures -- except at even greater expense. In the Open University we have been lucky to have access to the BBC's facilities, both for producing television programmes and for broadcasting them nationwide to students in their own homes. Notice, though, that this combines the disadvantages of fixed viewing times and lack of easy opportunity to discuss the material with others -- besides inhibiting the "video segments" approach.

Maybe within ten years, video-cassette players will be as widespread in people's homes as audio-cassette players are today. Even so, it might be prohibitively expensive to produce and keep track of multiple copies of videotapes -- especially if learners are numerous, and too geographically distant from one another to share. One alternative might be to arrange occasional viewing sessions at local centres, but that would raise all the problems I've already mentioned in connection with on-site learners.

Is Your Motion Really Necessary?

In view of the great expense involved in planning, producing and presenting moving pictures, we clearly need to ask this question. Is **motion** really essential in the pictures you want to show your learners? Or would a printed set of "still" pictures, perhaps with audio-cassette commentary, serve just about as well? (Figure 11.6, to which I referred earlier, shows how a series of such pictures can even illustrate change over time.) Could you

Figure 11.6:   Showing Change with Still Pictures
(Adapted from Open University course T352, Unit 10)

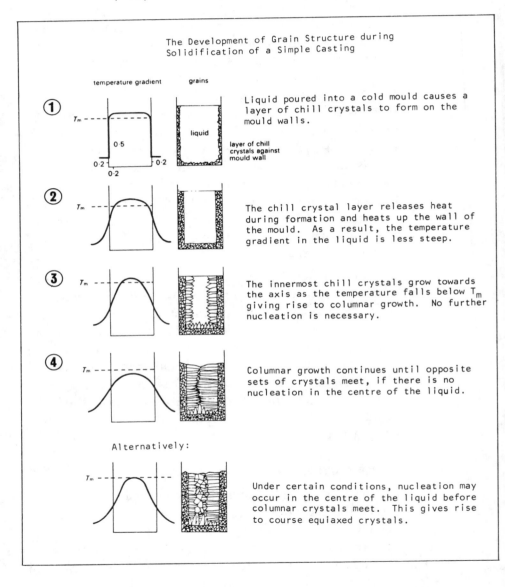

The Development of Grain Structure during Solidification of a Simple Casting

temperature gradient   grains

① T_m

0·5

0·2   0·2
0·2

liquid

layer of chill crystals against mould wall

Liquid poured into a cold mould causes a layer of chill crystals to form on the mould walls.

② T_m

The chill crystal layer releases heat during formation and heats up the wall of the mould. As a result, the temperature gradient in the liquid is less steep.

③ T_m

The innermost chill crystals grow towards the axis as the temperature falls below T_m giving rise to columnar growth. No further nucleation is necessary.

④ T_m

Columnar growth continues until opposite sets of crystals meet, if there is no nucleation in the centre of the liquid.

Alternatively:

T_m

Under certain conditions, nucleation may occur in the centre of the liquid before columnar crystals meet. This gives rise to course equiaxed crystals.

justify the additional expense, and maybe inconvenience -- for both teachers and learners -- of using video?

You will need to weigh your own decision in the light of your own special circumstances. Below you will see my suggestions for sample applications in which video might be justifiable -- provided your time and resources could not be expected to produce **greater** dividends of understanding and satisfaction by being invested in less expensive media:

Sample applications. Each of these possible applications for video assumes that **motion** is essential. I have not tried to avoid overlap, and my list is meant to be suggestive rather than exhaustive. Video might be worth using:

- To demonstrate the use of tools or equipment.

- To demonstrate activities that learners are to carry out -- e.g. interviewing or car-driving.

- To present experiments in which the processes (rather than, or as well as, the results) must be observed.

- To present a dramatic performance (e.g. a play or a ballet) or a musical performance -- if it is important to see as well as hear the performers.

- To analyse change over time, using animation, stop-frame, slow-motion or speeded-up pictures -- e.g. the movements of an animal or of the atmospheric belts on Jupiter.

- To suggest the spatial, three-dimensional qualities of a still object -- e.g. a building or a piece of sculpture -- by moving the camera around it, thus giving the viewer a sense of sharing space with the object.

- To show a discussion or interaction between two or more people in which "body language" is important and/or in which it is necessary (and would otherwise be difficult) for the learner to identify who is speaking at any one time.

- To take the learners into situations -- e.g. down a copper-mine or into the cockpit of a jet plane making its landing -- which they might not otherwise be able to enter (and which they could not properly experience through the medium of still pictures).

- To provide primary source material for the learner to explore or analyse, using principles or techniques developed in the course -- e.g. archive film of historical events or video recordings of naturally occurring situations (like classroom exchanges between teachers and children, or animal courtship behaviour).

Summary

This section has suggested caution in the use of moving pictures in self-instruction. If you are thinking seriously about using video material, here are four crucial questions to ask yourself:

1. For this particular course/lesson, could video material provide worthwhile learning experience that could not be provided more cheaply using other media?

2. Can I make it possible for my learners to view the video material?

3. Can I make my own video material, or obtain suitable material made by other people?

4. In view of the costs -- both to me and to the learners -- can we use video without having to economize on more essential media or neglect more worthwhile opportunities?

If you do decide that video is essential and justifiable, don't be persuaded that you must therefore make "television programmes". Most of the applications I listed above would have been served as well or better by the "video segments" approach.

> MUCH OF WHAT IS TAUGHT ON TELEVISION COULD BE TAUGHT AT LEAST AS WELL IN **PRINT** (TEXT PLUS STILL PICTURES -- WITH OR WITHOUT AUDIO SUPPORT..

MEDIA NOTES

This seems a good point to emphasize the need for **printed** support materials. Let's call them "media notes". I mentioned such materials more than once while discussing practical work and audio-cassette teaching. If you want your audio-casette learning, for example, to be closely integrated with the study of a tutorial-in-print, your audio notes might be anything from a few occasional paragraphs to a substantial section within the text of the tutorial-in-print. Alternatively, your audio-cassette lessons may be free-standing and the associated print materials may make up a separate booklet.

However, media notes are equally vital for serious study using radio, video, or computers. In fact, it may be the media notes that reveal to learners how the media lesson is meant to tie in with the rest of the course -- and thus persuade them to spend some time on it. In general, media notes might perform any of the following functions:

- Describing the content of the media "experience".

- Explaining its purpose -- e.g. its objectives.

- Showing how it links with ideas and methods taught in other parts of the course.

- Explaining how to use any special equipment or materials involved -- especially any safety aspects.

- Giving guidance on how to learn from the experience.

- Providing questions or activities for the learner to tackle before, during or after the experience.

- Providing feedback to these questions or activities.

- Reproducing "stills" from a video sequence or computer lesson to help the learner recall the experience afterwards -- or providing pictorial (and text) material for study during an audio-cassette or radio lesson.

- Summarizing the main points.

- Suggesting follow-up activities.

If you give too little information in such media notes, your learners may neither see the point of using the medium nor be adequately equipped to make the most of it if they do. Yet if you give too much, learners may either neglect to read the notes before using the medium or else read the notes **instead** of using the medium.

With the exception of Figure 11.6, every figure so far in this chapter shows an extract from media notes. For two final complete examples, look at Figures 11.7 and 11.8. Figure 11.7 relates to a geological field trip, Figure 11.8 to a television programme. (If the latter notes had been for a "video segments" tape, they would have mentioned several points at which learners should stop the videotape and the questions they should tackle at those points.)

Figure 11.7:   Media Notes for a Geological Field Trip (from Open University course S236.)

THURSDAY   Fossils and sediments, Staithes and Quarrington

Start 0830

Equipment required

These notes
Field notebook
Clipboard
Compass clinometer
Staithes field sheets
HARD HATS ARE VITAL
Hammers and goggles are useful for Quarrington.

Aims of the day

Staithes

1   Identify the sedimentary rock types, sedimentary structures, trace fossils and body fossils exposed in some Lower Jurassic strata.

2   Record the occurrence of these features in a sequence of strata on a partially completed graphic log, and complete the log.

3   Measure the orientations of palaeocurrent indicators in the strata examined.

4   Infer environments of deposition of the sequences and, in the case of that in the graphic log, how these changed over time.

Quarrington

1   Interpret the lithologies and sedimentary structures in the Permian strata.

2   Comment on the depositional environments, and the palaeoclimate at the time of deposition.

The route

The route leaves Durham on the A177, past the Science Site, passing over Coal Measures, hidden under drift deposits, to Bowburn and to Quarrington.

From Quarrington the route follows minor roads eastwards across the Permian strata to join the east coast trunk road, the A19, which is followed south through the Teesside industrial complex. Note the ICI Billingham works, which were originally developed to exploit anhydrite in the Upper Permian. Reserves are now exhausted and the mines closed. In the distance will be seen the British Steel complex at Grangetown and the ICI Petro-chemicals Division at Wilton. This area contains the biggest acreage of petrochemical works in the country.

South of Middlesbrough the route follows the A174 and the A171 through the town of Guisborough. The route skirts the foot of the scarp forming the northern edge of the Cleveland

Hills formed of Lower Jurassic (Lias) beds capped by sandstones of the Lower Deltaic Series. Skelton, Brotton and Loftus were centres of the now defunct Cleveland Ironstone mining district. Boulby is a deep mine from which potash salts from the Upper Permian Evaporite Series are extracted.

Staithes

Introduction

Staithes is situated some 12 km north-west of Whitby on the coast of County Cleveland. You will leave the coach at the top of the hill leading down to the harbour. *Please take all your essential equipment including your lunch as you will be away from the coach for the rest of the day.*

The visit consists of two exercises, both along the sea cliffs that flank Staithes harbour (Figure 4). You will be walking over the wave-cut shale platform, which in places is fairly slippery; so stout boots and care are necessary.

SAFETY NOTE

You must not linger on any part of the shore when your tutor asks you to return to Staithes. Timing is crucial since the incoming tide covers most of the platform, and can easily cut off stragglers. Do not go further than Old Nab when doing the graphic log exercise, and if you are unsure about your mobility along this stretch of shore, your tutor will show you the limits within which you should stay. Please keep within sight of your tutor at all times. You must wear your helmet when approaching the cliffs, since fine fragments drop down even in fine weather.

For the same reason you are advised not to hang around unnecessarily under the cliffs. Neither of the exercises at Staithes requires a hammer. Indeed, please refrain from hammering any part of the section, so that it can remain unspoilt for later students and also because loosening of the cliff wall by hammering may provoke rock falls.

In some weeks during the summer school period the tides may make this exercise impossible and an alternative exercise (described on separate sheets) will be done.

General stratigraphy

The section along the shore on both sides of Staithes harbour exposes strata of the Lower Jurassic (Lias), dipping gently to the south-east. Along this section four distinctive units can be seen; they are:

1   the Jet Rock Formation (youngest),

2   the Grey Shales Formation,

3   the Cleveland Ironstone Formation and

4   the Staithes Formation (oldest).

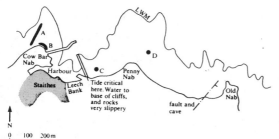

Tide critical here. Water to base of cliffs, and rocks very slippery

fault and cave

N

0   100   200 m

Figure 4   Map of the Staithes area.

Figure 11.8:   Media Notes for a Television Programme (from Open University course D102, Unit 8.)

12   TV STUDY GUIDE

TV8   THE END OF THE LINE

This programme looks at different explanations of the causes of economic crises – the explanations that arise in everyday conversations – and places them in the context of the theories that have been discussed in this unit. We again use the drama format of a dialogue between Steve and John: Steve is made redundant, and they argue over why their particular factory is being closed; but it becomes clear that the argument is, inevitably, about why the economy as a whole was in a crisis.

Before the programme

Try to ensure that you have reached this point in the unit. If you have not been able to find the time to get this far, you will still find the programme useful, but try to read Sections 4 and 7 quickly before it starts. Make sure you are familiar with the distinction between basic and immediate causes of crisis: it is elaborated in those sections.

During the programme

The programme is concerned with the causes of crisis, but while watching it you should look for the different levels of causes that are discussed. On the one hand, there is the question of whether John's or Steve's actions should be blamed for causing their particular firm to close or whether it resulted from structural causes beyond anyone's control. On the other hand, there is the problem of what causes crises in the economy as a whole: how do factors such as a collapse of demand, falling profits and conflict between labour and capital interact?

After the programme

Write down, briefly, your answers to the following questions. They are not meant to be a test, but instead a means to help you check your understanding of some of the points in the unit and programme.

1 Think of the argument between Steve and John. In the course of it several explanations for the factory's closure were put forward. Here is a list of some of them – try to complete the missing words with either 'much' or 'little':

Demand for the product was too . . .

The capitalist installed too . . . new machinery.

The workers put up too . . . resistance to the scrapping of traditional methods of working.

2(a)

Q   How might higher wages in John and Steve's factory have *increased* its difficulties?

A   By intensifying the fall in its . . . (fill in the relevant word).

2(b)

Q   How might higher wages in factories have helped to *ease* the difficulties of the economy as a whole at least temporarily?

A   By leading to an increase in workers' . . . for . . . goods and thereby weakening the . . . cause of crises. (Fill in the three words).

(If you found question 2(b) difficult, read through Section 8 and try again).

The answers are given at the end of the unit text (p 47 below).

COMPUTER TEACHING

This section will be just as cautious as that on video. In one form or another -- like Computer Assisted Learning (CAL) or Computer Based Training (CBT) -- computer teaching has been around for some time. During the 1970s and early 1980s, cynics were heard to remark that "Computer assisted learning is the medium of the future -- and it always will be".

That future now seems to have arrived for some, thanks to miniaturization, mass production, and the diminishing cost of powerful equipment. But the costs remain enormous -- especially the labour costs of designing suitably interactive learning materials -- and seem likely to severely restrict the worthwhile use of computers in education (and even in training).

Experience in the Open University suggests that between two and four **months** of professional time are needed to produce a CAL /CBT exercise that will engage learners of varied ability for one **hour**. Similar estimates have been heard from commercial computer organizations. (Producing computer-based interactive video is even more time-consuming.)

The delivery system is also very expensive. Even assuming your organization can allow your learners access to a suitable computer, there will be the costs of accommodation, telephone bills, and all the servicing and administrative costs I mentioned earlier in connection with on-site video.

As with video, the costs of equipping and administering a computer teaching system may become huge if your learners are studying at a distance and have to travel to a number of CAL/CBT centres to use terminals. Many of your learners will nowadays have microcomputers in their own homes, of course. But there are so many different models, each refusing to run programs written for other machines; and, in any case, most home computers are too underpowered to do anything very sophisticated, educationally.

Forms of CAL and CBT

Despite the problems, some institutions can justify using computers for **some** courses. The Open University, for example, operates a national network of some 250 computer terminals linked to its mainframe computer. It also has several courses that call for students to use computers in their own homes. So what can computers do for self-instruction?

In theory, a powerful computer should be rather proficient as an instructor. After all, it can:

- store considerable amounts of information;
- select from it at great speed;
- present the learner with print and animated diagrams;
- respond to contributions typed in by the learner;
- give immediate feedback to the individual learner; and
- deal differently with different learners.

Again in theory, computers can be programmed to use their teaching potential in three main ways:

1. Tuition. Here the program requires the computer to act as a patient, personal tutor. It leads the learners through a sequence of material which they are expected to master. The computer can discover in what areas each learner has difficulties -- then explain the ideas involved, using appropriate examples and exercises -- and test the learners at each step to check how well they have understood.

Different learners may be presented with different examples and test exercises, according to their earlier responses. And the program may "branch" different learners into different kinds of material according to the particular difficulties or interests they reveal.

2. *Simulation.* The second form of computer teaching uses the computer to simulate a particular situation or system with which the learner can interact. Thus the learner will be able to "experiment" in total safety with, let's say, a nuclear reactor, an ailing hospital patient, the processes of mountain-building, or the economic structure of the EEC.

Learners can call up the information that will enable them to run the reactor, treat the patient, and so on, as they think fit, trying out their interpretation of the underlying principles. The computer will tell them what effects their decisions are having -- especially if the reactor is about to go critical or the patient expire. (See Figure 11.9 for an extract from a simulation exercise.)

3. *Data-crunching.* Here the computer is used as a means of searching large amounts of data and/or of manipulating it at high speed. Thus the learner might ask the computer to search for certain figures or patterns in hundreds of census returns or to produce complex charts and graphs.

In seconds or minutes, the computer may be able to provide learners with data that might otherwise have taken them hours or days to work out. Relieved of this drudgery and delay, learners can get on with the more important task of making sense of the data.

So much for the theory. In practice, much that is offered in the name of CAL and CBT seems to concentrate on telling and testing (especially testing) rather than on teaching. Too often it makes little or no use of the

Figure 11.9: CAL Simulation -- Extracts from an On-screen Discussion between Computer (C) and Student (S) (from W.Feurzig's "Decision Making", in *Computer Assisted Learning in the Health Professions*, Harvard Medical School 1970, ed. L.M. Stolurow)

AFTER DISCUSSING THE PHYSICAL APPEARANCE OF A
CASE-STUDY PATIENT, THE STUDENT (S) AND COMPUTER (C)
CONTINUE THEIR ON-SCREEN DISCUSSION AS FOLLOWS:

S   *Laboratory reports ?*
C   Fine. Which lab tests would you like to have done ?
S   *X-ray.*
C   X-ray will be taken. Results will be sent to you
    as soon as possible.
S   *Urine exam.*
C   The analysis will be done.
S   *Rectal exam.*
C   You're not being careful. The patient is too
    acutely ill for a rectal examination.
S   *WBC*
C   The white count will be taken.
S   *Pulse ?*
C   Unchanged.
    Some of the first series of lab reports have just come in.
    Urine exam: Insufficient fluid for analysis.
    RBC: 5 million.
    WBC: 15500.
    Differential: Shift to left.
    When the other reports are in you'll be notified.

          (PART OF DIALOGUE OMITTED)

C   Perhaps you think it too early too arrive at any definitive
    conclusion. On the other hand, you may be prepared to
    make the diagnosis now. Are you ?
S   *No.*
C   Fine. Nevertheless we've got a fair amount of information
    -- at least enough to raise some, perhaps several,
    diagnostic possibilities. Have you any in mind ?
S   *Acute pyelonephritis.*
C   Unexplained fever, chills, malaise, and flank pain are
    certainly consistent with acute pyelonephritis. Do you
    think that the absence of dysuria reinforces the diagnosis ?
S   *No.*
C   Right. And isn't the white count somewhat high for
    this diagnosis ?
S   *No.*
C   You're wrong. The white count is high, though a later
    reading is indicated for substantiation.

          (PART OF DIALOGUE OMITTED)

C   Any other thoughts as to diagnosis ?
S   *Pneumococcal pneumonia.*
C   I see you're still interested in this diagnosis.
    Are you absolutely sure ?
S   *No.*
C   What would help you nail down the diagnosis ?
S   *Evidence from X-ray findings.*
C   Good. Anything else ?
S   *Evidence from blood culture.*
C   What you really need is evidence from the sputum smear
    and culture. Anyway, continue with your investigation
    and we'll see what happens.

computer's unique capabilities. Too often it could be done just as well (if worth doing at all) in the pages of a book.

> COMPUTERS ARE TOO EXPENSIVE TO
> USE AS ELECTRONIC PAGE-TURNERS

If you believe you can put computers to better use in your subject, here are some questions to ask yourself:

CAL/CBT Checklist

- Will CAL/CBT provide a learning experience that is both essential and incapable of being provided by a cheaper medium?

- Do we have the ability and the time to think out and produce quality teaching programs -- perhaps at the rate of 2-4 months per hour of learner time?

- If not, can we be sure of obtaining relevant programs of quality from outside sources?

- Where, when, at whose expense will learners use CAL/CBT?

- How can we ensure that learners do take up the opportunity to use CAL/CBT? (For example, by basing assessment activities on it.)

- Can we do enough teaching with CAL/CBT to make it worthwhile for learners to acquire the necessary skills?

- Can learners be given any form of human help -- e.g. by tutors/mentors -- if they get into difficulties?

- How will tutors or other helpers be chosen and prepared for their role?

- What printed back-up material (media notes) might learners need to help them get the most out of the learning experience?

- What arrangements can we make for evaluating and improving each CAL/CBT package in the light of experience?

Administrative footnote. Even if you decide not to use CAL/CBT, if your organization has a computer, you may appreciate its help in the **administration** of your course -- especially if you are dealing with large numbers of learners. For instance, you might use it to keep records -- e.g. How many of your learners are falling behind schedule? How many of your tutors are marking with undue severity? -- and to mark objective tests.

HUMAN MEDIA

This may seem an odd heading, especially in a book about self-instruction. But people can have some of their learning "mediated" -- that is, deliberately conveyed or at least supported -- by contact with other human beings, even when they are studying at a distance. This contact may or may not be face-to-face. Learners may be in touch with tutors or mentors (or other learners):

- by writing to one another;
- by telephone;
- by computer conferencing;
- by exchange of audio-cassettes; or
- by face-to-face contact.

Face-to-face contact is, of course, easier for on-site learners. But all five types of contact may be possible for distance learners also. They may, for example, be encouraged to meet together regularly, with a tutor, for group discussion or practical work based on their individual studies. Even very occasional contacts with other learners and/or with tutors or mentors may be invaluable to your learners and are worth considering in your course planning where possible.

Roles for Human Contact

We can identify a number of roles for human encounters in and around a self-instructional course. Not all of them demand the services of trained, paid tutors:

Encouragement and support. Self-instructional learners (especially those learning at a distance) may be prone to anxieties. They may worry about whether their approach to learning is appropriate; about whether they are reaching satisfactory standards; about how to reconcile their studying with the demands of family life and friends; about whether it will all be worthwhile for their career or other aspirations -- and so on.

The necessary encouragement and support can best be provided through "live" contact with another human being. A more experienced colleague (or mentor) can help learners talk through their problems. Trained counsellors may be needed for serious cases, especially where specialized knowledge is required. But even the learners themselves -- in "self-help" groups -- can help dissipate one another's routine anxieties.

Remedial tuition. However thoughtfully you prepare your materials, some learners are going to have difficulties with them. You may be able to arrange for learners to discuss such difficulties with a tutor. (But don't be like some course developers who assume they can therefore take less trouble with their materials and leave it to tutors to "tie up the loose ends".)

Inspirational teaching. Occasional face-to-face seminars can refresh the learner's spirits. Before each new stage of the course, learners might be brought together for a session at which the tutor sums up the course so far and sets the scene for what is to follow. Learners might thereby feel gratified at having covered so much ground already and heartened for the work that still lies ahead.

It is generally easier to stimulate your learners' motivation face-to-face than it is in print, or even on audiotape. Though, as with all these roles, an inept tutor could do your learners more harm than good.

Practical teaching. You may have been able to build all necessary practical work into your self-instructional materials. But, in some subjects, learners will need face-to-face demonstrations, and they will need to carry out their lion-taming or their open-heart surgery under the guidance of an expert who can give them immediate feedback while observing their performance.

Advice on options. Not all courses require every learner to follow exactly the same path. Some give learners considerable freedom to decide which areas they will concentrate on. Others have a substantial "project' component, in which -- perhaps after the course has given a grounding in the subject -- learners are expected to select and explore a topic of their own choice.

In such cases, the learners may benefit from access to a tutor who can help them not just with choosing topics but also with organizing their personal researches. Learners may also need advice on which bits of the course they can safely neglect if they start running out of time.

Marking and commenting. Marking and commenting upon learners' performance seems to me an essential feature that distinguishes a self-instructional course from a publishing venture. For one thing, the obligation to present their work at frequent intervals helps pace the learners' endeavours. Even more importantly, commenting helps shape the learners' learning. Without personal feedback on what they have accomplished, they might just as well be reading teach-yourself books.

Written comments on assignments for example, can be seen as **tuition by correspondence** and will be especially valuable to distance learners who are less likely than on-site learners to get any face-to-face discussion of their work. (More about commenting in Chapter 13.)

Tutors and Other Human Contacts

If you are running just one course, for a small group of learners, you may be able to perform all the above roles single-handed. Otherwise, you will need to think about how other people might be recruited and briefed to play their parts as tutors, mentors, or whatever.

Communication with tutors. Getting other tutors to work effectively with learners -- at least as effectively as you would do yourself -- depends on good communication. You will need to provide tutors with a full set of course materials and to make sure, perhaps at a briefing meeting, that they are familiar with the content and the rationale of the course. They will also need written information ("Tutor Notes") concerning any specific instructions or general guidelines you wish them to follow. (See Figure 13.4 on page 324 for an example.)

Once tutors have begun their work, you may ask them for regular reports about the good, bad and curious aspects of the course that they encounter in dealing with learners. Conversely, you will need a mechanism -- perhaps a regular meeting or a newsletter -- for sharing new information with then, and for passing on any revised instructions.

Teaching around other people's (your) course materials may not seen a very creative task. So how do you help maintain your tutors' interest? Human tuition is a rare and precious resource in a system that is chiefly to be self-instructional. Tutors need to know exactly how they are meant to complement (and not compete with) the self-instruction, or this resource may be squandered.

Learners as supporters. Let us not forget the other "human media" that might help our learners. In particular, learners can get help from one another. They may support one another through times of self-doubt. And they will help one another sniff out the limits of the system, identifying what the "hidden curriculum" really requires of them, and what's in it for them.

They can also help one another with course work. Each may understand points that fox another. And even if both are flummoxed, at least each may be reassured to find that he or she is not alone in confusion. With vocational or professional education in particular -- e.g. where farmers, or teachers or zoo-keepers are studying together -- the learners' diverse experiences, when fed into discussion, may actually form part of the **subject-matter** of the course. Each learner may see his or her own experience differently as a result.

Bringing about such collaboration may not be easy, especially if learners are studying at a distance. One thing you might do is provide names, addresses and telephone numbers of all learners in an area who agree to being on the list. Learners who have recently completed the course might also agree to be "contacts". If you could also arrange an informal gathering for learners to meet one another, this might overcome the reservation many learners might feel about making "cold contact" with mere names on a printed list.

"Self-help groups" might begin to evolve from such informal gatherings, or indeed in the social after-glow of more formal tutor-led sessions. If your learners are studying on-site, the self-help groups may arise spontaneously. Even so -- especially if learners rarely need to work in the same place at the same time as one another -- you may need to give each learner a list of all the learners on the course.

Mentors. Some self-instructional courses -- especially on-site ones -- use what are often called "mentors". These are more experienced colleagues, perhaps even the learner's line-manager or a specialist elsewhere in his or her organization.

Mentors may support the learners in a variety of ways. At the very least, they may act as a "resource" for learners to draw on and someone with whom to sound out ideas. But they may also take on a more tutorial role -- demonstrating practical work and supervising the learners' own practical activities, assessing and commenting on tests and assignments, and even giving informal coaching.

If you see a role for mentors within your course, don't forget to ask: "What's in it for the mentors?" Will it improve their promotion chances? Will they see it as worthwhile and rewarding for its own sake? Will they recognize it as relevant and helpful to them in other aspects of their jobs? You may need to look for ways of harnessing their motivation -- as well as giving them guidance and support in carrying out their roles.

Other contacts. Finally, in thinking about other human support, consider the possible roles of family, friends and workmates. Clearly, they can have a negative effect on the learners' studies if they are not supportive, or at least sympathetic. But they can actively help with learning also. In teaching some topics, you may give your learner certain questions to discuss with colleagues in order to gather a variety of experiences and viewpoints. In a more general way, learners might be encouraged to discuss what they are working on with anyone who seems at all interested. Even if the other person doesn't contribute much, the effort to articulate and put across the new ideas they are grappling with will help sharpen up their own understanding.

Checklist for "Human Media"

Finally, here are some basic questions to ask about the human media:

1. Does the course need tutors and/or mentors?

2. What roles must they perform?

3. Where can suitable people be found?

4. How can they be recruited and rewarded?

5. How can they be informed (and kept informed) as to what is expected of them?

6. How can they be kept motivated?

7. How can their work be monitored?

8. What other "human media" might learners usefully make contact with -- e.g. other learners?

9. How can we facilitate such contacts?

Remember:

> SELF-INSTRUCTION DOES **NOT**
> MEAN ALWAYS LEARNING ON YOUR OWN.

FINAL MEDIA CHECKLIST

To help you make sense of this chapter as a whole, let me remind you of a set of key questions which I posed in Chapter 4. You need to ask these questions about your whole course and about each individual lesson within it:

- Which media are available to me **and** to the learners?

- Do any of our learning objectives imply particular types of stimuli and particular media?

- If so, how and to what extent -- e.g. for what proportion of the learner's time -- would I wish to use each of the preferred media?

- What would it cost me **and** the learner (in money, time and convenience) to use those preferred media?

- Would less expensive media be **acceptably** effective?

- Do the chosen media offer the learner sufficient **variety** of stimulus and activity?

- How can I combine media (e.g. print and audiotape) for maximum interest and effectiveness?

Finally, my own personal opinion:

> OF ALL THE MEDIA WE HAVE DISCUSSED IN THIS CHAPTER, THE ONE WITH THE MOST **UNDER-USED POTENTIAL** FOR SELF-INSTRUCTION IS AUDIOVISION.

12. THE PHYSICAL FORMAT OF YOUR LESSONS

In what physical form is your lesson to be presented to the learner? This may be entirely your own decision. For all I know, you are not only writing but also illustrating, typing, reprographing and packaging the whole thing yourself. But that seems unlikely. Your material will probably be "processed" by a typist and a reprographics expert, and you may also be dealing with a graphic designer and even an editor.

Each of these specialists will contribute his or her own ideas as to how your lesson might be presented. And each may identify several constraints on what is possible. Some such constraints may arise from the physical limitations of the resources available. Others may be "house rules" imposed on all authors. Yet others may turn out to be simply the personal preferences of the specialist.

This chapter is meant to help you understand what might be possible for your lessons, and to decide what you would regard as desirable. In it, I discuss:

- How your lessons might be packaged.
- How the text might be reproduced.
- How your pages might be laid out.
- How typography might be used.

PACKAGING YOUR LESSONS

How is your teaching material to be packaged? If you have any choice in the matter, there are at least five factors to bear in mind:

1. How many different **kinds** of material are involved?

2. By what means are the materials to be **delivered** to your learners?

3. In what variety of **contexts** might learners need to use the materials?

4. Might learners wish to **add** materials of their own?

5. How long might they wish to store and **re-use** the materials?

Considering the Questions

Let us consider those five basic questions, one by one. In the process, I'll raise a number of new ones. But I must leave you to answer them as best suits your own needs and circumstances.

Variety of materials? Your learner may be getting not only your tutorial-in-print but also, say, textbooks or collections of readings, audio-cassettes, specimens, home experiment kit, filmstrips and viewer, and so on. If so, you will need to think out a way of putting the items together in a reasonably coherent and manageable fashion. You can't handle them all over separately, but nor can you simply throw them together in a paper bag.

Can you at least reduce the number of separate items? Can a number of separate lessons be bound together? Can audio-cassettes (and perhaps filmstrips and viewer) be fastened to a flat sheet of plastic or cardboard of the same size as your text? Do you need to provide a plastic wallet to hold certain items -- and/or a cardboard box to contain all of them?

Delivery? You may be handing the material to your learners personally. Or they may have to go to one or more other people to collect them. Or you may be sending them through the mail. Is the learner to get all the materials for the course at the outset? Or are they doled out, bit by bit, as he or she progresses?

Each of these delivery methods imposes different packaging restrictions. If you give learners a great pile of materials, they may have trouble carting it away. If a variety of separate bits and pieces have to be distributed to learners by other people, components of the course may easily get lost. If you are frequently mailing material to learners, they may find themselves unpopular with whoever delivers their mail -- or have materials stolen from their doorstep -- if many of your packages are too big to go through the normal letterbox.

Getting all the course materials at once may be daunting to some learners (though helpful to others). But getting them separately may make it difficult to provide for coherent storage -- and increases the risk that some learners will fail to get some of the components.

Contexts of use? In what variety of contexts might learners want/need to use your materials? How might this affect the packaging? For instance, learners who want to do some of their studying on the bus to work will not thank you for giving them a thousand-page volume to hump around.

Should each lesson be detachable from the rest -- e.g. in a slip-case or ring-binder? Again, if learners might want to use "other media" (e.g. audiotapes, practical work, video) somewhere other than where they keep their course material, should the media notes be detachable?

Adding material? You might expect learners to add material of their own to the course -- either during it or afterwards. They might add their own extensive notes, calculations, designs or essays. Or they might add up-to-date articles, photographs, newspaper reports, photocopies from books, and so on. Do you care how they store these? If you wanted learners to interleave such additions with the relevant sections of your text, then you could help by presenting your material in loose leaf form for a ring binder.

Storage and re-use? You will also need to think of how your learners might store the course materials. Unless you provide storage boxes or files -- or can rely on the learners doing so -- the more separate bits and pieces you provide, the more likely they are to mislay some of them.

Furthermore, if the materials are to be in long-term use, paper for a ring binder needs to be heavy enough not to tear where the poles are punched. If, instead, you are providing bound booklets, the binding must be strong enough to stand repeated opening and closing. Yet: booklets with glued spines (laughably called "perfect binding") often fall apart; stapled pages may prevent the book being opened flat; comb-bound books can be awkward to store and may not allow for an identifying title to be shown on the spine; and stitching is expensive.

Your Answers

There are, of course, no ready-made answers to the questions above. You will need to decide what is **desirable**, and listen to advice about what is **possible**, within your own organization. The over-riding question to bear in mind is:

> HOW DO I ENVISAGE MY LEARNERS
> **USING** THE COURSE MATERIALS?

FOUR METHODS OF TEXT PRODUCTION

Here I want to draw attention to four different methods of getting your lessons reproduced. Each has its own advantages and disadvantages. The four methods are:

- Photocopying
- Stencil duplicating
- Offset litho printing
- Letterpress printing

Photocopying

If you are producing materials for a small number of learners, you may well consider using a photocopier. The best known trade name is Xerox, but there are now numerous makers, between them offering a wide range of equipment of good quality.

Photocopiers will give good reproduction of typing, handwriting, line drawings, and facsimile pages from books. Some photocopiers can also give acceptable reproduction of photographs, and some may perform other useful tricks like over-printing in colour, copying on both sides of a sheet of paper, and producing copies that are smaller or larger than your original.

Photocopying is a process you can easily carry out yourself, without needing to rely on a technician. But, if you want more than a certain number of copies, it may be expensive compared with other methods.

Stencil Duplicating

With this form of reproduction, a typewriter is used to cut your text into a waxed stencil "master", and copies are made by a machine that presses ink through the master onto sheets of paper. The basic equipment is rather limited. Drawings and line diagrams have to be cut directly into the master with a stylus. Furthermore, although the stencil master should be able to produce as many good copies as you might want in one run, the quality of subsequent runs may be less and less satisfactory.

It is possible to use a thermal copier to make a master without having to type or draw directly onto a wax stencil. Indeed, the machine will make a stencil by copying any typewriting or print (text or line drawings) that contains print -- from an ordinary sheet of paper. The method is quick and easy, but the masters produce rather fuzzy copies.

An electronic scanner -- a more expensive machine -- allows you to cut stencils incorporating photographs and even full colour. The print quality is better than that obtainable from the first two types of stencil mentioned above; and, using special masters, you can print thousands of good masters.

Offset Litho Printing

The offset litho machine reproduces from a paper, plastic or metal plate onto which your text and pictures have been transferred by any of a number of different photographic or electrostatic processes. Your "original" can be typed, printed or handwritten. It can incorporate printed text from other sources. Line drawings, charts, and special headings of rub-down lettering can be stuck on the page wherever you need them. And it can even incorporate photographs after they have been "screened" (a process in which the shades of grey are converted to dots of varying sizes) using separate equipment.

In short, offset litho gives you enormous freedom in preparing your original -- often called "artwork" or "camera-ready copy". You can stick whatever you like on your page -- provided you make a clean job of it -- and alterations are easily made. Furthermore, the print quality will be good for thousands of copies and (at least if you use metal plates) later reprints should be no less good. Many commercial books, including this one, are now produced by offset litho.

Letterpress Printing

This is the traditional method that most people think of when "printing" is mentioned. It is done by a machine that prints directly from raised metal letters, each of which has been put in place, manually or mechanically, by a skilled technician known as a compositor. The machine can print thousands of excellent copies, with no loss of quality in a later reprint.

But compositors are extremely well-paid, and the labour costs make letterpress too expensive for print runs of less than a thousand or so copies. Furthermore, illustrations have to be prepared separately from the text, and the additional costs involved are likely to limit the number you can afford to use.

Which to Use?

You may or may not have a choice of method. If given a choice, I would usually opt for offset litho. It allows you so much scope in composing your own pages -- especially if you want to use frequent pictures and other visual devices. Letterpress might produce a more prestigious-looking text; but learners might not find it markedly more attractive, and it would certainly not be more legible. Yet you and/or they would pay dearly for it.

My general remarks above, however, are clearly not a sufficient basis for choosing. Find out what methods are available in your oganization. Look at examples of the material they can produce. Discuss the pros and cons with colleagues who have used them and with any technicians whose help you would need. Then decide which of the available methods best suits your needs at a price both you and the learners can afford.

LAYOUT

In this section I invite you to consider how you might want the pages of your tutorial-in-print to look -- e.g.:

- What page size and format to use?
- How many columns?
- How to use the margins?
- How might pictures be placed?
- Should colour be used?

Again, your institution may have its own "house rules", giving you little choice in these matters.

Page Size and Format

Page size. Ideally, this should depend on the kind of material you are presenting. Generally speaking, a tutorial-in-print can benefit from having pages even larger than this book -- allowing flexibility in arranging the frequent activities and pictures. If, on the other hand, you were presenting little but continuous text, a page smaller than this might suffice.

In the UK and the rest of Europe (but not in the USA), the A-series of paper sizes (promoted by the International Organization for Standardization) is now widely used. The system is pictured in Figure 12.1 below:

Figure 12.1:   International A-series Paper Sizes

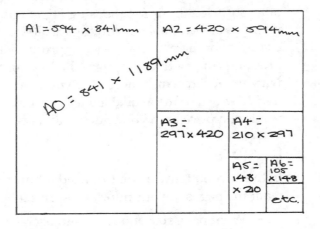

Each numbered size has one side in common with the previous size, but halves the other side. Thus it keeps the same shape but has half the area.

A4 is a very popular paper size for self-instructional courses. It gives plenty of space in which to lay out text, activities and pictures for maximum effect. Furthermore, ring-binders, files and wallets are all readily available in this size. So are pads of paper for the learners to write on and insert in the package if they so wish.

If you cut A4 in half across its long side, you get A5. This sheet has the same proportions as A4 but, of course, has only half the area. It would therefore restrict you in your layout but would still be a shade too large to boast the possible advantage of being "pocket-size".

Format. By this I simply mean which way up will you use the page? You may print with the short edge of the page uppermost ("portrait" format) or with the long edge uppermost ("landscape" format):

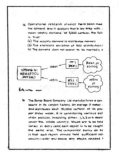

Portrait   Landscape

Even if you use the conventional "portrait" format for most of your text, you may well include a "landscape" page from time to time. Such pages can be useful if you wish to display a large photograph or table. If you want your learners to read some text along with the picture, however, you'd be wise to print both at the same angle lest they twist their heads off.

Columns and Margins

An A4 "portrait" page may be printed in one, two or even three columns. A "landscape" page can take three or four. Using more columns, with a smaller type-size, enables you to get more words on a page. The consequent saving in paper, however, is offset by the fact that readers may be depressed by pages that are too heavy with print. Apart from being more difficult to read, densely-printed pages can be dispiriting to learners in that they may feel themselves to be making very slow progress through the book.

Columns. The simplest approach (if you are producing camera-ready copy) is to use a single column. Multiple columns may be more difficult to manage, unless you are using a versatile word processing package.

If you use a single column, its width should ideally be no more than three quarters of the width of the page if you are using type of this size. With smaller type, don't let the column exceed two thirds of the width of the page.

If a line of type is too wide, reading becomes difficult because the reader's eyes are constantly delayed in locating the beginning of the next line, especially if lines are printed close together. Research suggests that 60-65 characters (letters and/or spaces) is about the maximum line-width that can be read comfortably. That is about a dozen words.

Margins. If you keep your single column of print to, say, two thirds of the page, you will have room for a wide margin on one side. The wide margin can be used for:

- side headings;
- paragraph numbers;
- repetition of a technical term that is being newly introduced in the text alongside;
- material that would otherwise be "footnotes";

Figure 12.2: Varying Line Widths and Spacing

Key: *The long lines in A are more difficult to read than the shorter ones in B. However, extra space between the longer lines, as in C and D, may somewhat improve on A's legibility. The spacing and line width used in D becomes even more legible with a larger type-size (E).*

A   Using more columns, with a smaller type-size, enables you to get more words on a page. The consequent saving in paper, however, is offset by the fact that readers may be depressed by pages that are too heavy with print. Apart from being more difficult to read, densely-printed pages

B   Using more columns, with a smaller type-size, enables you to get more words on a page. The consequent saving in paper, however, is offset by the fact that readers may be depressed by pages that are too heavy with print. Apart

C   Using more columns, with a smaller type-size, enables you to get more words on a page. The consequent saving in paper, however, is offset by the fact that readers may be depressed by pages that are too heavy with print. Apart from being more difficult to read, densely-printed pages

D   Using more columns, with a smaller type-size, enables you to get more words on a page. The consequent saving in paper, however, is offset by the fact that readers may be depressed by pages that are too heavy with print. Apart from being more difficult to read, densely-printed pages

E   Using more columns, with a smaller type-size, enables you to get more words on a page. The consequent saving in paper, however, is offset by the fact that readers may be depressed by pages that are too heavy with print. Apart from being more

- small illustrations;
- larger illustrations that occupy the full width of the page;
- captions for pictures that are set within the area of the block of print;
- visual signposts (see page 175);
- verbal instructions to the reader;
- the reader's own notes or comments; and so on.

Obviously, some restraint is called for. Any one margin that contained all these types of information would be an eye-sore. And even if some margins display side-headings, for example, while others display technical terms or captions, how will you enable readers to tell at a glance what kind of information you are offering them?

Your wide margin can be on either side of the column of type. Perhaps your choice will be determined by whether you want your reader to look at marginal items before or after reading the text. In the former case, your wide margin ought to be on the left; in the latter case, on the right. If you expect readers to do much writing in the margin, most would prefer the wide margin to be on the right.

Incidentally, although the left-hand edge of your block of type will form a straight vertical line ("justified" as the technical term has it), there is no need for the right-hand edge to do so. An unjustified, ragged edge, as on this page, may look rather "unprofessional" to you -- but readers are unlikely to notice, and it will not impede their reading. On the contrary, the ragged edge helps in distinguishing one line from another and thus aids the reader's eye in locating where it wants to be in the paragraph. The reader will also be saved from the peculiar spacings and frequent hyphenations that can result from justification. Even with a two-column layout, an unjustified right-hand edge is quite acceptable.

Placing Your Pictures

When a paragraph refers to a picture, try to place the picture as close to it as possible. Try to ensure that your reader can see both the picture and the words referring to it at the same time, without having to turn a page. The reader should certainly not be given another paragraph to read through before the picture comes into sight.

Small pictures can be placed alongside the paragraph in the margin, if it is wide enough. Larger ones will go into the body of the text. Try not to leave just one or two stray lines below a picture at the bottom of a page. The reader is likely to overlook them. Better perhaps to give the picture more space and move these lines to the next page.

If you have a two or three-column format, you can run a picture across one, two or three columns. If you run it across more than one column, you would do well to move it right to the top or bottom of the page, or the reader may lose the downward flow of the columns.

Ideally, you should design adjacent pages together as a "double-page spread". Thus, for example, you might be able to prevent two over-dense pages from falling opposite one another; but you might allow one fairly dense page if the opposite one were largely pictorial:

Double-page Spreads

Colour

There are two ways in which you might want to use
colour in a lesson:

- Coloured print or line drawings.
- Coloured photographs.
- Coloured pages.

Print. Black ink is easier to read than any other colours
and should always be used for the bulk of any lesson. A
second colour (contrasting with black but not so pale as to
be invisible in artificial light) can be both attractive and
useful in distinguishing one kind of text from another.
But a second colour does add to the expense, and its
signalling role can usually be fulfilled in cheaper ways. If
you must use it in illustrations, however, (e.g. in graphs
or maps), then you may be able to use it for print as well,
without extra cost. You may also introduce occasional
blocks of solid colour -- e.g. as a background to certain
sections of the text.

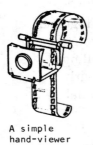

A simple
hand-viewer

Photographs. Colour photographs are especially
expensive to print. If you are producing only a few dozen
copies of your tutorial-in-print, it would be considerably
cheaper to take colour prints and stick them in by hand.
Alternatively, colour filmstrips can be provided cheaply
-- together perhaps with a simple hand-viewer costing
next to nothing.

Tinted pages. You may feel that certain sections within
your lesson might be presented on coloured paper. For
instance, test questions might be on blue-tinted paper;
media notes on green; and instructions for practical work
on pink. This can be quite effective, provided you don't
make your booklet too much of a bewildering rainbow.
Restrict yourself to pastel tints, and preferably no more
than two or three of them. Inserting occasional coloured

pages will not, however, be possible with letterpress printing -- and even with other methods it will add something, if only a little, to the costs of production.

TYPOGRAPHY

You've now given thought to the overall shape of your pages and the text that will be on them. But, in printing your text, you will need to decide how to use:

- typeface or font (style of lettering);
- spacing of type;
- headings; and
- rules and borders.

Let's look at each of these in turn.

Which Typefaces?

Your choice of typeface (or "font" in computer language) will depend on what equipment you will be using -- e.g:

- An ordinary typewriter (single typeface).

- A "golfball" or "daisywheel" typewriter (or a basic word processing printer) offering a limited range of typefaces.

- A word processing laser printer (numerous fonts).

- A printer's letterpress composer, offering an enormous range of typefaces.

Obviously, an ordinary typewriter will be the most limited, but there is still much that you can do with it. Such a typewriter usually offers one or other of the first two faces illustrated below -- either "pica" or "elite". Some typewriters may have, instead, a "san serif" typeface, or even "italic" or "script". Obviously, all of these will give you both upper case (capital) letters and lower case letters.

Figure 12.3: Comparing Typefaces

This is typed in PICA, a large face
giving only 10 characters per inch.

This is typed in ELITE, which is smaller
and gives 12 characters to the inch.

This is an ITALIC typeface (like ELITE,
but sloping) with 12 characters per inch.

This is SCRIPT typeface with 12 characters
per inch and meant to resemble handwriting.

This is a SAN SERIF typeface (no little
tails) -- again 12 characters to the inch.

Either of the first two or the last of the typefaces above
(or their letterpress equivalents) would be suitable for the
main body of your text. Italic or script, however, can
become tiresome to read if you use more than a
paragraph or two now and again for special effect. Your
learners are likely to be most accustomed to an upright
typeface with serifs; of the two shown above, Elite is
probably to be preferred. It is closer to the size of print
most often found in books ("10 or 11 point") and allows
you to get more words on a page without it looking any
more dense.

Occasional special typefaces. Whatever typeface
you use for the body of your text, you may occasionally
want something different. You may want to use more
than one typeface, so as to distinguish between different

kinds of material. You may, for instance, want to print instructions for activities in a different face from the main text, and the feedback comments in yet another.

A few "special effects" are obtainable with an ordinary typewriter. You can use <u>underlining</u> and CAPITALS. You can widen your S P A C I N G. You can even **embolden** a word or phrase -- either by inserting a thick piece of paper between type and ribbon or by backspacing and typing over the same letters several times. Such devices are adequate for picking out the odd word or phrase, or heading. But they would make for uncomfortable reading if allowed to occupy more than a couple of lines of print.

What if you want to distinguish between more **extended** sections of text -- e.g. feedback on activities, or guidance on how to study a section? There seem to be four possibilities:

- Keep a second typewriter with a different face -- e.g. italic.

- Use coloured type (discussed under "Layout" above).

- Use indentation -- and/or boxes -- and/or put a lot of space around the special item.

- *Write the section in your own fair hand* . (Handwritten self-instructional books are not uncommon nowadays -- like Mr Wainwright's celebrated fell-walking guides, Figure 12.4.)

"Golfball" and "daisywheel" typewriters and some word processors, make it possible to switch between pica, elite, san serif, bold, italic, and so on. You may also be able to use a photocopier to vary the size of your type. Word processing packages such as *Microsoft Word* allow for all the variety of font style and size you see within this book -- and much, much more.

Figure 12.4:   A Handwritten Text (from *The Southern Fells* by A. Wainwright, Westmorland Gazette, 1960)

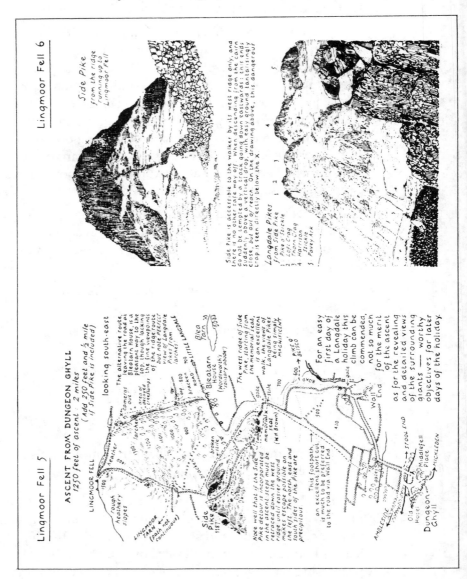

However, such versatility can be a dubious blessing. One can over-complicate a text with too much typographic razamataz. Few people ever fully exploit the potential of an ordinary (but imaginatively used) typewriter.

Spacing Your Type

Here we are concerned both with legibility and with how to make clear the structure of your lesson:

Legibility. Whatever typeface or font you choose, its spacing on the page strongly affects its legibility. The main problem is how to keep your reader's eyes moving smoothly from left to right, and yet be able easily to locate the beginning of the next line. As I have already shown, the longer the lines, the more difficult this becomes -- especially if there is too little space **between** lines. (See Figure 12.2.)

Revealing structure. The spacing of your type can also help reveal the structure of your teaching. Thus it acts as an "access device" (see Chapter 8). It can help your reader make appropriate approaches to different sections of the text. For instance, how will you use space to indicate the beginning of a new paragraph? You may leave extra space between paragraphs, or indent the first line, or do both. (I prefer to do both.)

You will also need to decide how much space to leave around headings. You will notice that my headings are closer to the block of text that follows them than to that preceding them. The latter space is the same as that between paragraphs. First and second level headings have space below them; but third level headings I have run directly into the first line of the text they relate to.

You may want to indent entire blocks of text -- e.g. quotations from other authors. Lists too may need space around them, as may text that you put in a box. After an indented section, it is better not to indent the paragraph that follows. Just make sure it has at least the normal line-space you are using between paragraphs.

Headings

Three basic grades. In Chapter 8, I suggest three grades of headings as the maximum that either you or the reader will be able to keep track of. These are fairly easily distinguished typographically, even using an ordinary typewriter. The three grades of heading in this chapter, for example, could have been typewritten as follows:

- "TYPOGRAPHY

  You've now given thought to the overall shape..."

- "Which Typefaces

  Your choice of typeface (or "font" in computer..."

- "Revealing structure. The spacing of your type can also help reveal the structure..."

Designers often advise against allowing one heading to follow directly below another, without any text between them. Notice at the beginning of this section, for instance, how "HEADINGS" is followed at once by "Three Basic Grades". Designers might suggest inserting a line or two of text under the first heading to introduce the material covered under the following sub-headings -- e.g. "In this section we shall look both at the basic grades of heading and at special display headings that we need only occasionally". Would those few words have been worth adding here -- and perhaps have prevented the word "HEADINGS" looking a little lost on the page? But such an overview can sometimes seem heavy-handed -- especially if the ensuing section is short.

Display headings. For major "display" headings -- e.g. the titles of your lessons or groups of lessons -- even letterpress might not produce lettering large enough to make a powerful impression. Many word processors could, but a typewriter certainly could not.

One alternative is to use a **headlining machine**. With some such machines you can impress letters onto sticky tape from a variety of typefaces; the type can then be cut up and stuck on your page. Other headlining machines work photographically.

Here is a sample of lettering on HEADLINING TAPE

The other alternative is to use a sheet of rub-down lettering -- Letraset is the best-known brand. These are available in a wide range of typefaces and sizes. See Figure 12.5 for samples.

Such lettering (and other graphic devices) is easy enough to apply to a sheet of paper. But it needs to be done slowly and carefully and requires a good eye for spacing -- even if one has taken the trouble to draw faint pencil guide-lines first. However, if you do apply one letter too close or too far from its neighbour (or too high or too low), you can easily rub it off and try again. For occasional use, it's worth the trouble. San serif typeface is easier to use -- e.g. Univers or Helvetica.

Figure 12.5: Some Rub-Down Lettering (Letraset)

Futura Black • Bauer

abcdefghijklmnopqrstuvwxyz
ABCDEFGHIJKLMNOPQRSTUVWXYZ
1234567890 ß &?!£$[.,;:]

Gallia •

A ABCDEFGHIJKLMNOPQRRS
STTUVWXYZ
1234567890 ÆØ &?!£$(.,;:)

Helvetica Medium Condensed • ○ Letraset © 1977

abcdefghijklmnopqrstuvwxyz
ABCDEFGHIJKLMNOPQRSTUVWXYZ
1234567890 æøßÆØ &?!£$(.,;:)

Sapphire • Stempel

ABCDEFGHIJKLMNOPQ
RSTUVWXYZ
1234567890 &?!£$[.,;:]

Schneidler Old Style •

abcdefghijklmnopqrstuvwxyz
ABCDEFGHIJKLMNOPQRSTUVWXYZ
1234567890 æøßÆØ &?!£$%(.,;:)

Univers 65 • ○ Deberny & Peignot

abcdefghijklmnopqrstuvwxyz
ABCDEFGHIJKLMNOPQRSTUVWXYZ
1234567890 æøßÆØ &&?!£$(.,;:)

Univers 66 • Deberny & Peignot

abcdefghijklmnopqrstuvwxyz
ABCDEFGHIJKLMNOPQRSTUVWXYZ
1234567890 ß &&?!£$(.,;:)

Rules and Borders

Rules (straight lines of various thicknesses) and decorative borders are a useful typographic device. They are available both on rub-down sheets for the do-it-yourselfer and in the "toolkit" of a letterpress printer. They can even be created on an ordinary typewriter. For example:

Some rub-down rules and borders (Letraset)

Some typewritten rules and borders:

You will notice that a rule has been used at the top of each page of this book -- just to separate the running headings from the rest of the text. Rules have also been used to enclose material presented as "Figures".

The more elaborate decorative borders can have a special role in a tutorial-in-print where they make useful "stoppers" for activities. (See Figure 5.2I on page 108 for example.) They can also be used, as in this book, to box certain kinds of recurring text. In both cases, restraint is necessary. Don't use a border so florid that it dominates the page. And don't use more than two or three different borders or their dramatic effect will be lost.

FIVE FINAL POINTS

- Don't leave thoughts about the physical format of your lesson(s) until after you have finished writing. Even if you have no choice of format, or have to reach agreement with colleagues, the sooner you know what possibilities and limitations await you the better. That way you may be able to write in such a manner as to make the best of them.

- Don't forget to apply the same standards of layout and typography to any materials you offer aside from the main text -- e.g. course guide, tutor notes, and so on. Also, if you want to include articles or book chapters written by other authors, would their layout and typography be acceptable if you printed facsimile copies? (Might this even be desirable, both in giving your reader a change of visual style and in marking them out as different from your text?) Or do you need to have them retyped in the same format as your own material?

- Do look critically at other people's layout and typography as well as your own. No book is perfect in that respect (not even this one). You can learn from other people's errors as well as from their successes. For a start, you might look again at the sample pages shown in Figures 5.2A-L (pages 92-117) -- and note the varied ways in which they do or do not embody the ideas discussed in this chapter.

- Do try to ensure -- if you have any influence at all in the matter -- that materials are **not** produced in so glossy (expensive) a version, or in such large quantities (several years' worth), that you cannot afford to dump some of them and rewrite if they later prove unsatisfactory in use.

- Above all, remember that physical format and design affect how learners will work with your materials and what they will get from them. If you don't make decisions about their format, other people will -- and their decisions may or may not be conducive to effective learning.

> EDUCATIONAL DESIGN IS TOO IMPORTANT
> TO BE LEFT TO THE DESIGNERS.

13. ASSESSING YOUR LEARNERS

In this chapter, we are concerned with how your learners' learning might be assessed. The kind of assessment demanded by your course can often determine how and what your learners decide to learn. So it is important to use the right kind of assessment for the kind of learning you want to encourage.

Of course, you may say: "But I've been teaching -- and assessing -- for years. What's new?" The vital difference is that self-instructional learners are working on their own. Your learners may be anxious about what assessment will require of them -- but they may be unable to question you about it, or negotiate how they would like to tackle it. They may not even know other learners with whom they might discuss it. Furthermore, you may not know until too late about how your learners' learning is being affected by your assessment demands. And you may be unable to do much about it, even if you do know. Hence, with self-instruction, assessment needs to be thought out more carefully, and spelled out more explicitly, than is usually the case with face-to-face teaching.

THE NATURE OF ASSESSMENT

What is assessment? I hope we can agree on one thing :

ASSESSMENT $\neq$ GRADING

Assessment is not to be confused with grading and marking. Certainly you can't grade or mark a learner's work without first assessing it. But it is quite feasible (and will sometimes be more appropriate) to assess **without** going on to award grades or marks.

Assessment is an attempt to gain knowledge of the learners' competences. In particular, what competences did they bring to the learning and what competences have they acquired as a result of your teaching?

THE PURPOSES OF ASSESSMENT

Why might we want to gain knowledge about a learner's competences? I would identify two main purposes for assessment -- according to the use that is to be made of the results:

1. To aid the learners in their subsequent learning.

2. To report on what they have already learned -- e.g. as a grade or as a written report on each learner.

The first use of assessment is sometimes called **formative** because it is meant to help form the learner's learning. The second is called **summative** because it sums up what each has achieved.

Formative Assessment

Formative assessment is involved every time you use what you have learned about a learner in order to decide what to say to that learner next. Similarly, your learner may assess his or her own strengths and weaknesses in order to decide where next to put his or her efforts. Such **self**-assessment is an essential part of the kind of "pre-recorded" teaching we are discussing in this book. We make use of "activities" (SAQs and ITQs) in order to help the learners monitor and develop their own learning. Sometimes this may involve their getting feedback from colleagues -- **peer** assessment.

We may also require the learner to tackle occasional tests and examinations; and these will be assessed by a tutor. Again, the tutor may provide comments that may help the learner to learn. One of the functions of these more formal exercises may be to let the learners know how closely their competences approach the standard expected by some **external** examining or accrediting body that they hope to satisfy.

Summative Assessment

The purpose of summative assessment is to report, or put on record, what is known of the learners' attainments.. What did they study? Did they pass or fail? What grades did they get? What competences did they acquire? Are they now fit to work without supervision? Such reports are usually for the benefit of other teachers, or of professional bodies, or of employers.

The traditional example of summative assessment is the end-of-course examination -- written or practical. Here, the prime purpose is to establish what the learners have achieved -- not to give them feedback that will help them learn. Mid-course tests and assignments can also be used summatively, however, if they contribute to the learners' final grades, reports or "portfolios".

Three General Points

- Any one act of assessment can be used **both** formatively and summatively

- Some courses may have **no** summative assessment -- e.g. "hobby" or "interest" courses on subjects like amateur bee-keeping or ragtime guitar-playing.

- **All** courses need formative assessment, preferably carried out by someone else in addition to the learner -- e.g. by colleagues or by a tutor.

The Timing of Assessment

When shall learners be assessed? As we have noted, their work can be assessed during the course, lesson by lesson, and/or at the end of the course. If any of the in-course assessment is used summatively, it is often called "continuous assessment". In some courses, the learner's overall course "result" depends on a combination of continuous assessment and end-of-course examination.

You will know what kind of assessment will be possible for your course. What I am talking about in this chapter will be applicable to any kind. My examples, however, will be related to the kind of test or assignment you might set the learner for checking by a tutor or mentor at the end of a lesson or series of lessons within a course. (The self-assessment activities you might set within a lesson are thoroughly discussed in Chapter 6.)

Thus, at the end of every hour or so's study, you might set your learners a little test on what they have covered so far. As a very rough rule of thumb, you might think 5-10 minutes of testing would be about right for an hour of studying. Of course, you could save these up and set your learners, say, a half-hour test after three hours -- or even have them spend a couple of hours on an assessed exercise after about 12 hours of study. Even if they were to tackle a number of smaller tests, you might require them to wait until several were completed before seeking comments from their tutor or mentor.

WHAT TO ASSESS?

What aspects of the learners' competence will you expect to assess in your assessessment exercises? Surely you will wish to assess their attainment of **lesson objectives** and their progress towards attainment of the **course objectives**. Indeed, in presenting your tests and assignments, you may wish to remind your learner of which objective each item relates to. (See Figure 8.4, on page 177, for an example of this.)

For many teachers, it is only at this stage -- when they start thinking seriously about how to assess -- that talk of aims and objectives really begins to make sense.

In a way, at least from the learner's viewpoint, the assessment tasks **are** the lesson objectives. For instance, whatever the lofty aims and objectives you may have in mind, if learners are eventually assessed merely on how well they have memorized certain details from the lesson, then recalling those facts is the **real** objective as far as the learners are concerned.

So, when you come to assess what learners have got from a lesson, it is essential to use methods that truly relate to **your** aims and objectives -- and not to some other possible aims and objectives. For example, it is all too easy to set out to teach people, say, how to repair a punctured tyre -- and yet end up by asking them not to do it but to write an essay about how to do it!

More subtle mistakes can be made by assessing a closely-related (but different) objective. If, for instance, our objective were to have the learners **interpret** a certain kind of graph, it would be an inappropriate form of assessment to ask them merely to **draw** the graph instead. We cannot necessarily infer possession of one competence from seeing the demonstration of another.

> THE QUESTIONS THAT ARE EASIEST
> TO ASK MAY NOT BE THE ONES
> YOU MOST NEED TO HAVE ANSWERED.

METHODS OF ASSESSMENT

What will you get the learners to **do** in order to show what they have learned from your lessons? Don't put the finishing touches to the first draft of a lesson before you've thought about this question. Some writers would say don't even start the first draft until you have.

For the sake of this discussion, I shall divide assessment exercises into two broad categories:

- *Product assessment* -- like essays, worked calculations, multiple-choice tests, project reports, drawings, 3-D constructions -- where there is a physical **product** to assess.

- *Process assessment* -- like performances, interviews, or displays of learners' practical competence -- in an activity or **process** that may or may not result in any physical product.

Product Assessment

The "paper-and-pencil" test is the most familiar form of product assessment, in conventional as well as self-instructional teaching. It may take the form of a so-called **objective test**, consisting of various types of multiple-choice question. Or it may require learners to construct their **own answers** -- e.g. in the form of a few words, a paragraph, an essay, or a report of several thousand words, perhaps with diagrams and calculations.

"Own answer" tests. The most basic kind of "own answer" question requires only words or brief phrases as answers. For example, to draw on the subject of Diet and Nutrition (as I shall throughout this section).

Q. What is the name of the disease affecting children who eat insufficient protein?

A. *Kwashiorkor.*

Q. Why is meat considered high quality protein?

A. *Because it contains amino acids in similar proportions to human tissue.*

Longer answers can be called for:

Q. Write a paragraph (not more than 200 words) explaining the importance of a balanced diet.

Q. Use your table of Average Energy Requirements to calculate the dietary needs of each of the two people whose daily activities are listed below. Then, using the Food Composition tables, evaluate the adequacies of their daily diets as given below.

The "own answer" required can be longer still. Learners might be set an essay of several thousand words on world food supplies. Or they might be asked to report at similar length on their own field study of how a group of workers exposed to advice about nutrition have altered their diets.

Questions requiring such extended answers will usually be asked when we want the learner to present an argument -- an analysis, interpretation or evaluation, reviewing the relevant facts and coming to some sort of conclusion about them. Such arguments need not be restricted to essays and reports. If the situation seemed appropriate, learners could, for example, be asked to write a letter on the subject as if to the editor of a newspaper, or a memo to their boss, or the script for a video, and so on.

"Objective tests". One of the problems with "own answer" exercises is that teachers cannot always agree as to the quality of the learners' answers. Thus, the same essay, or even mathematical exercise, might get a different grade from different teachers -- because they happen to value different aspects of the learner's performance.

With objective tests, however, the markers' subjective preferences cannot affect the grades. (That's why they're called "objective".) Marking could be done by someone ignorant of the subject -- or even by computer.

Objective tests are composed of multiple-choice questions of one form or another -- e.g. "one from several", "true-false", or "matching".

The most widely useful type of question (or "item") is the "one from several". Here, the item is made up of a question or an incomplete statement, followed by several alternative answers -- one of which answers the question or completes the statement correctly. The learner may be asked to ring or underline the correct answer. For example, here are two ways of asking the same question:

- Children whose diet is deficient in protein are liable to a disease known as:
  A. Beri-beri
  B. Marasmus
  C. Rickets
  D Kwashiorkor
  E. Scurvy

- What is the name of the disease to which children are liable if their diet is deficient in protein?
  A. Beri-beri
  B. Marasmus
  C. Rickets
  D Kwashiorkor
  E. Scurvy

Notice that the incomplete statement in the first version above has been replaced by a straightforward question in the second. Often this will be easier for learners to read, especially when the alternative answers are long ones.

A variation on this type of question is to let **two** of the answers be correct. In such cases, it is best to offer at least seven alternatives from which the two are to be chosen. (Otherwise, guessing is just too likely to be rewarded.)

Even with "one answer from several", it is unwise to use fewer than four "distractors" (as the **incorrect** answers are called). This rule is broken, for instance, by items that merely ask the learner to agree or disagree with a series of statements, e.g.:

- Children whose diet is deficient in protein are liable to Kwashiorkor. TRUE or FALSE?

Such true/false, yes/no, agree/disagree questions are best avoided in objective testing. After all, the learner has a 50-50 chance of guessing the correct answer. There are other drawbacks. It can be difficult to think up relevant statements that are indisputably right or indisputably wrong. In any case, you may think that directing your learners' attention to statements that are false is rather a dubious teaching technique.

The "matching" question is another type of item occasionally used in objective tests. Here the learner is given two lists of things and is asked which thing in one list belongs with each thing in the other list, e.g.:

- Here are the names of seven diseases:
  Marasmus, beri-beri, pellagra, rickets,
  heart disease, night-blindness, kwashiorkor

  Which of them do you particularly associate with each of the following dietary deficiencies?
  (Write one disease against each deficiency.)
  1. Vitamin A...
  2. Vitamin C...
  3. Vitamin D...
  4. Protein...
  5. Calory..

With this kind of question, it is important to have more things in the first list than in the second. Otherwise, the learner who knew all but one of the matches would get that one right automatically. But if we have, say, two or three more things in one list than in the other, the learner will still have to choose from three or four answers for the final match.

A variation on matching is the "ranking" question. Here the learners have to decide which thing on the list ranks first, second, third, etc. -- according to some stated criterion. For example, in the case of the seven diseases mentioned above, learners might be asked to pick out, and arrange in order, the three causing most fatalities.

Again, the element of guessing may worry some teachers. if you really want to be sure why the learners have chosen the answers they have, you can always ask them to add a note explaining or justifying their answers. This means, of course, that the test will now be a combination of "chosen answer" and "own answer" and must be marked by someone knowledgeable in the subject.

Nevertheless, such a combination may sometimes be valuable in distance teaching, where the marker may not necessarily meet the learner face to face. The need to explain their answers may reveal those learners who are somehow finding the correct answers in your teaching materials (or in other learners' work) but without really understanding them. Remember:

> "OWN ANSWERS" CAN HELP YOU SEE
> WHAT IS GOING ON IN THE LEARNER'S
> MIND -- "CHOSEN ANSWERS" CANNOT.

Which to use? Any one test or assignment can contain both "own answer" and "chosen answer" questions. For which purposes is each best suited? How do you decide when to use which?

Objective questions are most likely to be appropriate when your objectives require that the learner should be able to select from, discriminate between, or decide among a finite range of alternative possibilities. These alternatives might include terms, ideas, quantities, sounds, smells, pictures, actions, objects , and so on.

Thus, if you wanted to test whether your learners could discriminate between the symptoms of pellagra and those of similar diseases, you would need to present them with several "cases" to choose from. **How** to present those cases would be a further problem for you. Would you want the learners to distinguish between written accounts of signs and symptoms, pictures of patients, real patients, or what? The fact that learners could recognize a written description might be no indication that they could recognize the real thing.

On the other hand, when our objectives require learners to be able to recall, define, explain, justify, report, invent, sketch out, argue a case, or otherwise come up with their own ideas -- then multiple-choice questions cannot give an appropriate test of their abilities. For such abilities we need "own answer" questions -- even though different assessors may disagree about the quality of a particular answer.

As we've already seen, such own-answer exercises may ask for brief responses from the learner, or for extensive ones. In general, we should avoid asking learners for extensive written answers unless we are sure that either:

(a)   they already had the necessary compositional skills before beginning the course, or

(b)   we are providing tuition in those skills within the course itself.

Even professional adults often turn out to be quite inept -- and certainly unpractised and lacking confidence -- in the writing of essays. This is especially likely to be so in distance courses, where they may have little opportunity to compare their efforts with those of other learners. Short-answer questions (together perhaps with a few multiple-choice items) will often allow for just as thorough a test, and one that is less "contaminated" by calling on skills that you are not actually aiming to assess.

Process Assessment

Finally in this section, we must mention the kind of testing in which we assess on-going **processes** -- as when we assess a learner's ability to carry out an interview or to prepare a meal following principles of hygiene and nutrient preservation. To do so, the assessor must be present in the situation in which the learner is displaying the competence -- perhaps in the learner's workplace.

Such situational assessment is necessary when there is no assessable product resulting from the learner's activity. For instance, we might not be able to tell from the state of the interviewed person or completed meal (nor from any report the learner might make on either of these processes) whether the learner had or had not followed acceptable procedures.

If your objectives are concerned with **how** your learners do or make something, or how they interact with other people -- then there may be no proper substitute for watching them, or listening to them do it. For such assessment, it is useful to produce a checklist of the points you'll be looking for in their performance.

Checklists may be especially necessary if **someone else** has to do the assessment. Figure 13.1 opposite is an example of a checklist for use in observing a learner perform a trouble-shooting task. It tells the assessor how to describe the task to the learner, what to look for in the learner's performance, and how to arrive at a grade. With job-related lessons, such checklists could help line managers and others towards a realistic assessment of the competence that trainees gain from your materials.

In some cases, it may be possible to assess a learner's ability by listening to an audiotape, or viewing a videotape, of the learner carrying out a practical activity that you cannot observe "in the flesh". But such an alternative might be inconvenient and costly, and still not allow you to be confident about the learner's competence.

Figure 13.1: Checklist for a ProcessTest
(Reproduced by permission of British Coal)

STRICTLY CONFIDENTIAL — Not to be shown to Apprentices   C.198/28

NATIONAL COAL BOARD   COLLIERY APPRENTICE ELECTRICIANS   IT 8

TEST CENTRE.. NAME .... No. ....

DATE ....

Connecting up a three wire signalling system   **60 mins.**

Connect up the system comprising:

Two Bells
Two relays/relay unit
Two pushes or keys

Check for operation. If you cannot complete the wiring without a circuit diagram you should either draw the diagram yourself or ask the Examiner for one. If the Examiner has to give you a diagram he will deduct some marks from your score but you will not fail the test because of that alone. When checking any safety devices make sure that the Examiner knows you are doing it. Assume you are working below ground in a safety lamp mine. Do not spend more than ten minutes on drawing the diagram.

NB — One of the faults shown below must be prepared on the equipment prior to the test without the candidate's knowledge.

Show by X which of these faults the candidate was required to diagnose and rectify

☐ PUSH/KEY CONTACTS NOT MAKING   ☐ BELL NOT RINGING   ☐ SUPPLY FAILURE

SECTION A. Did the candidate make correct connections to: *(Enter in each box a tick for YES, a cross for NO)*

☐ Bells
☐ Relays/relay unit
☐ Pushes/keys
☐ Battery/transformer

SECTION B. Did he check that any intrinsic safety devices:

☐ Were in place
☐ Were correctly connected

If the system did not function satisfactorily, did he:

☐ Locate the fault
☐ Rectify the fault

SECTION C. Did he:

☐ Check the operation from both pushes/keys
☐ Connect all wires securely
☐ Make sure that wiring looked neat and tidy
☐ Replace and secure all covers and screws
☐ Carry out all connections without the aid of a diagram supplied by the examiner
☐ Have a systematic approach to fault location

GRADING. Enter in the box the grade awarded for this test

☐ Candidates should be graded as follows:

Grade A — Where ALL items in Sections A and B and at least 4 items from Section C are ticked
Grade B — Where ALL items in Sections A and B and at least 2 items from Section C are ticked
Grade C — Where ALL items in Sections A and B and less than 2 items from Section C are ticked
Grade D — Where ALL items in either Section A or Section B are ticked
Grade E — Where both Sections (A & B) include at least one item marked with a cross

Signed .... *Examiner*

Setting an Assignment

So what are the main points to bear in mind when setting a test or assignment for learners? Perhaps there are four main issues to make decisions about:

- *How big should the assignment be?* That is, how much time can you reasonably expect your learners to put into it -- bearing in mind the amount of time they have devoted to learning since the previous test or assignment? (If the assignment or test can be seen as contributing to the learner's learning -- rather than merely allowing its practice or application -- then proportionately more time might be allotted to it.)

- *What kinds of exercises might be appropriate?* Follow this guiding principles: Do not set any assessment question without asking yourself why you are setting it, what underlying knowledge, skill or attitude it is supposed to be testing, and how it relates to important learning objectives and competences.

- *What feedback might learners be given?* How can learners be provided with feedback that will help them learn from their attempt at the assignment? With objective tests, they can, at the very least, be told what the correct answers were (if not why). With "own answer" questions (and practical tests), they need a tutor's comments/advice on their performance. (More about this in the final section of this chapter.)

- *How to formulate the questions?* Many books have been written about how to design assessment exercises, and I have no space to paraphrase them here. However, to supplement what I have said on the subject in the preceding pages, let me add the following:

Writing own-answer questions. With questions (or
practical exercises) that require learners to produce a
response rather than choose among several they are
offered, we must make clear **what kind** of response is
required of them. Suppose, for example, you were asked
to answer this question:

> "Is it true that only psychology can provide us with
> valid explanations of criminal behaviour?"

It may occur to you that you could produce some sort of
answer without having a scrap of knowledge about
psychology. After all, you'd need only show that criminal
behaviour can **also** be explained in other terms -- e.g.
economic, social, or political.

But would your answer satisfy the markers?
Perhaps not -- because they might want you to answer it
from particular points of view, or in such a way as to
demonstrate your familiarity with certain approved
experts on the subject.

And even if you guessed what kind of answer they
wanted from you, you might still be giving them far more
of it than they required. You don't know how big your
answer is supposed to be. You could answer in one word
-- No! (or Yes! if that's the way you see it) -- or your
answer could fill a very fat volume of case studies and
analysis. Perhaps neither of these is quite what the
marker, or the setter, of the question is looking for.

But why should the learner be left to guess what is
required? Fortunately, the authors of the assignment
have anticipated our objections. They have provided
detailed notes of guidance for learners. As you'll see in
Figure 13.2 overleaf, they not only say what kind and
how big an answer is required, but also give guidance on
how to set about tackling the question. Will your learners
sometimes need such specific guidance?

Figure 13.2: Assignment Notes for the Learner
(from Open University course D101)

QUESTION AND STUDENT NOTES

This week's assignment consists of a short exercise based on
the four accounts which make up section 3 of Unit 2 (i.e. the
pieces by Sullivan, McIntosh, Worth and Stevens). In not
more than 500 words tackle the following topic:

Examine the argument that only psychology can provide us
with valid explanations of criminal behaviour.

1. Reread through section 3.3.2 'Explanations of behaviour',
    p.84, noting the ways in which explanations of behaviour
    may differ: selection of causal factors, levels of analysis,
    concepts, models.

2. Write about each of these differences, illustrating them
    from the four accounts in section 3. You might, for
    example, in discussing the second difference, show how
    McIntosh locates her explanation of the organization of
    thieving in the conflictful nature of society whereas
    Stevens includes genetic and personality factors.

3. When you have completed the analysis above, read the
    second paragraph of section 3.3.2 and try to relate what it
    says (i.e. that different explanations do not necessarily
    conflict) to what you have so far thought and written.
    Then go back to the original argument about psychology
    and try to come to a conclusion.

4. Finally, reread what you have written, making sure that
    your ideas are relevant, clear and expressed precisely.

For some assignment exercises -- e.g. if your learners are
not in regular contact with tutors or other learners -- you
may wish to give similarly detailed guidance. For other
assignments (and for learners who can discuss the
questions with other people), this will not be necessary.

Remember that the more guidance you give as to
what kind of answer is expected, the less chance your

learners have of showing they do not **need** such guidance. Where you draw the line must depend on your objectives. If you give your learners too many hints and clues, you may lead them to demonstrate achievement not of the objectives you initially had in mind but of some lesser, more restricted ones, instead.

As an illustration, look at the sequence of questions below. They all concern the Swedish political system. But each one is testing rather different abilities and insights:

Qu.1   What aspects of the political system of modern Sweden seem to you most worthy of comment?

Qu.2   Comment on the political stability of modern Sweden.

Qu.3   Explain the political stability of modern Sweden.

Qu.4   Identify and discuss three factors that might help explain the political stability of modern Sweden.

Qu.5   Identify and discuss three factors that might help explain the emergence of a stable political system in Sweden despite the massive social and economic changes engendered by processes of modernization.

Qu.6   Which *three* of the factors listed below might best help explain the emergence of a stable political system in Sweden despite the massive social and economic changes engendered by processes of modernization?

    (a)   Affluence
    (b)   Gradual economic development
    (c)   Traditional legitimacy
    (d)   Civic culture
    (e)   A homogeneous political culture
    (f)   Equality
    (g)   Congruent authority patterns
    (h)   Elite consensus
    (i)   The habituation of mechanisms of conflict resolution
    (j)   Political institutionalization

One by one, the questions become more specific -- leaving the learner less and less responsibility for deciding what is significant about the situation referred to, and in what terms to respond to it. For instance, the learner answering Question 1 may choose not to discuss political **stability**. The learner answering Question 2 may choose to describe political stability without **explaining** it. The learner answering Question 3 may choose to refer to more or to fewer than **three** factors. And so on.

Finally, Question 6 takes multiple-choice form. It tests merely whether the learner can recognize the three crucial factors when they are presented in a list. It could be followed by further multiple-choice questions taking each of the ten suggested factors in turn and asking "If this was one of the three factors you chose, which of the statements below best explains the contribution made by that factor". But such a sequence of multiple-choice questions would **not** be testing the same abilities as, say, Questions 3 or 4.

Writing multiple-choice items. Here I concentrate on the "one from several" items that are the staple of objective tests.

The aim of writing such a question is to ensure that learners who have the necessary understanding are able to answer it correctly -- while those without it are not.

To ensure the first of these, be careful not to introduce **irrelevant** difficulties -- e.g. don't ask "Which of the following is the eponymous hero of a novel by Charles Dickens?" when it is more appropriate to ask "Which of the following names refers both to the hero and the title of a novel by Charles Dickens?" (If you wanted to test the learner's understanding of the word "eponymous", this should be done in a separate question.)

To ensure that learners **without** the knowledge are unable (without guessing) to pick out the correct answers, you must be careful to avoid "give-aways". Let me illustrate this, in Figure 13.3 opposite, with a test that breaks every "rule" in the book. Glancing through it, you may feel that its subject-matter is somewhat unfamiliar. Don't let that worry you. The test contains a number of "give-aways" that should enable you to identify the correct answers despite knowing nothing about the subject.

Figure 13.3: Give-aways in an Objective Test

For each of the eight items, underline the one answer
you believe to be correct. Maximum time 15 minutes.

1. The main function of dingle-grabblers is to ruthe
    A.   dingles
    B.   growks
    C.   snitters
    D.   beegums

2. Regrallification becomes necessary when
    A.   the gudges noogle
    B.   the rakob flames telsate, and the vosts fail to flonce
    C.   the breg fribbles
    D.   the hooluphs elgage

3. Nuriles are trassed by yukhorrhoea because
    A.   all their obblers are sushed
    B.   their fleepers are always tolloidable
    C.   the ning-daphle is usually runged
    D.   their snares are never grovid

4. Non-abordal nittering usually involves an
    A.   dacklex
    B.   grumeld
    C.   telloid
    D.   ustbile

5. Which of the following are the results of sub-foping?
    A.   grazzed allops and mulced crips
    B.   rakols juckested by snallums
    C.   a bralious inflaction of plabsts
    D.   trass-loomphed vallicles in gled

6. Which of the following is/are essential for breg-slepping?
    A.   stost and rune
    B   rune
    C.   phyke and rune
    D.   rune and molp

7. The ustbile can be used in
    A.   slunthing
    B.   freeping
    C.   nittering
    D.   grunging

8. Which of the following is the correct alternative?
    A.
    B.   *Don't worry: there's nothing*
    C.   *missing here!   DR*
    D.

Answers (and comments) overleaf...

Here are the answers to the test items shown in Figure 13.1 -- together with advice on how to avoid the writing errors illustrated in that test:

1. **A** Don't allow the "correct answer" to contain an unintended clue -- e.g. a word (like "dingles") that is naturally associated with a word in the "stem" (the introductory statement or question).

2. **B** Don't let the correct answer be much longer or more detailed than the "distractors".

3. **C** Don't write distractors with qualifying terms that are too embracing (e.g. "never", "always") making the learner so suspicious as to reject it in favour or the more moderate correct answer.

4. **D** Make sure that all answers are consistent with any single or plural verb used in the stem.

5. **A** Make all the answers consistent with any single or plural verb used in the stem.

6. **B** Don't let one answer be an instance of (or be included in) one of the others. (Here, for example, if A, C or D were correct, B would have to be correct also.)

7. **C** Don't let one item in a test contain a clue as to how another item should be answered. (Compare item 7 with item 4.)

8. **D** Vary the placing of the correct answers in random fashion, so that there is no obvious pattern.

WHETHER OWN-ANSWER OR MULTIPLE-CHOICE, BE PREPARED TO **MODIFY** YOUR QUESTIONS AFTER TRYING THEM OUT ON LEARNERS.

HOW TO USE ASSESSMENT RESULTS

In response to the questions in our tests and assignments, learners say and do things. These "things" are the "results" of assessment. As I pointed out at the beginning of this chapter, we can use the results in two different ways. We can use them to report on the learner's work -- e.g. by grading or marking. Or we can use them as the basis for teaching -- for helping our learners learn something new. Or, of course, we can do both.

Reporting on Achievement

As I mentioned earlier, grading (or marking) is not a necessary part of assessment. That is, we can appraise our learners' work -- reporting to them or to someone else about what we find strong, weak or interesting in it -- without needing to attach a grade, percentage mark, or the like. That is, we can use words to **describe** what we see in the work. (Such a verbal report could lead into teaching the learner, as we discuss in the next section.)

In many situations, however, you will need to report in terms of letter grades or numerical scores rather than (or perhaps as well as) words. As an experienced teacher, you are unlikely to see much of a problem in marking learners' tests and assignments -- provided you do it **yourself**. However, with self-instructional teaching, you may need to share this task with other people.

At least some of your learners may have their work assessed by other teachers (call them "tutors") acting on your guidance. Or perhaps assignments will be marked by mentors or by more advanced learners. In all such cases, the question is: How do you ensure that the mark given to a particular piece of work is much the same as you would have given it if you had marked it yourself?

Impression v analytic marking. There seem to be three different approaches to marking an assignment:

1.   impression marking;
2.   analytic marking; or
3.   some sort of compromise between 1 and 2.

With impression marking (much used for essays), one gets an overall impression of the worth of the work, and gives an appropriate mark. With analytic marking, one follows a pre-arranged mark-scheme. The marker is asked to look for certain features in learners' answers and give so many marks for this point and so many marks for another. A clear example would be an arithmetic test where each expected answer is specified precisely -- and the marker is instructed to give one mark for each correct answer and no marks for working that is only partially correct.

When the assessed exercise consists of a number of short one-answer questions (or even a practical task), you may find it quite straightforward to provide assessors with an analytic mark-scheme. Suppose, for instance, you were setting items like these:

1. List the principal components of a balanced diet and describe briefly the function of each in the body.

2. Name five diseases caused by inadequate or unbalanced diet.

3. Calculate the amount of
    (a)   energy
    (b)   protein
    (c)   vitamins A, B, C and D
    (d)   calcium and iron
    in the attached recipe (using food composition tables).

4. Prepare a meal using the attached recipe, taking all necessary steps to minimize loss of nutrients during the preparation.

Here it should be possible to tell the marker what to look for (and reward) in each case. You could, in fact, give "model answers". Even with item 4 -- a practical test where the process rather than the product is to be assessed -- you could provide the marker with a **checklist** (like Figure 13.1 on page 313) against which to score the learner's performance. Furthermore, you could tell the marker that:

Item 1   is to be marked out of 12 (1 point for the name of each component, 1 point for its function);

Item 2   is to be marked out of 5 (1 point for each disease);

Item 3   is to be marked out of 20 (5 points for each correct calculation); and

Item 4   is to be marked out of 30 (with so many points being deducted for each step not properly carried out).

However, it is not so easy to devise an analytic mark-scheme when what you are expecting from learners is an extended "own answer", e.g. an essay. Look for example at the "Tutor Notes" in Figure 13.4 overleaf. They were provided for markers by the author of the essay question on explaining criminal behaviour that I printed in the previous section (page 315). (Incidentally, a question you may like to ask yourself when telling learners what to include in answers, and markers what to look for in them, is: How far are you justified in giving **different** information to each?)

The notes in Figure 13.4 seem to represent a compromise approach to marking. They are partly analytic in that tutors are directed to look for certain factors in the learners' answers. But much is left to each tutor's impressions as to how much weight to give to one factor compared with another. Thus, markers might not agree very closely as to a given learner's grade. (The "teaching" comments they give the learner might be quite different also.)

Figure 13.4: Tutor Notes for Assignment Marking

Assignment   <u>TUTOR NOTES</u>

This assignment is intended to get students to think about
the nature of explanation in social science by applying some
methodological principles discussed in Section 3.3.2. of
Unit 2 to the explanations of crime given in Section 3.

Typical answers that follow the suggested framework will
consist of a brief paraphrase of each principle (illustrated by
examples drawn from the four printed accounts). Direct
quotation from Section 3.3.2. is not excluded, though try to
check that examples reflect an <u>understanding</u> of the
principle that is being quoted. Reward students for clarity
and selectivity as against extensive coverage and
exemplification which neither reveal understanding nor
keep to the 500 words limit.

Students have been asked to come to a conclusion about the
explanatory power of psychology in comparison with the
other social sciences in question. The conclusion, on one
side or the other, or more probably that hinted at in the
student notes, is less important than the discussion that has
led up to it.

Other frameworks are admissible provided the student has
tried to answer the question set. Students may introduce
further ways in which explanations differ or want to question
what is noted at the beginning of 3.3.2. , that social science
explanation is based on a deterministic assumption. Reward
these provided they contribute to a coherent, relevant answer.

In general, with open-ended own-answer questions, it
is difficult to guide the marker very precisely without
exposing learners to the risk that their good (but
unpredicted) points will fail to get rewarded. Non-
specific guidance, on the other hand, means that a
learner's grade will be very dependent on who marks
his or her work.

Where you are relying heavily on impression
marking, it may be essential to get your markers together

for an "agreement exercise" -- letting them all compare the marks they would give to some sample answers -- before they start awarding grades in earnest. You may also need to monitor their marking by occasionally marking some of their learners' work yourself. You may also need to decide how far tutors can be allowed to diverge from what would seem to be the "ideal" grades.

An overall score. Finally, if you are setting a test or assignment or examination consisting of several different items, your markers may need to be told how to reach an overall score for each learner. Do they simply add up the marks for each of the separate items and give the "total achieved" as a fraction of the "total possible" score -- e.g. $5/10 + 8/12 + 11/15 + 9/15 + 16/20 = 49/72$? Or do they convert it to a percentage? Or do they arrive at a letter grade, using some such arbitrary conversion scale as: 1-14 = E; 15-24 = D; 25-44 = C; 45-59 = B; and 60-72 = A? If you are a member of a course team, the procedure will clearly need to be decided in discussion with your colleagues.

Discussing the marking. Will you and/or your markers be meeting learners face to face? Or will you merely be marking work that is sent in to you? In the former case, the marking might beneficially be discussed with the learner -- or even carried out in his or her presence. It would certainly be possible for markers to question their learners further about answers that were only partially correct. They could also ask learners to restate such answers, or explain them more fully, before deciding a final mark.

The possibility of such discussion -- which could take place by telephone or even, at a pinch, in writing -- leads us into the second way of using assessment results. Regardless of whether or not learners' work is to be awarded marks and grades, you will still need to consider how the learners might be helped by the comments and suggestions of a tutor.

Teaching Through Assessment

Assessment results reveal the learner's strengths and weaknesses. They therefore suggest where he or she might be helped by a teacher.

If the assessor is meeting the learner face to face after the assignment -- and especially if he or she is assessing in the learner's presence -- it is easy to move from assessment into teaching. A faulty answer or performance will give rise to discussion; the assessor will attempt to elicit the cause of the weakness and can, there and then, help the learner to overcome it. The marker becomes **tutor**.

If tutors are not meeting learners face to face (or talking with them on the telephone), they must do rather as you are doing -- that is, teach the learner in **writing**. Here they will have an advantage over you, however. They will be teaching a limited range of points to a particular learner whose specific difficulties they have already seen evidence of in his or her completed assignment. Even if they are also talking with their learners from time to time, tutors should be encouraged to make the most of their opportunity to teach through written **comments** and **advice** when they return assignments to their learners.

They should be encouraged to direct their comments at what they believe to be the chief strengths and weaknesses of each "performance". They have to decide their teaching **priorities**. In order to most benefit the learner, they may ignore some minor weaknesses in order to help the learner remedy the major ones. For example, a particular learner's written report may strike the tutor as poorly organized, factually inaccurate, full of spelling mistakes, and missing the point of the assignment. Yet the tutor might choose to disregard the first three weaknesses in order to comment and advise solely on the last one. Here the tutor might be conscious that there is a limit to the range of criticism and advice a learner can take at any one time -- and that even the best organized, most accurate and perfectly spelled report is wasted if it is not what the assignment asked for.

Types of tutor-comment. If you want your markers to provide this tutorial feedback on learners' work, they will need guidance on appropriate types of comment. Essentially, you will be asking them to write down remarks and suggestions that will help their learners think again about what they have done, and about how they might do differently another time. The tutor's written remarks need to convey what he or she would have had to say if it had been possible to meet the learner face to face. With distance learners, it's no good scribbling "See me!"

Nor will it be sufficient merely to pepper the learner's work with ticks and crosses and question-marks, underlining or circling a word here and there. Verbal comments are not sufficient. Suppose the following remarks were all that a tutor had written on a learner's script:

> This is quite a fair piece and you make a number of points well. But some are rather less well illustrated than others and the argument is sometimes weak or not fully expressed.

These remarks may well be true, but they are unlikely to help the learner improve. They are too general. The learner needs to be told precisely **where** and **how** he or she has illustrated less well, argued weakly, or expressed less than fully. The learner might also be told what he or she might have done to avoid these faults.

However, we must at least commend the above tutor for starting off with some words of encouragement. Some tutors seem to notice only the faults in a learner's performance and neglect to mention its positive aspects. Learners won't thank you (or learn much) if all the comments bring them is unrelieved gloom. They need to be told their work has some redeeming features -- or at least some realistic prospect of improving.

Here are some of the ways in which tutors might teach through their written comments on learners' performance. You will no doubt be able to identify many more in your discussions with your own tutors or in your own tutoring. Written comments may:

- Draw the learners' attention to facts they have overlooked or misinterpreted.

- Suggest alternative approaches or interpretations.

- Suggest new sources (e.g. other people) from whom learners might get feedback.

- Draw attention to gaps in the learners' reasoning.

- Suggest how learners might present their ideas more effectively.

- Offer comments that will help learners sharpen their practical skills.

- Ask for further explanation of muddled answers.

- Demonstrate useful short-cuts in procedure.

- Help learners reflect on how a piece of work might have been improved.

- Point out relationships between the learners' present work and their earlier work.

- Commend the learners for any unexpected insights, special efforts or improvement in competence.

Adopting the right tone. The tone of the tutor's remarks is very important. For instance, such comments as those below (all authentic) might be expected to do more harm than good to the tutor-learner relationships:

This just won't do.
Style!
Disorganized and inchoate.
Your spelling is atrocious.
Clap-trap.
You must get your facts straight.

Yet the tutor-concern behind such impulsive remarks can be turned into positive guidance -- without sounding either condescending or threatening. Below, for example, are some further comments collected from learners' written assignments. Each has the flavour of **dialogue**, with the tutor seeking clarification, evidence, or amplification -- trying to stretch the learner's thinking:

- *The meaning is not very clear here. I find what it appears to mean very unlikely. Can you quote the figures?*

- *Important point but needs broadening out from the specific example. Also did any benefits accrue for schools and children?*

- *If you had given the electronic structures of neon and sodium it would have helped show the essential difference between them.*

- *Your answer is OK as far as it goes but you do not explain why the drop in IE is so large. Look again at Figure 7 of the unit and ask yourself what is so special about the electronic structure of neon and how does it differ from that of sodium.*

- *Yes it is very difficult to assess the effectiveness of the party, either locally or nationally, in this role. I would have welcomed an example on a local issue known to you.*

- *Comment on the results, Chris. Why is there, do you think, such a difference between the least and the greatest? Should these be taken into the average?*

Notice that good tutor-commenting may depend more on asking stimulating questions than on providing ready-made answers. As a final example, here is one tutor's response (a kind of mini-tutorial) to a learner's mathematics assignment. The tutor's questions lead the learner in a new approach to the set problem -- which is to decide, given that Set (i) $\{\wedge, \vee, \sim\}$ is an adequate set of connectives, whether Set (ii) $\{\square, \sim\}$ is an adequate set:

> *What does* $\{\wedge, \vee, \sim\}$ *being an adequate set of connectives mean? All connectives can be written in terms of* $\{\wedge, \vee, \sim\}$
> *How do we show that* $\{\square, \sim\}$ *is an adequate set?*
> *By showing all connections can be written in terms of* $\{\square, \sim\}$.
> *Knowing Set (i) how do we show Set (ii)? In other words, how can we replace Set (i) by Set (ii)? How do they differ?*

Guiding your assessors. So, if other people will be marking your learners' assessment exercises, or just offering comments on them, what can you do to help ensure those people giving useful advice. Here are five ways of helping:

1. Discuss with assessors the importance of teaching-type comments, and how they might usefully be made. Draw their attention to types of comment, tone, and the need for learners to receive the assessor's response as quickly as possible.

2. Show the assessors some examples of good and bad commenting on typical learner's work.

3. Ask each assessor to examine a few pieces of learners' work and record the comments he or she would make to each learner to aid improvement. (You should do this too.) Then compare notes and seek consensus as to how best such learners might be helped.

4. Produce general notes of guidance about assessing learners' performance on your course. But also produce specific guidance notes about each separate exercise that is to be marked and/or commented on. (See the examples on pages 313, 323 and 324.)

5. Monitor your assessors' marking and commenting, from time to time. Find out how the learners feel about the kind of feedback (written or spoken) they are getting. Have "refresher" discussions with any assessors whose commenting is not as helpful as it could be -- or whose marking is too tough, too lenient, or too inconsistent.

Final reminder. Don't forget that learners also have a right to expect feedback on their practical performance in process assessment. So too with objective test items (multiple-choice questions) -- learners can still be given valuable feedback that will help them review their work and improve it. Even with an end-of-course examination, it is worth considering how learners might be given feedback that might help consolidate their learning or aid their approach to future courses.

SUMMARY

Here, to sum up, are the main questions you will need to answer when planning your assessment strategy:

1. Is there any necessity for occasional tests or assignments? Or will the self-assessment encouraged by "activities" be sufficient?

2. If you do need tests or assignments, how frequent should they be? And how time-consuming?

3. Which of them can be self or peer-assessed, and which should seen by a tutor for marking and/or comments.

4. Which lesson or course objectives will each test or assignment be aimed at?

5. What kinds of question -- e.g. objective or own-answer (short or long) -- are appropriate?

6. How can questions best be posed so as to give a true picture of the learner's competence?

7. If certain competences need "process" assessment in the presence of an assessor -- perhaps in the workplace -- how can this be arranged?

8. Must some assessment be carried out under controlled conditions -- e.g. to a time-limit, in the presence of an invigilator, and without access to reference books or consultation with colleagues? (In other words, is a formal examination needed?)

9. How can learners be provided with appropriate feedback that will aid their learning?

10. How can the marking and/or commenting of assessors be made as effective as possible?

DO ALL YOU CAN TO MAKE EACH ASSESSMENT
A **LEARNING EXPERIENCE** -- AND NOT JUST
A FORMAL CHECK-UP ON WHAT HAS BEEN
LEARNED ALREADY.

14. EVALUATING YOUR LESSONS

However carefully you design a lesson, you can't expect to produce perfection in your first draft. It will be capable of improvement -- either in its content or in teaching effectiveness (or both). Hence the need for evaluation.

WHAT IS EVALUATION?

Evaluation is the process of getting various people's reactions to your course or lesson -- with a view to improving it. What do people think of your lesson? What is it like to work with? How effectively does it teach? What are the results of your course? What unexpected problems arise? What needs changing? These are the kinds of question that evaluation might answer.

Why Bother?

There are many reasons why you should care about evaluation. One reason is that many people may need **convincing** that your new approach to teaching is worthwhile -- especially if self-instruction is not yet well-established in your organization. You may need to prove to sceptical administrators, managers and other teachers that the results can be as good as, if not better than, those obtained by more traditional approaches.

Also, you may need convincing yourself that all your planning and preparation time has been well spent. The chief and educational reason for caring about evaluation, however, is that it can lead to noticeable **improvements** in your teaching -- and therefore in your learner's learning.

Types of Evaluation

In this chapter, I discuss three types of evaluation, the second of which has two forms. I list them below in the order in which you would normally carry them out:

- Critical commenting.
- Developmental testing -- including face-to-face tryout and field trials.
- Continuous monitoring.

CRITICAL COMMENTING

In this form of evaluation, you get people to read your draft lesson carefully and offer you their critical but, let's hope, constructive comments. Who might usefully read it and offer such comment? You might ask:

- subject-matter experts (see Figure 14.1);
- tutors who are familiar with learners like yours;
- your learners' managers (if appropriate); and
- learners who have recently studied the subject.

Such "critical friends" may take issue with you over fundamental matters of content, style and teaching strategy. Or they may find nothing to suggest but minor enhancements. Either way, their response may well be sufficient to renew your own incentive to take a fresh hard look at the material -- and do more critical commenting of your own -- before trying it out on some learners new to the subject.

Course Team Discussions

If you are working in a course team, it is essential that **at least one** of your colleagues should be persuaded to provide critical comments on your lesson. These can either be put in writing or be spoken face-to-face, privately or in a course team meeting. Course team discussion of each draft lesson can be valuable. Matters of general principle often emerge and lesson authors can **learn** from discussion of one another's drafts. However, such group analysis can be threatening to the individual author unless the working relationship is a sympathetic and mutually supportive one.

Figure 14.1: Expert's Comments on a Lesson

Page 30

I was very impressed by the organization chart. But do make clear that this is just an example (and not very typical).

Page 31

Para 7.8 will get you shot! If you go to press suggesting that the Chairman is the political adviser to the Chief Education Officer you will be slaughtered -- quite rightly. The CEO is the professional adviser to the Education Committee. You have it back-to-front.

Page 33

There are LEAs which are not *Counties. Please try not to make students think their County Council representative is automatically an LEA representative, or that all Counties are LEAs and Districts are not. I know it is complicated, but it is important.*

Page 35

What a nice Authority your Mr Edwards works for. In most Authorities I have known, a letter like that from an AEO would produce apoplexy all round. Formality is still the order of the day. You may not like it, but it is so, and the course should reflect it.

Page 41

The management of the Council as a body (rather than as a collection of separate enterprises) is a fairly simple concept which you seem to have hidden behind jargon ('corporate management') that the student will not understand.

Areas of Commenting

There are two main aspects upon which you might invite critical comments:

- subject-matter content; and
- likely teaching effectiveness.

You may ask all your commenters to consider both; or you may ask some to concentrate on one aspect and some on another. For instance, you might send your lessons to subject-experts (inside and outside your institution) to comment on content; while you get tutors and experienced learners to speculate about the likely teaching effectiveness of your materials. Figure 14.1 shows the kind of useful comments that may come in from a subject expert -- in this case, an expert on educational administration.

You may wish to offer your commenters a **checklist** to guide them as to the kinds of issue you'd like them to address. Here are two checklists, one for subject-matter content and one for likely teaching effectiveness. They are simply examples; you may have more appropriate questions of your own that you'd want to ask.

Subject-matter Content -- Checklist:

- Are the aims and objectives sufficiently explicit?
- Do they seem worthwhile and relevant to what learners (and others?) perceive as their needs?
- Do the objectives support the aims?
- Are there any additional aims and objectives that should be included?
- Is the content appropriate to the objectives?
- Is it factually correct?
- Is it up-to-date?

- Are there any important omissions?
- Is there any redundant material?
- Does the material hang together logically?
- Does it avoid over-simplification and over-generalization?
- Is it balanced, and careful to recognize opposing viewpoints where appropriate?
- Does it use evidence responsibly?
- Does it contain any unsatisfactory examples, analogies or case studies?

Likely Teaching Effectiveness -- Checklist:

- Will learners understand what is expected of them? (Is there enough study guidance?)
- Do you think learners will have difficulty achieving any of the listed objectives?
- How long would you expect learners to take over each section?
- Does the material seem pitched at the right level of difficulty and interest for the intended learners?
- Do the examples, analogies and case studies seem relevant to learners' interests and are they sufficiently illuminating?
- Can you suggest any additional examples, analogies and case studies?
- Can you comment on any sections that are likely to cause problems for learners (or support staff)?
- Are all new terms adequately explained?
- Is the number and distribution of activities and/or self-tests about right?
- Are all the activities worthwhile and practicable?

- Does the assignment or suggested follow-up activity (if any) seem appropriate?

- Can you suggest any further ideas for activities, tests or assignments?

Summary

So, there is a rough order of events concerning the type of evaluation we've discussed so far:

1. Decide who might offer useful comments.
2. Finish your first "public" draft.
3. Send it to the "critical friends" named in 1.
4. Revise your lesson in the light of comments.
5. Proceed to next stage of evaluation
   -- developmental testing.

DEVELOPMENTAL TESTING

So far you will have collected opinions about the content of your lesson and **speculations** about its likely teaching effectiveness. These latter speculations do remain guesswork -- even when you have "critical friends" who are brilliantly intuitive and frequently correct. You won't know definitely whether, what and how well your material teaches until your lesson is studied by learners who are new to the subject.

It will then be no good saying "Well, I taught them; but they just didn't learn". If they don't learn, or otherwise find the experience uncongenial, then your lesson is at fault. It needs revising. That is the purpose of developmental testing.

Developmental testing involves us in trying out our lesson on "sample" learners and revising it before we publish the final version. Clearly, these sample learners should be as like our intended learners as possible in background, motivation, etc. But they will not necessarily be studying the lesson under exactly the same conditions. For example, an individual sample learner may not even be asked to read all the lessons in your course. Nevertheless, such sample learners can give us invaluable help in improving the lesson for the benefit of future learners.

There are two main forms of developmental testing:

- Face-to-face tryouts
- Field trials.

Face-to-face Tryouts

For this kind of developmental testing you will need two or three sample learners with whom you will work, **one at a time**, through the second draft of your lesson.

How to begin? Sit down with your learner in a quiet place where you can avoid being disturbed for an hour or two. Check -- with a test if necessary -- that he or she is competent to begin on the lesson. That is, has your learner already acquired whatever prerequisite abilities you are expecting of learners? (These may have been acquired by reading previous lessons in your course.)

It may also be worth testing your learner on the concepts you are covering in the present lesson. It is just possible that he or she is (somehow) already competent with them. If so, this learner's responses will not imply much about those of the learners it is eventually intended for. (In short, the learner who knows it all already -- like the learner who doesn't know enough to begin -- will not be typical of your "target audience".) There is another reason why it is worth your finding out about the learner's **prior** perceptions of the ideas in your lesson: it may help you understand how he or she reacts to your handling of them.

Make sure your learner understands the purpose of your collaboration -- that the lesson is on trial, not the learner. Admit that you expect there to be weaknesses in the teaching and that you hope, with the learner's help, to eradicate them before it goes into wider circulation. Clearly, the more lessons a particular learner tests with you, the more relaxed he or she will be -- and the more "natural" will be his or her approach to the material.

So, get your learner started. Observe how he or she works through the lesson. What sequence does your learner follow -- and from what starting point? How does he or she respond to your activities? And are there passages that seem to bore or annoy or cause your learner undue difficulty? If you have to explain anything orally, make a note of what you say, because you may decide you need to write it into the next version of the lesson. You may also want to make a note of any comments your learner offers about the difficulty, relevance, interest or effectiveness of various parts of the lesson. And how long is your learner taking to work through the various sections?

When your learner has finished, test again to find out what he or she has learned. This should lead you into a critical discussion of your lesson. Which parts has your learner learned most from? And from which parts has little been learned? Can your learner suggest why this might be? How does the learner's present understanding compare with what he or she already knew about the topic? What changes would he or she suggest in the lesson?

How such a discussion might go, and the kinds of improvement that might be suggested, will vary according to you, your learner, and the sort of learning materials being tested. Much depends on your rapport with the learner and on your ability to get him or her to level with you -- rather than holding back for fear either of being thought "thick" or, alternatively, of hurting **your** feelings about your precious lesson. (Some authors prefer not to mention that they wrote the lesson being tested.)

Once you have corrected any glaring errors or weaknesses revealed by your first learner, you can try the lesson out with one or two more. Take particular note of any reactions they have **in common**. They may all make similar mistakes on a certain activity, for instance; or all may suggest that a certain passage is patronizing, sexist or at odds with their experience.

Weigh the words of your try-out learners carefully. Some comments will seem trivial; others richly insightful. Remember, they are most unlikely to have revealed all the weaknesses in your lesson. But at least the responses should help you seek out further weaknesses yourself. Consider whether or not your learners' comments are likely to be typical of future learners. Are some of them personal and unlikely to be repeated? Do some of them suggest areas of weakness that would crumble under general scrutiny?

When you have digested all your learners' comments, do what seems necessary to amend your lesson:

- Cut out irrelevant material.
- Expand any explanations that are too terse.
- Insert more practice exercise where called for.
- Allow for additional summaries or reviews.
- Shorten your elephantine sentences.
- Sharpen your analogies.
- Insert more effective examples.
- Tie your pictures more closely to the text.
- Make better use of additional media.

In short, improve your lesson.

You may feel, of course, that face-to-face tryout is too time-consuming or difficult to arrange for every lesson. Nevertheless, I would strongly urge you to evaluate at least your **first few** self-instructional lessons in this way -- even if you need to work with two or three learners at once. Also, you may want to return to face-to-face testing for any subsequent lessons in which you are trying out novel approaches or are presenting learners with unusual learning problems.

The fact is, face-to-face tryouts -- in which you can **observe** the learner at work on your material -- can contribute a great deal, not just to the development of a particular lesson but to **your** development as a "teacher in print". Many competent practitioners of self-instruction will admit that much of their expertise derives from the insights and awareness developed in their early experiences of trying out materials face-to-face. It can be a disturbing experience -- "How can they possibly be having trouble with such carefully written material?" -- but one with a lot to teach the teacher.

However, such a tryout will not give you all the information you need. After all, the situation is rather artificial. Your eventual learners will not have you sitting alongside them as they work through your lessons. So, having revised your material in the light of a face-to-face tryout, you may then evaluate it more "realistically" in what I have called a **field trial**.

Field Trials

For this you will need a large group of sample learners, say 20 or 30. You will have them use the lesson in much the same circumstances as the learners for whom it is eventually intended. For example, this may mean their reading it in their own homes at whatever time best suits them. Or it may mean they must tackle the material in their work-place, with or without a tutor or mentor to call on in emergencies. Aim to create whatever would be the normal working conditions.

How are you to find out how learners use your lesson and what they have got out of it? Can you find out without being with them while they are learning? Yes, to some extent. You can, for example:

- Require them to tackle a test on the lesson, before and after working through it, and assess their performance.

- Ask them to fill in a "log sheet" and/or questionnaire (see Figure 14.2, 3 and 4 for examples) -- in which they might comment, for instance, on:

  (a)   How long they took over the lesson.
  (b)   How easy/interesting/useful it was.
  (c)   What they liked and disliked about it.
  The answers to (a), (b) and (c) may be illuminating in their own right. But they are likely to be even more so when compared with learners' responses to other lessons in the series.

- Interview some of the learners afterwards to discover their general impressions of the lesson and how they think it might be improved.

None of the procedures mentioned above makes the situation of the field trial learners very much different from what might be the "regular" working conditions. However, they do fail to collect one kind of useful information that is richly available in face-to-face tutorial tryouts. That is, field trials may give us little information about **how** the learner tackles the material. Even if it were realistic to have all learners working together in one room -- and that seems unlikely -- we could not follow each one's minute-by-minute progress.

The nearest we can get is to ask the learners themselves to record their reactions as they work. This does, of course, make their situation different from that of the learners for whom the material is intended. Nevertheless, you may feel that the "artificiality" of writing down reactions is worth enduring for the sake of the insights that may be forthcoming.

Free comments. The simplest way of getting moment-by-moment reactions is to invite learners to write their comments in the margin of the text as they read -- or in a separate notebook with non-book materials. Below are some comments of this kind I have had from learners. (Some are quite similar to the comments one may get from experts.) As you will notice, such remarks are likely to persuade one to take another (evaluative) look at one's lesson:

> *I've lost the drift of the argument.*
>
> *Too many technical terms all at once.*
>
> *Sexist!*
>
> *This paragraph is contradicting itself.*
>
> *I am getting quite intrigued now.*
>
> *So dull, I don't want to go on.*
>
> *This doesn't apply in my work.*
>
> *We need photographs to appreciate this distinction.*
>
> *What is this supposed to be an example of?*
>
> *Beautifully clear and logical.*
>
> *Can't you give another worked example before this exercise?*
>
> *What has this paragraph got to do with the topic?*
>
> *Superficial -- nothing to think about here.*
>
> *How is this different from the word's everyday meaning?*
>
> *I could do with a summing-up about here.*
>
> *I'd need to try this out in the workshop to be convinced.*
>
> *What am I supposed to do with this information?*

Figure 14.2: A Tester's Log Sheet

TESTER'S LOG SHEET				
1. YOUR NAME *C.B. Russell*				
2. TITLE OF COURSE UNIT *KANT, Units 17, 18*				
SECTION	STARTED AT	FINISHED AT	TOTAL TIME	YOUR COMMENT ON THE SECTION AS A WHOLE
1.1 – 2.8 (pp. 1–20	4.20	5.0	.40	Clear & well presented
	6.40	7.30	.50	Since I have no experience of philosophy, I am glad that you are introducing it gradually
3.1 – 3.6 (pp. 21–57)	7.30	9.30	2.	The difficulties started when you asked me to read long passages from Kant. I did not feel properly prepared for this.
	11.15	1.00	1.45	
	2.30	3.45	1.15	
	6.30	8.00	1.30	
4.1 – 6.2 (pp. 57–97)	2.	3.20	1.20	I became saturated, and lost the thread of your commentary. I was not sure what the Exercises required me to do.
	4.50	6.30	1.40	
	9.	9.45	.45	
Assessment Exercise (p. 98)	9.30	11.15	1.45	My problem was whether to confine myself to the Autonomy of the Will, or to try a broader approach. The latter seemed to give me a better chance of showing what I know.
	1.30	3.40	2.10	
	7.00	9.00	2.	
	10.00	1.20	3.20	
TOTAL TIME (INCL. ASSESSMENT)			21.40	

Figure 14.3: End-of-Unit Questionnaire (Part One)

END OF UNIT QUESTIONNAIRE (Part One)

1. Name: 2. Unit title/No.

   J. Brodie   *No. 19*

3. What did you particularly like about this unit?

   The examples discussed are basically interesting but

4. What did you particularly dislike? *Most of my time and effort was spent struggling with the sociological terms & the writing style of sociologists. The overall themes & concepts are difficult to master because of the language barrier.*

5. Were there any sections, concepts or words that you found particularly difficult, or not well explained? If there were, please give details.

   The terms were copiously explained but with definitions that were hard to recall during later reading. Repeated re-reading & refreshing of memory was necessary during difficult & complex passages, e.g. first paragraph of section 3.1

6. Can you suggest what might have helped you in these cases?

   Use the same definitions in self-assessment questions as are printed in text: 'action', 'role', 'norms', etc.

7. Do you have any other comments about this unit?

   As with other sociologically-based units, my difficulties stem from the terminology. Other disciplines' approaches to the same topics (crime, unemployment, immigration, etc.) seem to overcome this difficulty & get their message across using more familiar, or at least more clearly defined terms.

Figure 14.4: End-of-Unit Questionnaire (Part Two)

END OF UNIT QUESTIONNAIRE (Part Two)

1. NAME.... *K. Mitchell* .... 2. Course Unit.. *Unit 12* .....

Put a tick in the appropriate box for each of the questions below:

3 How much of the subject matter of the unit was already familiar to you?
- [ ] All of it
- [ ] Most of it
- [ ] About half
- [ ] A small amount
- [✓] None at all

4 To what extent did you enjoy working through the unit?
- [ ] I liked it very much
- [✓] I quite liked it
- [ ] I felt indifferent to it
- [ ] I rather disliked it
- [ ] I disliked it very much

5 How difficult did you find the course unit?
- [✓] Very difficult
- [ ] Fairly difficult
- [ ] Neither too difficult nor Fairly easy   too easy
- [ ] Very easy

6 How difficult did you find the assignment exercise which followed the unit?
- [ ] Very difficult
- [✓] Fairly difficult
- [ ] Neither too difficult nor Fairly easy   too easy
- [ ] Very easy

7 Do you think the unit gave you enough practice in using the ideas it contained?
- [ ] Too much practice
- [✓] Neither too much nor too little practice
- [ ] Too little practice

8 In view of the amount of time the unit required of you, do you feel you learned as much as you might have expected from it?
- [ ] I learned a great deal
- [✓] I learned a reasonable amount
- [ ] I learned too little

9 If this course unit were considered typical material from the course for which you have applied, how would your experience of it affect your desire to take this course?

My desire to take the course would be:
- [✓] Very much increased
- [ ] Somewhat increased
- [ ] Unaffected
- [ ] Somewhat decreased
- [ ] Very much decreased

10 Are you willing to test further units?
- [✓] Yes
- [ ] No

11 Please give overleaf any other general comments that you would like the author (or illustrator) to take into account when revising this course unit for publication.

Field trial questions. As well as, or instead of, inviting free commenting, you can include special "field trial questions" in your lesson. That is, in addition to whatever activities and exercises your eventual learners will be asked to tackle, you can ask questions that invite your test learners to give information about their use of your materials.

For example, at the beginning of the lesson, right after your statement of aims and objectives, you might print the following:

In the space below, say what is your reaction to the author's aims and objectives. (e.g. Are they clear to you? Do they seem relevant? etc.)

At the beginning of each section within a lesson, you may have a box as follows:

Time started	

-- and a "Time finished" box at the end.

After each major activity, question or exercise -- especially one that relates to a major objective -- you may ask a set of questions such as the following:

1. Write down your answer to Exercise X in the space below.
2. How long did the exercise take you?
3. Was it clear what you were supposed to do?
4. How easy was it?
5. Did you consider it a worthwhile exercise?
6. How similar did you think your answer was to the author's?
7. What was your reaction to the author's discussion of answers?
8. If you were not satisfied with your answer,
   (a) what did you do about it? And
   (b) how do you account for your getting it wrong?
9. If you didn't tackle Exercise X, please say why not.

Thus, when you get back the printed lesson at the end of the field trial, you will get not only the learners' written answers to the key activities but also their comments on those activities.

After each section of the lesson you may include such questions as:

1. How long did this section take you?
2. Without referring back, summarize the author's main points in not more than 100 words.
3. How difficult was the section?
4. How interesting was it?
5. Did it seem clearly related to the aims and objectives of the lesson?
6. How useful or relevant were the diagrams, cartoons, tables, etc?
7. Can you suggest any ways of improving the section?
8. Do you have any other comments about the section?

N.B. With all such "field trial questions", make sure you **leave sufficient space** on the page for learners to write in their answers.

Group discussion. When learners have completed their work on the lesson and returned their annotated copies to you, you can analyse their reactions along with their test results. This will give you an overall picture of how they responded to the lesson, how long they took over it, and what they learned from it. You may then be able to meet with a group of them to discuss common reactions and suggestions for improvements. Key questions to ask in such a discussion (or in a questionnaire if you cannot get together with your field trial learners) are:

- What did you like most about the lesson?
- What did you dislike most?
- What changes would you recommend?

You can then put the finishing touches to your lesson and have it printed up for regular use by the learners it was always intended for. However, those learners may still respond differently from your developmental testers. So evaluation needs to continue.

CONTINUOUS MONITORING

Once your lessons are in regular use with your intended learners you'll need to keep them under review. Despite developmental testing, surprises do happen. Learners who are studying "for real" may reveal new weaknesses or peculiarities in your materials. This is especially likely if you use the same lessons again and again over several years, perhaps with the learners gradually coming to differ from those you originally wrote for.

Remember too that what learners learn depends not just on the quality of your materials but also on many other aspects of the **system** within which they are being used. So, your evaluation may eventually need to cover aspects of management, organizational politics, funding, learner-support, marketing, record-keeping, and so on.

Continuous monitoring takes two forms:

- Casual evaluation.
- Deliberate evaluation.

These may lead to changes not just in the lesson materials but also in many other aspects of the learning system.

Casual Evaluation

This kind of evaluation arises from things we "just happen to notice" during the life of the course. Here are some examples of things we might happen to notice, or have brought to our attention:

- Learners are dropping out of the course.

- One of our set books has gone out of print.

- Learners are getting increasingly late with their assignments.

- Other teachers are complaining about our learners.

- Some of our lessons are unpopular.

- Learners are not turning up for practical sessions.

- Some of our tutors feel constrained by the assessment system.

- Bad weather ruins an important field trip.

- Work done by previous learners is being plagiarized by the present group.

- Learners' managers are not providing the support they promised.

- Learners are spending far too long on the audiotapes.

- A new piece of legislation has made part of the course out of date.

- Assessment results indicate ineffective teaching in certain sections of the course.

Such items may arise from our own observations -- e.g. of assessment results. Or they may be reported by learners, tutors, or anyone else (e.g. line managers) with whom our learners and tutors have contact. We may not be able to do anything about the problem (or opportunity) indicated, but we should aim to be aware of it.

Deliberate Evaluation

Deliberate evaluation differs from casual evaluation in that we are actively seeking answers to specific questions about our lessons and the course. For example: Can the written guide to the course be improved in any way? Are learners without previous experience coping reasonably well? Is the home experiment kit being used? Do mentors feel that the workplace practical sessions are serving their purpose? Is the course leading to improvements in learners' job-satisfaction or productivity? And so on.

If you are not meeting all the learners who study your lessons yourself, it is essential to keep in regular communication with people who do. In the Open University, the central course team thus keeps in touch with the regional tutors who assess learners' assignment work -- and obtains from them evaluative reports on the course and how learners are coping with it. (See Figure 14.5 for tutors' comments on one block of a course.) Even with on-site courses, mentors or line managers may see more of the learners' work than do the people who devised the course. They should be encouraged to report regularly, either in writing or in discussion.

Discussions and interviews. Deliberate evaluation can often be conducted in group discussion with tutors and/or learners -- provided you can get them together for the purpose. With an on-site course, tutors might usefully get together weekly to discuss progress. Mentors and/or line managers might also welcome an

Figure 14.5: Tutor's Comments on Part of a Course

Tutor Number	*Comments*
86	Unit 10 reading, Deutsch in particular, seemed to cause students some difficulty, in spite of the summary in Unit 10. The article is good, however, and I found that a tutorial session cleared most of the problems. New tutors might be alerted in advance next year.
58	My own criticism is directed at Unit 10 which I consider to be far too vague and pitched at far too high a level of generalization. It appears to be out of keeping with the course so far. Perhaps a more interesting exercise would be to look at some situation in more detail. This would enable the incorporation of section 4, the controls of politics on communication, to be brought out in an integrated way rather than as a postscript.
26	Some of my students are critical of what they describe as the 'jumping about' nature of the course, i.e., a tendency to spend too little time on one topic area before switching to a distantly related theme. I think they would prefer more discrete blocks of emphasis on a particular social science.
28	This is the best block to date.
11	Unit 07 seems excessively technical containing matter not of obvious interest to social science students. This is my reaction with which students appeared to agree (out of politeness?). Unit 09 again seems too technical and more appropriate to a course in physical transport rather than social science aspects. Also appears totally to fail to integrate with earlier Units concerned with natural resources—so that there is no discussion of relative efficiency of fuel usage of different transport modes nor of fossil fuel constraints on transport technology and usage. These are topics most likely to interest D101 students I feel. Also are D101 students likely to be so interested in location of Turkish Railways?
44	07: written work by students showed that they had not grasped the significance of the concept of 'deep structure', despite the SAQ and CMA questions. Suggest that SAQ4 (p. 39) be broken down so as to draw out separately the elements of the definition given on p. 72. Unit 10 looks deceptively short and coming at the end tended to be rushed. I think that the Unit would come better after 08. The spatial factor is less demanding in comprehension because more concrete.

opportunity to discuss how they feel about the course. If participants cannot be brought together, perhaps you can interview them instead (on the telephone if necessary).

Using questionnaires. However, both discussions and interviews may be difficult to arrange, especially with distance courses. As an alternative (or as a supplement) you might collect information from course participants by means of a questionnaire.

The design of questionnaires is an art in itself, and I have no space to go into details. If you do need advice, it may be worth considering whether there is a colleague within your organization who has experience in questionnaire design and survey techniques.

To get you started, it is worth noting that the questions used in questionnaires normally fall into three basic categories.

1. A question, together with several alternative answers expressing different ways of rating some aspect of the course. The learner is asked to choose whichever one he or she agrees with. For example:

    How clear do you feel about what the project will be demanding of you?
    (a) Very clear
    (b) Fairly clear
    (c) Rather unclear
    (d) Very unclear
    (e) I've not thought much about it yet

An alternative approach is to pose the question as a statement with which learners are asked to indicate the extent of their agreement or disagreement. For example:

> Would you agree that the demands likely to be made
> on you by the project are now clear to you?
> (a) Very much Yes
> (b) Yes
> (c) Haven't thought about it yet
> (d) No
> (e) Very much No

2. A question inviting the learner to look at several answers and choose whichever ones apply to him or her. For example:

> For lesson 12, which of the following aspects
> do you believe might have been improved?
> (i)   Aims and objectives
> (ii)   Study guide
> (iii)   The case study
> (iv)   Activities
> (v)   Feedback on activities
> (vi)   The practical exercise
> (vii) End-of-lesson test

3. Open-ended questions inviting learners to make a free response, writing down their comments. For example, as a follow-up to the last question mentioned above, one might ask:

> What do you believe should be done to
> improve those aspects you have picked out?

Clearly, what you ask questions **about** will vary from one course to another. It will also vary according to the point within the course at which your questionnaire is to be completed, and according to the kinds of decision you hope to be able to make in the light of the answers.

The best way of ensuring that your questions are as clear and ambiguous as possible is to try them out on a few people in draft form. That is, give it a tutorial tryout. If you cannot find appropriate learners to vet your draft questionnaire, then friends, spouse or colleagues may be able to oblige by pointing out weaknesses and obscurities that have escaped your notice.

Even the best of questionnaires, however, may produce answers that are hard to interpret. What do learners **mean** when they identify a particular lesson as "difficult", "too long", and "very interesting"? Do they all mean the same thing? Ought we to do anything about it?

> IT CAN BE VERY ILLUMINATING TO **INTERVIEW** SOME OF THE LEARNERS WHO HAVE COMPLETED YOUR QUESTIONNAIRE.

USING EVALUATION DATA

The ultimate and over-riding question in evaluation is "So what?" That is, what are we to **make** of the information we collect? How are we to use it?

The aim of evaluation is to understand our course and how learners interact with it -- with a view to sustaining it, developing it and where possible, **improving** it. (Check the four aspects of course planning depicted in Figure 3.1 on page 36.) The improvements you make to your lessons, and other aspects of your course, will ideally benefit learners who are **currently** working with it. Some changes cannot be made fast enough, however, so some improvements will benefit **future** learners only.

Examples of Course Improvement

Let us look briefly at the kinds of improvement that might be made in the light of evaluation findings:

A distance course. This first example, In Figure 14.6, is a set of recommendations compiled for one distance learning course by my colleague, David Hawkridge.

Figure 14.6: Evaluation Recommendations for a Distance Learning Course

Evaluation findings	*Recommended changes*
1. 40% of students consider workload on Lessons 3 and 4 to be at least 50% greater than for other lessons.	Remove the exercise on p.64. Eliminate items (c) and (f) from the reading list.
2. 30% of students report that local resources are not available for carrying out the mini-project in Lesson 7.	Replace the mini-project with an essay so that no students are placed at this kind of disadvantage.
3. 52% of students do not find the tapes for Lesson 3 to be useful.	Change the third assignment so that is is based on both the printed material and tapes, or eliminate tapes, or revise tapes so that they are more useful
4. Students (12%) want additional material on the mathematical aspects of Lesson 9.	Recommend appropriate remedial text if available, *or* prepare suitable material
5. Academic colleagues (5) want inclusion of alternative material to counter allegations of bias in Lesson 9.	Do not alter materials. Include summary of their allegations. Add an alternative text to list of recommended books.
6. 70% of students want fewer assignments.	Replace the project with an essay (see 2 above) and replace essay C with a quiz-type test, self-marked.
7. Less than 30% of students tackled either of the two integrative 'course-as-a-whole' questions in the examination; and marks on those two questions averaged 20% below those gained on the questions of more limited scope.	Make the tackling of one integrative question compulsory in the examination; re-write final section of last lesson so as to give students practice in reviewing course to establish overarching principles and general insights.

An on-site course. The second example, in Figure 14.7 overleaf, is an extract from a lengthy report by Will Bridge on the evaluation of an on-site course in mechanics. It is particularly interesting here in reminding

Figure 14.7:   Evaluation Improvements to an On-site Course

The outstanding problems in the initial trial in 1972/3 had been the hurried and crowded nature of the test sessions, the students' slow overall progress which resulted from this, and the lack of a steady routine for them to keep to. To tackle the first problem, it was decided to use a larger classroom (seating approximately 50 students), and to try using fast students on the course to test their colleagues on those units the fast students had passed. The problem of slow progress was tackled by fixing deadlines for passing each of a minimum number of eight units throughout the course. A course-work mark scheme was arranged so that students were given one mark (equivalent to just less than one percent in the final grading) for being a 'tester', and one mark for each test passed before a deadline.

Another changes was made to the course for 1974. The units were re-arranged in a branching pattern, so that after a student had covered two introductory units, he was given some freedom as to which units he studied. This change was partly because the needs of the electrical engineers differed somewhat from those of the physical scientists, and partly because it was thought that different students might choose different sequences through the course.

With these changes the course was re-run in 1974. The staffing continued at the same level, but was supplemented by between two and four student testers employed at any one period. There were a number of improvements. A majority of the students completed at least the core of eight units, and there was no drop-off in attendance attendance over the two terms. This time I was the evaluator. I interviewed one third of the students, and looked for the reasons for these improvements. Overall, it seemed that the guidance the deadline provided did help students, particularly the weaker ones, to work steadily. They were also influenced by the (small) credit given for this.

It emerged from two questionnaires that, although throughout the year the student testers were found to be approachable and adequately knowledgeable, early on in the year they had not been sure about exactly what to do. For example, they did not know whether or not to accept correct answers which were not got by the same means as the answers provided by the model solutions, and they were not sure whether or not verbal explanations of written answers could be accepted. Some of the testers learnt by experience what to do, and in consequence became more acceptable.

The branching pattern was popular, although many chose the same sequence as the previous linear one.

However, there were still problems. Complaints about the workload continued, now coming also from weaker students who had previously dropped out. Also, students were still not convinced that they thoroughly understood units they had passed, some thinking the test questions not deep enough, and others thinking that tests did not cover all of each unit ...

from:

Bridge, W. (1977) 'Changes in a self-paced course' in *Individual Study in Undergraduate Science*, W. Bridge and L. Elton (eds), Heinemann, London.

us that evaluation can suggest changes in many aspects of the course besides the teaching quality of the materials.

The evaluation and improvement of that on-site course continued year by year. Some intended improvements turned out to have the opposite effect -- e.g. giving learners extra credit for passing units regularly may have been responsible for the cheating that was detected in some tests. Continuous monitoring is a continuing necessity.

Towards Re-making Your Course

Each time your course runs, ask such questions as these:

- Did the course attract enough learners?
- Did enough of them finish the course?
- Did they gain sufficiently in competence?
- Were the learners satisfied?
- Were the tutors/mentors satisfied?
- Were others (e.g. line managers) satisfied?
- What were the long-term effects?
- What needs to be changed?

Some changes you will be able to make from one year to the next -- supplementing this text, replacing that audio-cassette, briefing new kinds of people to support learners -- in a kind of "rolling re-make" of the course. But, eventually, the answer to that final question above may well be PRACTICALLY EVERYTHING. Sooner or later, evaluation may suggest you need to start on designing a new course entirely. Back to Chapter 3!

FINAL CHECKLIST FOR LESSON EVALUATION

In case you think I've wandered too far away from the evaluation of individual lessons, the checklist below should remind you of what might be done. Go through as many of the following steps as possible:

1. Criticize your first draft yourself, using a checklist like those shown on pages 336-338.

2. Send your second draft for critical commenting by friends, colleagues and other experts, using similar checklists.

3. Repeat your own critical reading in the light of their comments and suggestions.

4. Carry out any improvements indicated by critical commenting.

5. Tutorially try out your lesson on a few learners individually.

6. Carry out any improvements suggested by the tutorial tryout.

7. Insert "field trial questions" after major activities and at the end of sections, and compile any necessary questionnaires ready for field trial.

8. Run field trial with twenty or thirty learners.

9. Discuss possible improvements to lesson with field trial learners after analysing their responses.

10. Carry out "final" revisions to the lesson.

11. Print it -- but be prepared to revise it yet again, and eventually perhaps replace it, in the light of continuous monitoring of the course as a whole.

> DON'T JUDGE A SELF-INSTRUCTIONAL COURSE BY THE ELOQUENCE OF ITS DEVELOPERS OR THE GLOSSINESS OF ITS PACKAGING -- THE PROOF OF THE PUDDING IS IN THE EATING (AND IN HOW WELL IN STAYS DOWN).

15. STARTING, KEEPING GOING, AND FINISHING OFF

This brief final chapter consists chiefly of a few tips to get you started on your lesson-writing; some guidance about certain editorial chores you'll need to carry out while the work is in progress; and some suggestions about how to bring it all to a satisfactory conclusion.

STARTING TO WRITE

Here are some practical tips, most of which have helped me at some time or other. Perhaps some of them will be useful to you also:

- Allow yourself just so much time for preliminary reading and research (hours or days, according to the number of lessons and the newness of the topic) and be strict about deciding the day on which you will actually start writing your first draft of the lesson.

- If you do not already have an official deadline for completion, set yourself one. Preferably arrange it in such a way that you will suffer some inconvenience or embarrassment if you fail to meet it. For example, you might agree with some "critical friends" that you will have the first draft of your lesson available for them to read by a certain date.

- Don't feel constrained to write the lesson in the sequence it will be read by learners, if this doesn't suit you. If you find the beginning difficult, start somewhere else. Begin, perhaps, by writing an exercise or case study, or any part of the lesson that seems particularly interesting or "of the essence". The rest can then be written around it.

- Don't aspire to perfection in your first rough draft. Aim to cover the ground as fast as possible, getting the broad flow of ideas and activities established. Only then should you let yourself go back to your sources to check on any dubious details.

- Try to arrange a period of writing time -- several hours or, better still, a couple of days -- when producing your lesson will be your only task. If possible, find a place where no-one can burst in for an impromptu meeting and where no phones ring.

- If your lesson-planning and writing spreads over several days or longer, you may find you do a lot of "writing" in your mind while walking the dog or in the intervals of attending to other business. Always keep a notebook on you, so as to record the sudden "brainwaves" that might otherwise be forgotten.

- As you write, keep in mind one or two people you know who might be typical of those for whom your material is intended. Ask yourself, page by page, how Sid or Sue (or whatever their names are) might respond to your words (and pictures) of wisdom.

- Never assume that just because you've spelled out the information on the page it will necessarily mean anything to your learners. Unless you constantly ask yourself "Why am I telling them this?" and "What do I want them to do with it?" -- and reach satisfactory answers -- the information may remain inert.

- Resist the temptation to do the job less well than you know you could -- e.g. when you realize that a vivid example or pictorial representation or practical exercise would be far more telling than a verbal explanation (however clear) but would involve you in extra thinking time.

- If you get stuck on one section of your lesson, don't give it all up and go off to attend to whatever other duties you might be neglecting. Instead, try turning your attention to some other aspect of the lesson (or another lesson) and come back to the troublesome section later on.

- When you break off writing for the day, try to do so in the middle of a "good patch" -- so you'll find it easy to get started again next time.

- And, in general:

> AIM TO **ENJOY** WRITING YOUR LESSON: IF YOU DO, YOUR LEARNERS MAY ENJOY READING IT.

EDITING YOUR FIRST ROUGH DRAFT

Your first draft may well be handwritten and full of corrections, additions and crossings-out. But don't hand it over to your typist as soon as (let alone before) you have written the last word. Before you do so, **criticize** it -- preferably after having put it aside for a few days.

To focus your criticisms, consider your lesson in the light of each of the following questions (or work out a checklist of your own):

- Does the structure of the lesson seem sensible and coherent -- with introductions or previews, and summaries or reviews used where appropriate, and will learners be able to appraise it as a whole before tackling it in a detailed way?

- Have I taken adequate steps to motivate the learners and make clear to them how they might tackle the material and what they might expect to get from it?

- Have I pitched the lesson at the right level of difficulty -- challenging without being inaccessible -- and consistent with the prerequisite abilities I say I am assuming of learners?

- Is the tone that of a friendly but rigorous tutor, lively and interesting, light of touch, and with humour (and humanity) admitted where appropriate?

- Is my language plain and straightforward (e.g. what is my Fog Index?) -- with words and sentences reasonably short, and technical terms used only when essential (but properly defined and explained) and gobbledygook excluded altogether?

- Have I avoided sexist language -- language that seems to include people of one sex only when, in fact, either might be involved? For example, writing "he/him/his" when I might more accurately have written "he or she", etc. (or recast the sentence so as to avoid the pronouns altogether).

- Have I used analogies, examples (and non-examples), case studies, and pictorial illustrations wherever they might make a worthwhile contribution to the learner's understanding?

- Does my argument contain any unexplained gaps or redundancies or illogical jumps that might irritate or confuse learners?

- Have I included sufficient questions, exercises and activities to encourage learners in self-assessment and enable them to develop their understanding towards the objectives of the lesson?

- Does the lesson incorporate non-print media -- e.g. practical work, listening to audiotape, discussion with other learners or mentors -- where these might be more appropriate than print?

- Are any assignment exercises related to the aims and objectives of the lesson, clear in what they demand of the learner, and can I ensure that any given learner's competence would be judged in much the same way, whoever assesses it?

- Is the learner's likely workload (in terms of learning time) reasonable for the topic of the lesson?

Once you have made any amendments to your lesson suggested by these questions, **read it aloud** -- and tidy up any passages that still sound pompous, long-winded or unduly complex. Watch out also for jarring repetitions of a word or phrase -- e.g. you may have begun two or three paragraphs on the same page with "However".

One final point: Never let your one and only copy of the first draft (or any other draft) out of your possession. Much good material has been lost that way. As your handwritten or roughly typed draft swells and changes -- and especially before you hand it over for professional typing or word processing:

> **PHOTCOPY** IT -- AND STORE THE COPY
> SEPARATELY FROM THE ORIGINAL.

And if you're using a word processor yourself-- make frequent paper copies of the material you hope is still stored safely on disc.

TYPING YOUR DRAFT

Unless your lesson is one of a series and your typist already knows how to lay it out on the page, don't just hand over your manuscript and hope for the best. Give your typist **written** instructions and/or some sample pages typed as you would like your lesson to be typed.

Figure 15.1 overleaf, for example, shows the guidelines I prepared for the typist of the camera-ready copy for this book. Your requirements, of course, will be different, but you will have equal need to make them clear. If your material will eventually be printed, you may need to develop guidelines for your printer also.

Figure 15.1: Guidelines for My Typist

- Use A4 paper (for photo-reduction).

- Lay out the body of the text within the margins marked on the attached specimen.

- Leave right-hand margins unjustified.

- Type body of text in 14 pt Palatino (one-and-a-half spacing), except where otherwise indicated.

- Type running heads in 12 pt Helvetica italic with rule under.

- Type headings in 14 pt Helvetica bold, distinguishing between A, B and C headings as shown on specimen.

- Leave extra 12 pt space between running head and first line of text on page.

- Leave 12 pt extra space before headings and 6 pt after..

- Leave extra 12 pt before and 18 pt after boxed items.

- Leave extra 6 pt space between paragraphs.

- Indent each new paragraph as shown, unless preceded by an indented list, a box or figure, or an A- or B-heading.

- Do not hyphenate words at the end of a line.

- Do not strive to have the same number of lines on each page. If necessary, a page can over-run by up to two lines (e.g. to complete a section) or can be two or three lines short.

- Do not start a new paragraph or have a heading on the last one or two lines of a page.

- Do not end a paragraph on the first line of a new page.

- Insert attached illustrations exactly where shown in the sequence of text. Where the illustration is not attached, leave the amount of space indicated in my draft.

- Treat boxed items as illustrations. That is, do not split one between two pages unless it is too big to fit on one page.

While your typist is typing your lessons, keep in touch. Your guidelines may not be as clear or as comprehensive as you think. (Mine for this book certainly were not.) Check whether your typist is having trouble interpreting them. Amend them where necessary. Even if you are typing your own lessons, it is sensible to think out your own guidelines in advance, rather than trying to make them up as you go along.

GETTING COPYRIGHT PERMISSIONS

Will your lesson reproduce any materials -- e.g. words, pictures, recorded sound -- for which someone else holds the copyright? If so, you will need to obtain written permission from the holder of the copyright. You can send off for this while your typist is at work on your lesson, if you have not already done so.

Actually, it is best to start requesting permission as soon as you are reasonably sure you want to use any particular material. You will sometimes have difficulty tracking down the copyright holder (who may be the author, or the author's employer, agent or "estate"). A reply may be slow in forthcoming; and you may, in any case, be refused permission to quote or else be asked so high a fee that you need to consider whether the material really is all that essential.

What is Copyright Material?

It is wise to act on the assumption that any piece of writing (even a letter or a shopping list) is protected by the laws of copyright. That is, during the period of copyright -- 50 years from first publication or from the death of the author (whichever is the later) -- permission to reproduce it or any "substantial part" of it, can be given only by the holder of that copyright.

The same is true for pictures (e.g. diagrams, photographs and paintings, etc.) and for recorded speech or music and moving pictures. If you use any such material without permission you could be involved in an expensive court action for infringement of copyright.

What is Infringement?

The Copyright Act of 1956 indicates that infringement occurs when more than a "substantial part" of a work is reproduced without permission. Unfortunately, "substantial part" is not defined. However, some general rules of thumb are widely followed by publishers. If, for example, you are quoting an author's **prose** merely because it expresses something more elegantly or more forcefully than you think you could do yourself, then 50 words is about the most you should use without seeking permission. Though, of course, you must still place those words within inverted commas and name their author -- and somewhere mention the work from which the quotation came, together with its publisher and date.

With **poetry**, even 50 words may be too many to quote without permission, since they would form a "substantial part" of a short poem. One court case held that four lines were a "substantial part" of a 32-line poem. Better not to quote more than three or four lines or one-tenth of the whole poem, whichever is smaller.

If, on the other hand, you are using other authors' words not as a decoration to your text but in order to comment on or criticize their ideas (as in a scholarly article or a review), then you are safe in quoting much more. In such cases, it is widely regarded as "fair dealing" to quote, without permission, a single prose extract of up to 400 words, or a series of shorter extracts (none more than 300 words) totalling a maximum of 800 words -- provided this does not amount to more than 10% of the total (as it might, for instance, with a newspaper or journal article).

In reviewing or criticizing poetry, quoting up to 40 lines -- or 25% of the total, which is less -- is generally considered "fair dealing". Nevertheless, as mentioned above, you should give a full reference to the source of your quotation.

So, unless you are confident that your use of the quotation would be seen as criticism or review:

> SEEK PERMISSION FOR ANY QUOTATION
>
> OF MORE THAN 50 WORDS.

With copyright illustrations, recorded sound, and video or film material, the idea of "fair dealing" is not recognized. So you should seek permission for even a fragment of a picture or of audio or visual recordings.

Nevertheless, it is worth remembering that there is **no copyright protection for ideas or facts**. Copyright applies only to the actual words or pictures through which these ideas or facts are expressed.

On the one hand, this means that you would risk infringing copyright if you were to use the same words or pictures, without permission, in another medium -- e.g. making an audiotape of a written text. But, on the other hand, you may avoid infringing copyright by re-expressing an author's ideas in your own words, or re-drawing an illustrator's pictures in a different style. If you followed them too closely, of course-- without mentioning the source of your inspiration -- you might be accused of plagiarism instead.

Who Holds the Copyright?

To obtain permission, you will need to identify the copyright holder. If you are wanting to quote from a book, you will probably find the name of the copyright holder among the small print on the **reverse** of the title page. Usually it will appear in a "copyright notice", naming either the author(s) or the publisher, e.g.

Copyright © 1990 Winifred Smith.

Write to the author at the publisher's address. If you want to use illustrations and the illustrator is not given a separate copyright notice, assume that the publisher is the copyright holder. With articles from newspapers or journals it is safest to assume that the publisher is the copyright holder, unless the article carries a separate copyright notice.

The copyright in photographs, engravings, etchings and prints (as in painted or drawn portraits) belongs to the person who commissioned them. (If no-one paid for them to be produced, then the artists are regarded as having commissioned themselves.) With other paintings and drawings, copyright belongs to the artists, unless they have specifically assigned it to someone else. You can never assume that the present owner of the work is also the copyright holder -- even though they may think they are. If you are wanting to use a photograph of a painting, you may need to obtain permission not only from the person who commissioned the photograph but also the person who holds the copyright for the painting.

Incidentally, if you plan to print photographs you have taken yourself, and they include recognizable images of any living persons, you will need to seek their permission first.

The copyright of all radio and television material will belong to the broadcasting company. Films, audio-recordings and video-recordings should identify the copyright holder by means of some kind of copyright notice on the packaging and/or on the material itself. Needless to say, as with illustrations, the fact that you may own a copy of the material does not give you the right to reproduce it.

Writing for Permission

Write to the copyright holder, keeping a copy for your files. Give the following information:

- Full details of the work from which you wish to copy.

- A photocopy of the extracts or illustrations you wish to reproduce (or a tape of audio/video extracts).

- Any deletions or amendments you might want to make.

- The author(s), title, publisher -- e.g. a college or a commercial organization, expected date of publication of the work in which you wish to quote the material.

- If you will be publishing to a small number of learners, especially if you will not be charging for the materials, this might be worth mentioning to deter any copyright holder who might be tempted to ask a huge fee.

- An assurance that you will acknowledge the source of your quotations (on the relevant pages and/or on an introductory page, whichever you intend). Incidentally, illustrations are usually acknowledged in the caption by saying "from" (whatever the source) if the illustration is reproduced in its original form, or "after" or "based upon" if it has been re-drawn.

Protecting Your Own Copyright

In the UK, copyright is automatically established the moment a work is written (whether published or not). It may be vested in your organization if you are writing as part of your job; in you, if you are writing as a freelance or spare time activity. (The accepted test of whether you or your organization is the copyright holder is to ask whether you could reasonably be dismissed for refusing to produce such material). Despite the automatic protection, it is sensible to print the copyright notice on your work, i.e.

Copyright © 19XX Name of Holder.

Further Guidance

Copyright is undoubtedly a complicated business. Yet the development of self-instructional courses can be much eased by incorporating already published material. If you believe you need further guidance on how to do so without breaking the law, and if there is nobody in your organization who can offer specialist help, you should be able to obtain advice from the National Council for Educational Technology in London.

CORRECTING YOUR PROOFS

The word "proofs" normally refers to a sample copy of your finished text, provided by the printer so that you can check its accuracy before multiple copies are run off. However, we can use the same term also for a photocopy of the draft your typist has just finished typing.

If you can, try to ensure that at least one other person besides you and the typist reads the proof copy. You are the best person to ensure that your typist has followed the layout you intended. However, authors have a tendency to "see" the word they intended, regardless of what has actually been typed. So, mis-spellings, incorrect numbers, and the like, may be spotted more readily be more someone else who can compare your typist's draft, word by word, with your original.

Points to Check

The main points to check are these:

- Have your instructions about layout been followed?
- Are pages numbered correctly?

- Does the text contain any errors (e.g. spelling mistakes or missing words) that need to be corrected? If so, make your corrections on the photocopy, not on the original.

- Has the cold clarity of type revealed anything in the text that learners would find offensive, confusing or incomprehensible? If so, change it -- but resist the temptation to fiddle about with minor "improvements". Any extensive alterations now will waste the typist's time and may cause layout problems. (Better to save them for the perhaps extensive re-typings that may result from developmental testing.)

- Do you need to paste in any illustrations, draw any boxes or arrows by hand, or add any Letraset headings? (Don't do this until your typist has completed any necessary corrections.)

Symbols for Correcting Proofs

Your aims in correcting proofs must be to communicate clearly with your typist and/or printer. You need to draw their attention to points in the typewritten (or printed) text where they are to make a change -- and tell them exactly what that change is to be. This you will do by marking the proofs with symbols **agreed** between you. Any agreed symbols would do; but those I give in Figure 15.2 are very widely used.

Notice that the nature of your corrections should be indicated in the left-hand **margin** of the page. Within the text itself, it is preferable to indicate only the **place** where the correction is to be made. (Your typist may or may not be able to decipher corrections made between the lines; printers generally discourage them.)

Figure 15.2: Proof-reading Symbols

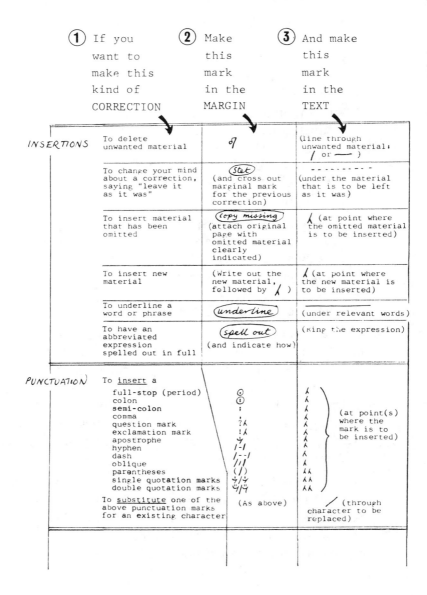

Figure 15.2: Proof-reading Symbols *(Continued)*

	CORRECTION	MARGIN	TEXT
TYPESTYLES	To change one typestyle for another:		Make this mark under letter/words to be altered Ring the letter/ words to be altered
	Change to:		
	italics	*(ital)*	—
	upright (Roman), not italics	*(rom)*	
	capital letters	*(cap's)*	≡
	lower case (small) letters	*(l.c)*	
	bold type	*(bold)*	‿‿‿
	another named typeface (e.g. san serif)	*(san serif)*	
SPACING & LAYOUT	To start a new paragraph	*(np)*	⌐ (before the word that is to begin the new paragraph)
	To run two paragraphs together as one	*(run on)*	⌐ (linking the last word of the first paragraph to the first word of the second)
	To move a line of type:		← left-hand edge of type)
	to right	⌐|	(enclosing material to be moved and showing how far)
	to left	|⌐	(up to beginning of material to be moved)
	To centre material on page (or column):	*(centre)*	(around material to be centred)
	To move a letter or word from:		
	end of one line (or column or page) to beginning of next	*(take over)*	(around letter/word)
	beginning of one line, etc., to end of previous	*(take back)*	(around letter/word)
	To transpose (change places of letters/words)	*(trs)*	(between letters/ words to be transposed -- number to show order if necessary)
	To transpose lines:	*(trs)*	(around lines)
	To insert space:		
	between letters or words	#	⋏ (between letters or words)
	between lines	# (Can also say how much, if not obvious)	(between lines to be spaced)
	To close up space:		
	between letters or words	*(less #)*	(between characters to be joined)
	between lines	*(less #)*	(linking the lines that are to be closed up)

If you have several corrections to make on one line, they should be indicated in order from left to right in the margin, each being separated from its neighbours by the oblique mark (/). If, heaven forbid, you have so many corrections that you can't indicate them all in the margin (or even both margins), write them on a separate sheet and staple it securely to the page.

When your instruction to the typist/printer is given by a word or phrase, e.g. "stet" or "take back", put a ring around it so as to decrease the possibility of its getting incorporated into the text by mistake.

MAKE ALL YOUR CORRECTIONS ON A **PHOTOCOPY**

— **NOT** ON THE ORIGINAL TYPESCRIPT

If some of your corrections seem too complicated for these symbols, use a separate sheet of paper to write or type out exactly how you want the relevant piece of text to look -- and attach it to the proofs with a marginal note to your typist or printer.

Figure 15.3 opposite illustrates the use of the symbols in correcting much of the text that now appears on pages 353 and 356 of this book.

Figure 15.3: Proof-reading Symbols in Action

TOWARDS A FINAL DRAFT

So you have finished proof-reading what will be the first "public" draft of your lesson. This you will take to perhaps two further drafts, improving your material in the light of evaluative comments -- first from colleagues and then from "guinea-pig" learners. I can sum up these final stages of producing your lesson by referring you to the advice and checklists given in Chapter 14. That is, once you are in a position to turn out multiple copies of Draft 1:

- Get critical comments on Draft 1.
- Correct and re-type where necessary to produce Draft 2.
- Developmentally test Draft 2.
- Correct and re-type where necessary to produce the final draft.

Of course, one could go on titivating a draft lesson for ever -- especially if one has a word processor. But, in these final stages, one has to struggle with what may seem like a dilemma -- viz, to get it **right** or to get it **finished**.

You are no doubt working to a deadline, and you **must** get your lesson finished. But will it ever be "right"? Yes, but only so long as you accept that "right" does not have to mean "perfect". In this imperfect world, right may often be less than perfect -- but will still be good enough. (And still sufficiently hard to attain!)

Better to settle for producing a succession of 90%-perfect lessons than to refrain indefinitely from publication in the hope that one day you'll turn out a hundred-percenter. If you ever do, you'll be the first!

INDEX